Wilderness Basics

The Care and Enjoyment of the Western Wilderness

Edited by Jerry Schad

Published by the Sierra Club
San Diego Chapter

SIERRA CLUB

MDCCCXCII

THE SIERRA CLUB

The Sierra Club, founded in 1892 by John Muir, has devoted itself to the study and protection of the nation's scenic and ecological resources—mountains, wetlands, woodlands, wild shores, and rivers. There are some 50 chapters coast to coast, in Canada, Hawaii, and Alaska. Participation is invited in the club's programs to enjoy and preserve wilderness everywhere.

National office address: 730 Polk St., San Francisco, CA 94109.

San Diego Chapter office: 3820 Ray St., San Diego, CA 92104.

First Edition

Cover illustration by Bob Frost

International Standard Book Number 0-9628677-0-5

Manufactured in the United States of America

This book is dedicated to the hundreds of volunteers, past and present, who have kept the San Diego Chapter's annual Basic Mountaineering/Wilderness Basics course running smoothly since its inception in 1957.

PREFACE

The many volunteers who made this book a reality have perpetuated a tradition stretching back more than three decades. In 1961, the Sierra Club San Diego Chapter published the first edition of *Basic Mountaineering*, a handbook for students taking the club-sponsored Basic Mountaineering Course. Perhaps better known as the "Red Book" for the distinctive color of its cover, that book was made possible through contributions of text, art work, and clerical work by more than two dozen Chapter members, and through the able efforts of Henry I. Mandolf, who served as chief editor.

Mandolf stayed with the project through a second (1965) and third (1970) edition, by which time the Red Book's influence was felt among a population far larger than the captive audience of Basic Mountaineering Course students. As a neophyte outdoorsman and newcomer to San Diego in 1972, I learned of the book through a classmate at San Diego State who helped me discover the joys of peak bagging and snow camping in southern California's mountains.

By the early '80s, it became necessary for the San Diego Chapter to rework the book in its entirety. The expanded, reorganized, and extensively rewritten book *Mountaineering Basics*, edited by Lynne Foster and published in 1982, again featured many contributions by Chapter members.

In the decade of the '90s, it has once again become necessary to recast and rewrite the handbook that has long been a standard reference in the field. The interests of Sierra Club members and Basic Mountaineering Course students have shifted and broadened over the years. There are several reasons for this: The increased pace of contemporary urban life has left many people with less leisure time but more of a need than ever to escape to the wild spaces. Day hiking, and visits to areas closer to home,

are becoming more popular. Women and families are taking to the outdoors in greater numbers. The use of regional parks, open spaces close to metropolitan areas, and formerly ignored expanses of desert are on the rise. There is an increasing concern that our remaining wild spaces are falling victim to onslaughts as direct as urban development and as indirect as air and water pollution. There's a greater awareness of the impacts that all travelers impart to the areas they visit.

The above-mentioned broadening of interests and concerns have led to an expansion of subject material in both the course and in this handbook. To reflect this, the course and the book now share the new title *Wilderness Basics*.

Although the content of this book overlaps to some degree that of its predecessors, almost all material in this book is freshly rewritten. New chapters on wilderness ethics, physical conditioning, coastal travel, special concerns of women, and traveling with children have been added. The chapters on outdoor equipment and wilderness medicine reflect changes in those fields. The trip planning chapter covers such newer issues as restrictive regulations, trailhead quotas, and planning for groups. The chapter on wilderness travel addresses a new and controversial way of exploring the open spaces—mountain bicycling.

Although this book was designed to serve as a reference for students taking the San Diego Chapter's Wilderness Basics course, its geographical scope is not limited to southern California. It is designed to serve people who want to explore wild places all over the western United States.

As in previous incarnations of this book, dozens of volunteers contributed text and illustrations, and helped during various phases of editing and review. The key player in this effort was Dave Moser, who as "project manager" solicited and brought together over a period of 18 months the writers, illustrators, and editors who made this book possible. My role as chief editor was to cement together into a coherent whole the diverse contributions of the 22 authors and seven illustrators. The authors (whose short biographies can be found in this book's appendix), were encouraged to speak in their own voices, and it is my hope that their individuality still comes through after so many electronic "cuts" and "pastes."

Aside from the authors credited in the individual chapters, Bart Ward made important contributions to the Foods and Cooking chapter, and Nick Soroka's contributions were incorporated into the Mountain Travel chapter. Bill Alley and Dan Anderson contributed material about cross-country skiing to the Winter Mountaineering chapter. Other additions and helpful comments were made by those (other than authors) who reviewed the manuscript, including Joyce Alpert, R. J. Arnold, Ric DeVan, Jo Getchen, Jim Kiefer, Cinde Nowicki, Sandy Sanders, René Schad, and Howard Williams. Comprehensive reviews of the entire manuscript and much technical editing of some chapters were the work of professional wordsmiths Bev McGahey and Karen O'Connor. Bev also made valuable suggestions concerning the production of the book. Ric DeVan helped prepare the index, and Nelson Copp assisted with production chores.

The illustrators whose work complemented our authors—Laura Cramer, Bob Frost, Clare Henkel, Paula Huddleston, Chris Lepre, Jim Rockoff, and Carolyn Wood (who also wore an author hat)—are gratefully acknowledged. Bob Frost also did the artwork for this book's cover, which was based on his silkscreen design for the official Wilderness Basics Course T-shirt.

Last but not least, thanks goes to computer wizard Cal Williams for converting a variety of word-processor formats submitted by the various authors into files that could be edited on my machine, and to Glen Conklin and Peggy Richards at Conklin Litho, the printers not only of this edition of Wilderness Basics, but also of its ancestor, the Red Book.

Jerry Schad
January 1991

TABLE OF CONTENTS

Chapter 1

The Western Wilderness: An Introduction

Olive Wenzel and Jerry Schad

"We travel together on a little space ship, dependent on its vulnerable supply of air and soil; all committed for our safety to its security and peace, preserved from annihilation only by the care, the work and I will say, the love we give our fragile craft."

—**Adlai Stevenson**

Our earth, the third planet from the sun, is the mildest and softest of the nine. It holds together more than five billion people and millions of species of plants, animals, and insects. It drifts through space with all of us on it, like a pale, delicate bubble. It's all we have.

All our lives, and for countless generations before us, humans have been transforming the earth to satisfy our physical needs and our desire for comfort. Today, it's clear that we cannot continue to exploit earth's resources at current levels without unraveling its life-support systems. We're also becoming increasingly aware of the importance of the dwindling number of places we call wilderness—places largely untouched by direct human intervention.

Almost everyone feels the need sooner or later to cast aside the trappings of civilization and escape to the wilderness—if only for a few hours or a few days. We take to the hills for relaxation, inspiration, education, and excitement. And we bring back memories that enrich our lives forever.

In the wilderness we glimpse the natural world as it once was on a global scale. On mountains, in deserts, along wild coastlines, our senses drink in simple pleasures: clean air scented with the nectar of a thousand blossoms, muffled silence in the heart of an old-growth forest, the blast of icy air off a glacier, the grace of a bighorn sheep moving on stone, the thunder of breakers felt as well as heard.

In cities we usually live apart from the natural environment; in wilderness we discover that everything is a part of everything else. We learn how plants and animals attain an elegant state of balance independent of most human influences. We become aware of the fragility of each component of the natural world and hence the ecosystem of the earth itself. We become aware of our responsibility as stewards of our remarkable world.

In the western United States—a microcosm of our fragile earth—the contrast between wilderness and the human-altered landscape is more extreme than in most parts of the world. The West is vast enough to retain enormous stretches of undeveloped land, yet populous and economically robust enough that the tendrils of urbanization, agriculture, mining, and timber-harvesting have encroached upon nearly every easily exploited acre. But it's the less accessible, less hospitable, and in many cases the most beautiful acres that are the West's best treasures. These areas can continue to be a source of basic needs such as clean air and water, as well as provide recreational opportunity, as long as we give them the care—and the legal protection—they deserve.

It's hard to speak of the western wilderness without rattling off a litany of superlatives. Few coastlines around the world surpass the scenic grandeur of our Pacific coastline, where mountains sweep dramatically down to the sea. No western state has to settle for a high point less than 11,000 feet in elevation, and most can claim part ownership of at least one of America's three most spectacular mountain ranges—the Rocky Mountains, the Cascade Range, and the Sierra Nevada. Consider, as well, the hot-tempered Cascade volcanoes, the geologic fairyland of Yellowstone, and the incomparably sublime Grand Canyon of the Colorado River. California's forests alone harbor the world's tallest trees—the coastal redwoods; the world's most massive trees—the giant sequoias; and the world's oldest trees—the bristlecone pines. California also claims Death Valley, the Western Hemisphere's lowest and hottest spot.

These and other stellar attractions in the West are distinguished by their inclusion in the National Park system. But national parks are only part of the story. While California, for example, has 21 parks and other units in the National Park system, it also includes 19 national forests; 285 state parks, beaches and recreation areas; plus vast chunks of public land administered by the federal Bureau of Land Management (BLM). In total, California contains 35 million acres of parks and recreation lands, fully one-third of its total area.

Nevada, Utah, and Arizona consist of an even greater percentage of public land, much of it formerly regarded as worthless desert. The recent establishment of Great Basin National Park in eastern Nevada has focused public attention on high peaks, lush meadows, and alpine lakes existing in the middle of a region generally thought of as being desolate and unfriendly. Not far from the much-touted Grand Canyon, Zion, and other national parks in the Southwest are a multitude of other worthwhile places to visit and enjoy. These include Monument Valley, the hidden canyons of the Colorado plateau and Mogollon Rim, and vast stretches of *de facto* wilderness under jurisdiction of the BLM.

The Rocky Mountain and Pacific Northwest states have their unique virtues as well. The Continental Divide, watershed of the nation, links together four states along a rocky cordillera. The Columbia River cleaves the Cascade Range, passing through the recently designated Columbia Gorge National Scenic Area. The Snake River forms the deepest canyon in the nation at the Oregon-Idaho border. Wyoming's Grand Teton and Yellowstone national parks crown a huge region best described as a hiker's, photographer's and climber's dream. All over the West, tracts of virgin forest still thrive, some by virtue of their protected legal status, others by virtue of their sheer inaccessibility.

Lovers of the western wilderness have worked for decades to improve access to remote areas without damaging them. The Pacific Crest National Scenic Trail stretches 2,600 miles along the roof-line of California, Oregon, and Washington. Concepts for other national trails include a route across the northwestern states, and a route along the Continental Divide.

It is not only the grand and remote landscapes and the famous trails that are worth a wilderness traveler's attention. Some of the West's most surprising wild areas lie just beyond the fringes of the biggest cities. Only 20 air-miles from downtown Los Angeles, black bears and bighorn sheep roam the canyons and crags of the Angeles National Forest's San Gabriel Wilderness. A climber living in Denver can take a shot at any of several alpine summits only an hour's drive away. Just over the Golden Gate Bridge from the skyscrapers of San Francisco, serene Muir Redwoods National Monument beckons those weary of jarring city life. In fact, nearly every sizeable Western city can boast of some remarkable natural landscape nearby.

Wherever they lie, the wild, unexploited lands of the West deserve attention and care. This book was written to help you, the outdoors enthusiast, prepare for wilderness outings. We hope you'll enjoy the wilderness, and at the same time protect both yourself and the environment from injury of any kind.

Chapter 2

Wilderness Ethics

Eugene A. Troxell

"Consider yourselves only as members of a biological species which has had a remarkable history, and whose disappearance none of us can desire."

—Albert Einstein

Wilderness is where we go to be closer to our roots. In the words of J.T. Whipple: "All America lies at the end of the wilderness road, and our past is not a dead past but still lives in us... Our forebears had civilization inside themselves, the wild outside. We live in the civilization they created, but within us the wilderness still lingers. What they dreamed, we live; and what they lived, we dream." [1]

The Wilderness Act of 1964 [2] defines wilderness as: "An area where the earth and its community of life are untrammeled by man, where man himself is a visitor who does not remain... It is a region which contains no permanent [human] inhabitants, no possibility for motorized travel, and is spacious enough so that a traveler crossing it by foot or horse must have the experience of sleeping out-of-doors." Wilderness, by this definition, included most of the earth's surface as recently as one hundred years ago. Today, as the global human population rapidly approaches six billion, wilderness is rapidly disappearing. Most modern Americans live their entire lives with no real experience of wilderness.

Many of us, however, still dimly recognize the wilderness as home, and we feel comfortable there. After all, the land that "generally appears to have been affected primarily by the forces of nature, with the imprint of man's work substantially unnoticeable" [3] is the environment in which all forms of life have evolved over eons. In this chapter we'll explore some of the reasons why wilderness is important and worth preserving, and discover how our ethical sensibilities—

our codes of behavior—are crucial to its preservation.

First, let's identify several "practical" reasons for preserving wilderness areas:

• *Scientific value.* Wilderness areas are invaluable as laboratories for scientific study in many disciplines. From an ecologist's point of view, for instance, a thorough understanding of undisturbed ecosystems is essential in the effort to recognize and hopefully stem the tide of human-induced species extinctions. The wilderness environment provides an absolute standard to which we can compare the health, or deterioration, of the particular environments we live in.

• *Archaeological value.* Humans once occupied some areas that today are uninhabited. Preserving such areas for current or future study keeps open the possibility of understanding cultures that preceded ours.

• *Wilderness as a storehouse.* Wilderness areas are storehouses of genes. Genetic diversity keeps ecosystems functioning properly. Plants, in particular, are important sources of raw material for future agricultural and pharmaceutical applications.[4]

• *Wilderness as a playground.* Wilderness areas are inherently fun and challenging in their capacity as natural playgrounds or gymnasiums. As an alternative to structured exercise, we can hike a canyon, climb a peak, tour a river by kayak, or explore the woods. The psychological confidence acquired on a wilderness trek often carries over into other areas of life as well.

These practical reasons aren't the only good reasons for wilderness preservation. In a philosophical context,

---

[1] Whipple, J.T., *Study Out the Land.*

[2] The Wilderness Act of 1964 was the first major act of the U.S. Congress to reserve large plots of undeveloped land as federal wilderness areas. Before that, certain lands were set aside as "primitive areas," but there were no officially designated and protected wilderness areas.

[3] Wilderness Act of 1964.

[4] Human-induced species extinctions are now estimated to be occurring at more than ten thousand times the normal (evolution-driven) rate of extinction. The biggest culprit is the expansion of the human population and the consequent usurpation of habitat.

wilderness—and all that is in it—is part of the creative force which has produced everything that exists. Our culture, our thought, and even our technological ability ultimately derive from the creative force that also manifests itself as wilderness. We can call that force "God," "nature," "evolution," "Gaia," or any number of other names. But no matter what we call it, it created us all. We, and all plants, animals, and inanimate matter are brothers and sisters in the family of creation, connected at junctures in the streams of evolution.

Most of us can best appreciate our connections with nature when we're cut off from the human-altered world. Wilderness is a cathedral, a sacred space—a spiritual state of mind—in which we can acknowledge, appreciate, and thus honor the creative force to which we are intimately bound. We become, in a sense, more complete.

Metaphorically our individual identities are like discrete droplets in the spray cast off by an ocean wave. Any drop separate from the larger body of water has an individual identity. *If* it had self-consciousness (which humans have achieved) it might experience fear, hope, suffering, success, defeat, and possibly love while in that state of separation. But the drop soon coalesces with the creative force from which it emerged, becoming again an integral part of the larger whole.[5]

In the cathedral of wilderness, it is not uncommon to reach a clear awareness of what we have recently come from, and of what we will soon return to. As John Muir put it, "I only went out for a walk, and finally concluded to stay out till sundown, for going out, I found, was really going in."

Despite our deep roots within the whole of nature, humans have evolved into something quite distinct from Earth's other inhabitants. Only humans need ethics.[6] This is because we are social animals. Our survival depends on the existence of societies, and societies depend on cooperative behavior. Other social animals behave socially because they have virtually no choice but to do so. Behavior essential to their existence is genetically programmed. This was true for *homo sapiens'* ancestors as well. But we acquired the ability to choose, which released us from many genetically determined behaviors. As our behavior became increasingly subject to conscious control, rules evolved—particularly for those types of behavior necessary for social living, and thus for survival. Ethics filled the void created by the power of choice.

Ethical regulation in the past centered on social behaviors necessary for the existence of clans, tribes and nations, with disregard for the welfare of other societies or other species. That made sense when the only behavior threatening to the continued existence of the human species was that which endangered the stability of social life.

Today it's not hard to imagine how the inappropriate use of technology could so radically alter the biosphere that Earth could become incapable of supporting future generations of human beings. Of course, most humans have not and are not intentionally trying to damage the biosphere. But it's now clear that the unintended consequences of some applications of technology have been wreaking environmental havoc around the world. There's a new category of human action, different from

---

[5] This metaphor has been adapted from a common Zen concept.

[6] The term "ethics" has different uses. One use is to refer to an area of study, commonly regarded as an area of philosophy. Thus one might take a college philosophy course dealing with ethics and study the ethical theories of major philosophers. Another use is to designate specific evaluations of types of conduct, as when one speaks of business ethics, or of ethics in government. The term is used in both senses in this chapter.

those threatening our ability to live in societies, which may directly influence our survival.

Previous generations of human beings never realized that mistreatment of the physical environment could lead to self-extinction. Consequently, there was no eleventh commandment "Thou shalt not place personal convenience, comfort, or profit over the health of the biosphere." When the Ten Commandments and other moral precepts were recorded, it was neither possible nor even imaginable that human actions could so damage the environment that it might become incapable of supporting future generations.

Einstein wrote, "Our world faces a crisis as yet unperceived by those possessing the power to make great decisions for good or evil. The unleashed power of the atom has changed everything save our modes of thinking, and thus we drift towards unparalleled catastrophe... A new type of thinking is essential if mankind is to survive."[7]

That new kind of thinking should take into account two salient facts: The first is our exponentially increasing technological power. Even if we don't have an unparalleled catastrophe, misapplied technology today may well affect the environment for generations. The second is our explosive population growth. In a ten-year span, at the current rate, the number of humans in the world *increases* by a number greater than the total global population at the time of the American Revolution. The increase in human population is squeezing gorillas, cougars, pandas, tigers, eagles, and millions of other organisms out of existence. Our sheer numbers place limits on what used to be ordinary behavior. Our ethical viewpoint must change to acknowledge these limits.

An essential feature of ethical thinking is the realization that *what is all right for one person to do must also be all right for other people unless there is some reason for distinguishing their respective actions.* For example, if in the wilderness it is acceptable for you to wash your dishes in a running stream, hide trash at a campsite, or cut corners when hiking a trail, it must also be allowable for other people to do the same things. When we use consequences of actions as a basis for determining the ethics of actions, we cannot just consider the rather negligible consequences of only one person doing the action. What may be negligible consequences arising from an individual action can become immensely harmful when a hundred or a thousand people repeat the action.

A hundred years ago, a camper could cut brush for a campfire, remove tall grasses and saplings to make camp beside a stream, and wash up in the clear, flowing water. The camper would expect that a few others might repeat the same actions in the same area in a year's time, with no appreciable harm done. The natural environment has sufficient regenerative power to heal the wounds inflicted by a few people each year changing things around for the sake of their personal comfort.[8] But if the number of people likely to camp in the same area each year jumps to a dozen, a hundred, or a thousand, the cumulative impact may be well beyond the regenerative powers of the natural environment. Even John Muir, a pioneer in the realm of wilderness ethics, would need to alter his wilderness behavior were he to camp today where he camped less than a century ago.

This is why it's so important to observe rules for hiking or camping in park and wilderness areas—even if the

---

[7] Quoted by O. Nathan and H. Nordin (eds.), *Einstein on Peace.*

[8] This does not mean there would be no evidence of people having been there. Desert environments heal even the smallest scars very slowly.

rules don't seem to be applicable in individual cases. The seemingly negligible effect of one harmful action introduces a moral dilemma: If it is all right for you to bend the rules, it is also okay for others.

As usage of parks and wilderness areas soars, managers are forced to impose unpopular regulations to minimize the cumulative impact of large numbers of people. We will surely see more of this—permit systems, trailhead quotas, and rules regulating actions as personal as toilet behavior and as sacrosanct as building a campfire.[9]

Of course, even if there are no official rules imposed on the area you visit, you should still regulate your own behavior. Be aware of your own impact, and think especially about the consequences of dozens, or hundreds, of people repeating the same acts.

The staggering numbers of human beings, as well as our advanced technology, provide good reasons for rethinking and recasting traditional ethics. We need an ethic based upon an awareness of the interconnections among all things. John Muir put it nicely: "When we try to pick out anything by itself, we find it hitched to everything else in the universe." This ethic should enhance, not destroy, the creative process of evolution by supporting the web of life. If we temper our actions with concern, and tread lightly upon our delicate and beautiful natural world, we can carry that same ethic back into our everyday lives.

We must adopt a conscious effort to leave every site we visit in a more pristine condition than it was when we arrived. We can cultivate an attitude of appreciation and respect for each plant and animal whose home we enter or pass through, taking care to disturb them as little as possible. Our respect can extend not only to the natural surroundings, but also to other people we encounter. Our wilderness experience should not diminish the quality of their experience.

In this chapter, we have explored some reasons why wilderness preservation is important, and reviewed the need for a wilderness ethic. In the following chapters you'll find abundant hints on how to apply that ethic.

---

[9] At the time of this writing, the Boy Scouts of America acknowledged population pressures in their announcement that campfires are to be avoided on future Scout outings. The reasons given for this unpopular announcement were similar to the considerations expressed here.

Recommended Reading:

Soft Paths: How to Enjoy the Wilderness Without Harming It
Bruce Hampton and David Cole
Stackpole Books, 1988
   (An excellent account of specific "do's and don't's," covering a wide range of
   outdoor activities.)

How to Shit in the Woods: An Environmentally Sound Approach to a Lost Art
Kathleen Meyer, Ten Speed Press, 1989
   (A lighthearted, but serious account of how to take care of toilet needs while
   enjoying the outdoors.)

Wilderness As Sacred Space
Linda H. Graber
Monograph Series, Association of American Geographers, 1976

Chapter 3

Physical Conditioning

Mary Engles

"He who rests, rots."

—Andrew Taylor Still
(founder of American Osteopathy)

It's a wonderful feeling to be strong and enduring—to trek up a steep ridge or down a boulder-tossed canyon with the greatest of ease. On the other hand, it's not much fun to set out on a hiking or backpack trip, only to realize part of the way through that you're in pain or too fatigued to enjoy the rest of the trip. So, don't use your first backpacking trip to get in shape—be ready before you go!

With today's emphasis on sports and fitness, many people are already pursuing some sort of regular exercise program. Fitness is "priority one" for some; others slack off during busy periods or during the winter months. Regardless of your particular situation, you can only start to improve from where you are right now. In this chapter you'll learn how to gauge your present physical condition, and discover some of the ways to attain or maintain the level of conditioning you desire.

Wilderness travel involves *aerobic* exercise. While exercising aerobically, your heart beats faster and you breathe more rapidly to satisfy the energy demands of your muscles. Aerobic exercise does not consist of short-duration bursts of energy that leave you "out of breath," but rather of longer periods of sustained energy output. You must increase your heart and your breathing on a regular basis to improve your aerobic capacity. That means getting your heart pounding and those lungs working several times weekly.

First, let's see what condition your "condition" is in. Good indicators of aerobic fitness are:

• resting morning heart rate of 60 beats per minute or less.
• stable morning weight.
• stable and repeatable "12-minute test."
• rapid return to normal heart rate after exercise.

The 12-minute test[1], developed by Dr. Kenneth Cooper in the 1960s, is one yardstick by which you can measure your aerobic fitness. It refers to how far you can walk, run, or jog in 12 minutes (see Table 3-1). For example, if you can cover 1.25 to 1.49 miles in 12 minutes you are considered to be in "fair" condition. At this point you may need about 10 weeks of regular aerobic exercise to get into "good" condition. "Good" means that you can cover 1.50 to 1.74 miles in 12 minutes. At that point, you're ready for most kinds of vigorous activity, and a maintenance program may be all that you need to stay in that condition.

A still-higher level of conditioning may be required if your goal is to tackle the likes of Mount Whitney. At high altitudes, your lungs and heart are under greater stress due to the reduced oxygen content in the air. And because of the long distances and steep climbing required for such a feat, you'll need more than just the ability to run for 12 minutes. Your training program would in that case include occasional sessions involving moderate to vigorous exercise lasting for a number of hours. Long-duration exercise, coupled with frequent, short exercise sessions, will help you attain your highest level of fitness.

If you're under 35, and free of significant risk factors (like smoking, high blood pressure, elevated cholesterol, hereditary heart disease), you can begin an exercise program without medical testing. Even so, you should progress slowly and be alert to the development of unusual signs and symptoms. Beyond age 45, you should have a "maximal exercise" (treadmill) test under professional supervision before embarking on any strenuous exercise program.[2]

---

[1] *Aerobics*, Kenneth Cooper, Bantam Books, 1968.

[2] American College of Sports Medicine: Guidelines for Exercise Testing and Prescription, 3rd edition, Lea & Febiger, 1986.

IF YOU CAN COVER IN 12 MINUTES	YOU ARE IN FITNESS CATEGORY
Less than 1.0 mile	Very Poor
1.0 to 1.24 miles	Poor
1.25 to 1.49 miles	Fair
1.50 to 1.74 miles	Good
1.75 miles or more	Excellent

Table 3-1: Kenneth Cooper's 12-minute test

Contrary to popular belief, you do not have different sets of muscles for different exercise activities. You use the same muscles in different ways and in different amounts. However, exercise does have a very specific effect on those muscles. The best way to improve your ability to hike up hills is to hike up hills on a regular basis. Not all of us live in places where this is possible or convenient, but there are alternatives. Some folks like to jog or take brisk walks regularly. Even donning a full daypack and taking a brisk walk at noon or before or after work can improve your aerobic capacity immensely.

In the broader arena of activities, any rhythmic action maintained for a prolonged period that involves large muscle groups (the legs, for example) is beneficial. Some examples are swimming, skating, bicycling, jogging, rowing, and cross-country skiing. Stop-and-start sports such as tennis, racquetball, and basketball are also effective if maintained for longer periods. The important thing is to do something regularly that increases your heart rate and breathing.

Your regular and frequent exercise sessions (as opposed to the occasional very long sessions that will prepare you for major expeditions) should be repeated at least three times per week and last for 20 to 30 minutes. During those sessions, you should aim for a level of activity that is within your personal "training zone." Figure 3-1 will help you determine the "training-sensitive" range of your heart rate for these sessions.

Your heart rate can be quickly determined by feeling your pulse in your wrist (or elsewhere) and counting the number of beats in 10 seconds as indicated by a digital or sweep-second-hand watch. Multiply the number of beats by six to find the number of beats per minute. For example, if you're 40 years old, you should keep your heart pumping at between 21 and 27 beats every 10 seconds, which corresponds to 126 to 162 beats per minute.

Before you start exercising, you'll need to consider any aches, pains, or other problems you now have. Some of these problems may be helped by exercise and some may be worsened unless remedial measures are taken. Lower back or knee pain, for example, can be eased by the strength and range of motion gained with exercise, or it may be intensified as a result of a particular kind of action that disagrees with you (like running on hard surfaces, going downhill, or twisting your body to put on or take off a heavy backpack). If you know you have a problem, check with an appropriate health professional for some preventative measures before attempting any strenuous workouts. Talk with sports-minded people or with those who have been injured to find an orthopedist or sports-oriented physician or physical therapist. Professionals such as these can assist you with a strengthening program that addresses your specific problem.

Regardless of any problem areas, you'll need to strengthen the large muscle groups of the buttocks, thighs, calves, abdomen, and back to be in peak condition for a backpack trip. The abdominals are particularly important as they help support the lower back. A program can be designed for you to carry out at a local fitness club or at home. You can use weights or exercise machines. You can climb steps or walk inclines at increasing speed to prepare for the elevation gains and losses inherent in mountaineering. Strengthening the shoulder and chest muscles will help you support the dead weight of a full backpack.

Muscle-strengthening exercise tends to tighten the muscles. The antidote is stretching—both before and after a workout. Stretching improves your leg and back flexibility and reduces your susceptibility to musculoskeletal injury. Good flexibility also maximizes your ability to climb over rocks, hop small streams, and stretch where you need to without fear of injury. When out in the wilderness, don't leave your stretching routines at home. Stretching should be part of your wake-up ritual on trips, especially on those beautiful, cold mornings in the mountains when you emerge

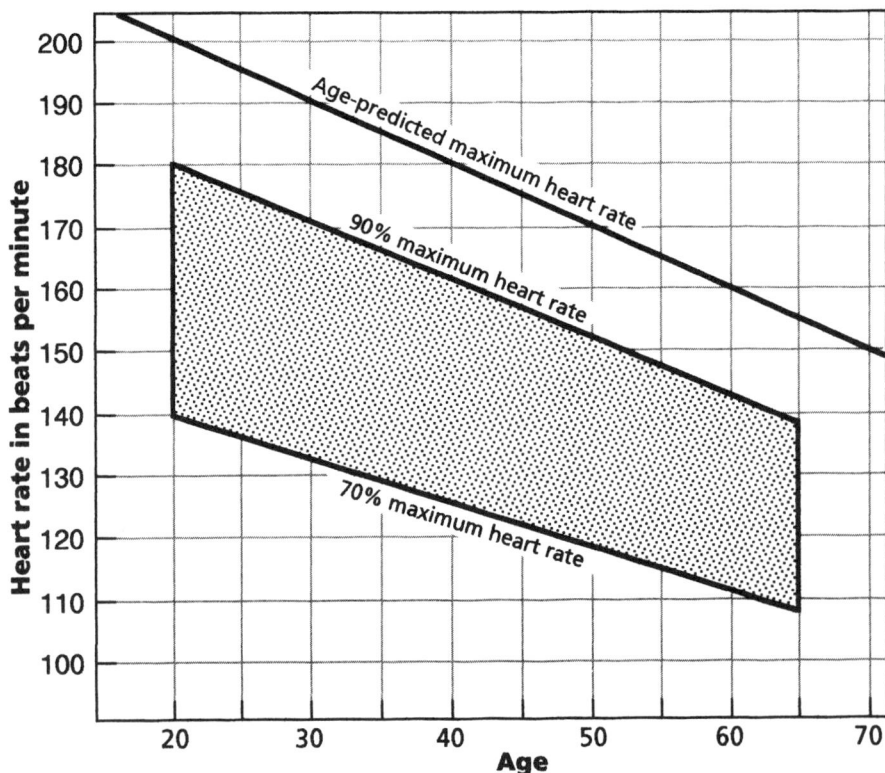

Figure 3-1: Your target heart rate for aerobic exercise should fall within the shaded range shown. This graph assumes that your maximum heart rate is 220 minus your age, and that aerobic exercise (for 20 to 30 minute periods is most effective in the range of 70 to 90 percent of your maximum heart rate.

from your warm sleeping bag. Browse through the illustrations in this chapter, or use Bob Anderson's book *Stretching* as a guide.

Your feet deserve some special attention before you begin your program and before you encase them in those hiking boots! Lubricate your skin with lanolin (unless you're allergic to it), file calluses with an emery board or pumice stone, and keep your nails clean and trimmed.

When you select a boot, you should know your foot type. Do you have a high arch, or is your foot "flat"? Are your feet flexible or rigid? Also be

Lower back "pressure reliever"

Hamstring stretch

Lower back stretch

Inner thigh/adductor stretch

Hip/gluteal muscle stretch

Side stretch

aware of the kind of terrain you'll be hiking. Not every foot or situation demands a stiff, high-top leather boot.

If your feet are subject to pronation (inward rotation at the ankle) or other irregularites of motion, you may need an orthotic (shoe-insert) device. A qualified health professional, such as a podiatrist or physical therapist specializing in foot problems, can help you solve your problems as well as help with boot selection.

One final note—an important caveat. Don't pretend you can whip yourself into shape in the last two weeks before a strenuous trip. Last-minute, rigorous exercise will surely deplete your body's energy stores and leave you too exhausted to enjoy the trip. Instead, do as marathoners do: train vigorously for 10 weeks, then ease off on the training for seven to ten days before the big event. A short period of rest on top of a good training base will have you literally exploding from the starting line . . . er, trailhead.

Good luck with your fitness program!

Recommended Reading:

Aerobics, Kenneth H. Cooper, Bantam Books, 1968.
(A classic work on aerobic testing and conditioning.)

Stretching, Bob Anderson, Shulter Publications, 1981.
(A well-illustrated reference with stretching exercises for various activities.)

The Complete Book of Running, James F. Fixx, Random House, 1976.
(Well-researched, practical, and easily read advice on running and sports performance.)

Training for Sport and Activity: The Physiological Basis of the Conditioning Process, Jack H. Willmore, Allyn & Bacon, 1982.
(A technical, but readable explanation of the body's response to physical activity.)

Neck/shoulder stretch

Calf stretch

Thigh/quadriceps stretch

Chapter 4

Trip Preparation

Dave Moser

"To me, adventure is planning to deal with whatever nature deals you"

—Galen Rowell

P lanning a trip can be almost as much fun as the trip itself. Reading books and spreading maps on the floor gives you a thrill of anticipation. The time and effort you put into your plans will result in greater enjoyment and increased safety.

Although most of this chapter applies to trips of overnight or longer duration, you can benefit by carefully planning even a short day hike. Some of the material below is geared to those in a leadership role. Even if you never take on the responsibility of guiding a large group, you'll profit by a knowledge of the detailed planning incumbent on the leader.

RESEARCHING THE TRIP

To help you plan your trip, rely on four primary resources: friends, guidebooks, maps, and rangers.

The first and most obvious resource is your friends. Wisdom gained by experience is the best kind. Ask them which areas they liked the best. Ask them how difficult each trip was, and whether they would do things differently another time around. If you want to get a second opinion, get the names and phone numbers of others who have visited the same areas.

Of the dozens of guidebooks published for wilderness areas in the West, there's probably one or more just right for the area or region you'd like to visit. Keep in mind, however, that conditions and trails may have changed since the books were written. Note copyright dates and verify information with the local authorities. You may want to follow up on some of the books and articles that are listed in the bibliography or "recommended reading" appendix of some guidebooks.

Obtain detailed maps of the area so that you can meticulously follow any verbal or printed description of a trip you want to take. Road maps, especially county maps, are good for showing the

major and minor roads leading to the trailhead. Topographic maps allow you to visualize in great detail the topography and trails of the area you plan to explore. Different maps will show different features of the same area, so try to obtain as many as possible. Remember that even the most current maps may not show the newer trails, and that existing trails can become eroded or overgrown so as to be unusable. Outdated maps are not necessarily useless—they may indicate old mines, defunct trails, historic towns, and other features erased from the newer maps that you may want to explore. A complete research effort might involve a trip to a public or university library for a look at old maps in the historical collection.

Rangers are another excellent source of information and are generally helpful. However, you should do some homework before contacting a ranger so you can ask intelligent questions. A "cold" call to a ranger asking for a good place to hike may waste both your time and the ranger's. When calling a ranger, have your maps and guidebooks in front of you. Ask to speak with someone who is familiar with the specific area you plan to visit. The office worker who answers the phone may not have the information you need. You may have to wait for a backcountry ranger to return your call, but the information will be worth the wait. Describe your plans and don't hesitate to ask for any additional information or suggestions. In some instances, the ranger may recommend an alternate trail that would better suit your needs.

If you're the trip leader, it's best to scout the trip in advance. That way you'll get first-hand information on road and trail conditions and the availability of water. Make notes on your maps for further reference. You may discover an interesting side trip, or you might end up deciding the trip is somehow not appropriate for the group you intend to lead.

DESIGNING THE TRIP

Designing a trip itinerary is exciting! Using your topographic map, you can mentally "walk" along and visualize your intended route. Take the time to study and "see" the elevation gains and losses, the distances to be traveled, the meadows, lakes, forests, and other features. Identify the best overlooks and the best spots for lunch or snack breaks. When choosing camp sites, try to visualize where the sun will rise and set. In a similar vein, you may want to plan your trip around a full moon. Or go when the moon is new to enjoy zillions of stars in an inky black sky. Consult an almanac or calendar to determine the moon's phase and the times it rises and sets.

Rather than having to retrace your steps on the trip, try to design a loop route. Or you can design a point-to-point trip using a car-shuttle or a drop-off-and-pick-up service. Using these strategies you can enjoy twice as much scenery as you would on an out-and-back trip.

When deciding how many cars it will take to carry people and gear, keep in mind that backpack equipment takes up a lot of space. Most compact cars can carry only two people and two backpacks. If someone in your group has a van or pickup truck, consider using it to haul the bulky gear while the participants ride in passenger cars. If you employ a car shuttle for point-to-point trips, remember that everything and everyone may have to fit into half the vehicles.

For a long drive to a distant trailhead, include time for rest breaks or meal stops at least every couple of hours or so. Plan to arrive early enough so you can get plenty of sleep before hiking in. If caravaning, CB radios can be very helpful. If you don't have a CB, try to borrow one—they can be installed quickly and easily. You can chat on the way, reducing the boredom of a long drive. If one vehicle needs to pull over, other drivers can be easily notified. You can also make decisions about when to stop for lunch, whether to take side trips, and the like. (Note: In Mexico you need a permit to operate a CB. Call your local Mexican Consulate.) Always carry extra water in the car on extended drives.

Anticipate what the weather will be like on the trip. You should know, for example, that snow flurries can occur above timberline in July and August. Or that the desert winds can hit 50 miles per hour or more anytime. Rivers swollen with snowmelt can be a problem in the mountains in spring and early summer. Sudden rains may turn dirt roads into quagmires of mud. Flash floods may lash the desert and canyon country during the thunderstorm season. Discuss any potential hazards with the rangers. A call to knowledgeable folks at the area's local weather bureau can result in a wealth of information. Hope for the best, but plan for any eventuality.

How much water will you have to carry? That depends on where the nearest streams are and whether or not they are flowing. Check this out with the ranger when you call. Decide how you'll treat the water. Some trips may require caches of water (and/or food) placed in advance. These supplies must be well hidden, animal-proofed, and protected from the elements. Leave a note, with date indicated, stating that you are depending on these supplies for your survival. If your trailhead is remote, you may want to leave some food and water in your vehicle (except in bear country).

When hiking at altitudes over 6000 feet, most people benefit from an acclimation period just before. A day or two spent at high altitude usually does the trick. Do some walking or easy hiking to adjust your body to the thinner air.

To organize all the details of your trip, develop a complete itinerary starting with the departure. List times and places, and allow a little slack for unforeseen circumstances. Consider the abilities of the slower participants when estimating times of arrival. Plan to arrive at camp with some daylight left. Much of the pertinent planning data can be summarized on the sample Trip Planning form on the opposite page.

PERMITS AND REGULATIONS

Permits are required for entry—day use and camping—into most of the federally designated wilderness areas (some require permits for overnight camping only). Many nonwilderness national parks and forests require camping permits as well. The permit system serves several purposes. In some cases it is used to limit the number of people using a particular area. That helps lessen the impact of too many people, and guarantees a better wilderness experience for visitors. Also, in going through the permit process, wilderness users are notified of the appropriate regulations. By issuing permits, agencies can collect data needed to carry out effective management of the area in question. Finally, permits allow the authorities to keep tabs on your whereabouts in case of an emergency.

Permit policies vary widely. Whereas in most areas permits are free, some agencies do charge a reservation fee. Permits for visiting many parts of the Sierra Nevada now require a $3 fee. Find out, well in advance, what the permit policy is for the area you're interested in. Permits are usually obtained by mail or in person. Sometimes permits can be issued as the result of a phone call. Guidebooks usually cover the nuts and bolts of permit application, but make sure the information is current.

Quite often, the key to getting the permit you want is to apply early. Permits for the most popular wilderness and park areas may become available only during a very limited time several months in advance. Some are granted "first-come, first-served" on a postmark basis; other permits are granted by lottery. Be flexible about dates of entry, and try to avoid the most popular days—Friday and Saturday. Consider group-size restrictions before you invite group-size restrictions before you invite too many of your friends or accept too many participants. If all else fails, remember that many areas reserve a fraction of their permits for people who seek them on the day of entry. You may have a second chance if you missed the first time around (although a lot of your effort in planning can go down the drain if you fail to get one).

Fire regulations vary widely in the western recreation areas. In some, campfire permits are required; in others campfires are banned altogether because of wildfire hazards or a scarcity of fuelwood. Some jurisdictions allow fires as long as you bring in your own wood. Wild areas in Southern California may have various fire restrictions imposed on them during the hot and dry summer and fall seasons. During extremely hazardous conditions, visitors may be prohibited from using any open-flame device at all, or they may be prohibited outright from entering certain areas. Although they're a traditional part of the outdoor experience, campfires are not always needed for comfort, especially in summer. Campfires draw attention inward to a small world only a few feet across; while the lack of a campfire opens up to sight and mind the infinite majesty of the night sky.

CHOOSING TRIP COMPANIONS

If you're the leader, and you aren't familiar with the prospective participants, it's your responsibility to screen them. Each person should have the proper equipment and skills. Each should be in good physical condition and possess the confidence and attitude necessary to handle the trip without depending unduly on other members of the party. In evaluating a large number of prospective participants, the use of a questionnaire is a good idea. Query them on:

- Their regular exercise program.
- Similar trips they've taken in the past.
- Equipment owned or available.
- Physical limitations or medical disorders that may affect their performance.

TRIP PLANNING SHEET

AREA _____   DATES _____

Personal Contacts	Phone	Comments

Road Maps _____   Trail Maps _____

_____   _____

Guidebooks	Date	Comments

Rangers	Phone	Comments

Permit Requirements _____

Maximum Group Size _____   Fires Allowed? _____

Water Availability _____

Weather Bureau Location _____   Phone _____

	DAY										
	1	2	3	4	5	6	7	8	9	10	Total
Destination											
Elev. Gain/Loss											
Mileage											
Hiking Time											
Sun Rises											
Sun Sets											
Moon Rises											
Moon Sets											
Phase											

A sample Participant Information form appears on the opposite page. You can screen participants initially over the phone. At the planning meeting (see next section) you can do more screening. Even after someone has been accepted for an outing, something could come up that would change that status. A participant's recent injury or illness might be reason for you to carefully reconsider their participation. It's your duty as leader to continue screening right up to the beginning of the trip. Dropping an obviously unqualified individual is both fair to the group, and fair to the individual who might otherwise end up having a miserable time. If the trip is to be a backpack over rough terrain, effective screening might include a pre-trip day hike over a similar kind of terrain. Those who seem to be having trouble should be informed gently that the trip is not for them.

PLANNING MEETING

Planning meetings are effective for almost all trips, especially those lasting two or more days. At the very least, the participants get to know one another beforehand. During the meeting the leader explains the general trip plan and the objectives including the
• driving route
• hiking route
• number of miles hiked each day
• elevation gains and losses

The following details should also be worked out:
• car pools/drivers
• equipment sharing—tents, stoves, etc
• cook groups or "central commissary" (all share in the same menu and cooking/cleaning responsibilities)
• food purchases; participants' dietary restrictions
• sharing of costs

All participants must understand what the trip entails and acknowledge that it's something they want to do. The leader should encourage questions and discussion. The following checklists and printed information should be passed out:
• trip description or summary
• itinerary
• map of the driving route
• map of the hiking route (USGS topographic and other government maps can be photocopied without violating copyright laws)
• list of the required and/or optional maps (if maps aren't provided)
• water requirements
• equipment required
• important phone numbers; numbers to call in case of an emergency

The more of this the leader puts on paper, the more prepared the participants will be before the trip.

Leaders should also collect the following information about each participant for use in the event of an emergency:
• name and address of a contact person
• name and phone number of personal physician
• disclosure of medical conditions or allergies that may affect participant's welfare
• current medications
• health insurance company and policy number

The above items are included on the Participant Information form on the opposite page.

At the planning meeting, drivers should be reminded to take along an extra car key. That simple precaution could save the group countless hours of wasted time. The extra key can be hidden outside the car or carried along on the trip in a secure place separate from the driver's key ring. Someone else in the party can be told where the extra key is located so that he or she can drive the car if necessary. Before leaving, all drivers must have their vehicles checked to be sure they are in good working order.

PARTICIPANT INFORMATION

Name _____

Address _____

Birthdate _____   Phone _____   (home)

_____   (work)

Regular Exercise Program _____

_____

_____

Recent Trip Experience:

Location	Dates	Reference	Phone

Physical Disorders _____

Allergies _____

Medications _____

Physician's Name _____   Phone _____

Health Insurance Company _____

Policy Number _____

In Emergency, Contact:

Name _____

Address _____

Phone _____   Relationship _____

We're all forgetful to some degree, which is why a checklist is a must for every participant. The leader can hand out a list of special equipment needed, but it's up to every participant to develop his or her own own personal list. After every trip taken, add to the list any items you wish you had taken. You'll end up eventually with a very long list—too much for any one trip—but a least you won't overlook anything on future trips. It's also helpful to include the weight of each item on your list. That way you can make make intelligent decisions when it comes time for the inevitable task of deleting nonessential items that are too heavy or bulky to carry.

SAFETY

While safety is everyone's business, there are several things the leader can do to assure that trip participants are prepared in the event of an emergency.

Familiarize everyone with the location of the nearest emergency telephones, and the appropriate emergency numbers. In addition to 911, this would include the numbers for the nearest sheriff, ranger, and fire department. An awareness of evacuation routes is invaluable in the event of an emergency.

Tell someone where you are going, when you expect to return, and what to do if you don't return on time. This is vitally important if you'll be hiking alone. Be sure that you tell someone you can depend on. While it may be a good idea to give a ranger your itinerary, rangers are accustomed to people who forget to check in when they return. It's best to leave full written details with the folks back home. You should include phone numbers of the local sheriff and appropriate rangers, vehicle descriptions, and license numbers. Ask them to report you missing if you are not back by a certain time.

LAST-MINUTE DETAILS

Some things can't be done until the final day or hours before the trip starts. Fill up the gas tank. Check under the hood. Check the weather—call a ranger or the weather bureau nearest the area you're going to visit. If the weather's been nasty, ask the ranger about trail damage and hazardous stream crossings. Check road conditions by calling your auto club or your state's highway patrol.

On some trips, you must sign in and sign out at a ranger station. After the trip, don't forget to sign out! If you don't, you may be responsible for an unnecessary search effort.

Finally, if you notice anything during your trip that the authorities should know about, be sure to report it. Those who follow in your footsteps may have a better wilderness experience because of it.

Chapter 5

Outfitting:
The Basic Equipment

Jan Craven and Mike Fry

*"A Book of Verses underneath the Bough,
A Jug of Wine, a loaf of bread—and Thou
Beside me singing in the Wilderness—
Oh, Wilderness were Paradise enow!"*

—The *Rubaiyat* of Omar Khayyam

L ife is basic, simple, and clear in the wilderness. A minimalist existence—making do with the least possible possessions—renews a weary spirit and reveals simple pleasures neglected in our hurried lives.

In the wilderness we can: Gaze at the silent stars. Listen to a bird's solo recital. Watch the pogo-stick ballet of a deer. Marvel at the wondrous forms and colors of the flowers, rocks, meadows, valleys, and forests. Concentrate on a thought without interruption. Dream a dream through to its end. Appreciate the sharing of a simple meal cooked over a tiny stove—a culinary masterpiece even with a few twigs or grains of sand thrown in. Listen for the mouth-watering call that energizes even the most weary of campers, "Hot water!"

Such idyllic experiences amidst nature require either lots of luck or careful preparation. This chapter, like the last one, focuses on preparation, not luck. Good choices of equipment are an integral part of preparation for a trip.

NEEDS AND PREFERENCES

Seasoned wilderness travelers always strive to pack the least and the lightest gear that can ensure their survival and comfort. The core items, or essentials, include those items necessary to achieve a reasonable measure of safety and comfort in the event of a delay or an emergency. The particular items considered essential will vary depending on where, when, and how long a trip is, but each essential item would fall into one of the 10 categories listed below.[1] Use the ESSENTIALS mnemonic to help you remember them:

Emergencies

Sustenance

Shelter

Extras

Navigation

---

[1] Many people are familiar with an earlier scheme called the "10 essentials." This list of items consists of: map of area, compass, flashlight with extra bulb and batteries, sunglasses, extra clothing, extra food and water, pocket knife, candle or fire-starter, first-aid kit, and waterproof matches.

Toiletries

 Incidentals

Attitude

 Light

Something to
carry all of it in

Emergencies
- Waterproof matches
- Candle—or flammable material (to assist in starting a stove or fire under adverse conditions)
- First aid kit (don't forget foot care)
- Whistle and/or signal mirror

Sustenance
- Food (including cooking gear if appropriate) to meet planned itinerary
- Water, and/or water-purification device

Shelter
- Sun protection: Sunglasses, hat, sunscreen
- Rain- and wind-resistant outer clothing
- Clothing for expected temperatures
- Footwear appropriate for the terrain
- Overnight gear (sleeping bag, pad, tent)

Extras
- *Extra* food
- *Extra* water
- *Extra* warm clothing

Navigation
- Map(s) of the area
- Compass
- Pencil and straight-edge
- Altimeter (if needed for critical navigation)

Toiletries
- Toilet paper
- Trowel (to bury solid waste)
- Sanitation/personal items

Incidentals
- Knife
- Nylon cord (for securing items or holding a delaminated shoe or boot together)
- Needle and thread or dental floss (for mending cloth, eyeglass frames, etc.)

Attitude
• A *positive* attitude—the ultimate essential!

Light
• Flashlight with fresh batteries
• Extra batteries and spare bulb

Something to carry all of it in
• Fanny pack, daypack, or backpack
• Stuff sacks (for compressing bulky items and organizing gear)

Essential equipment prepares you for the unexpected. If you do encounter adverse conditions on a trip, then having the right equipment will keep you comfortable. In the worst of circumstances, the essentials can mean the difference between a safe outcome and a tragic one. Never lighten the load you carry at the expense of essentials, lest you threaten your safety and that of others in your group.

How to fill your list of essentials, as well as non-essentials, for a given trip is up to you. Your personal preferences will change with time as you gain experience.

KEEPING THINGS LIGHT

A loaf of bread and a heavy coat equipped John Muir. He toughed out the elements, lived off the land, trusted the water, and was so at home in the wilderness he couldn't conceive of being lost. Times have changed, and so have our needs and desires.

When camping out of a vehicle, there's almost no limitation on the weight of gear. Just stuff everything in and go. But when your RV of choice is boots and backpack, every ounce counts. One of the challenges of backpacking and hiking is minimizing the weight you carry. Weight must be considered for every purchase you make. When packing for a trip you can use a small food scale to weigh and evaluate items. Ounces add up fast! Be clever and let one item serve multiple functions. A stuff sack can double as a pil-

low case, and your extra clothes can be the stuffing. Your rain parka can serve as a wind jacket, your cooking pot can be your bowl, and your bandana can play the role of towel, napkin, bandage, and dust shield.

Pack only the amount of sunscreen, contact-lens solution, or peanut butter you're likely to use on the trip. Eat breakfast out of the plastic bag that holds your cereal. Don't lug the bottle along with the wine! (Wine and alcoholic beverages are heavy, and a little goes a long way.) Leave the radio behind—you can catch up on the latest scores when you get home. Bring only part of your paperback book if you know you won't read the whole thing. Sleep in your clothes for warmth so you can carry a lighter sleeping bag or tent. But don't get carried away on the quest for lightness—you and every other participant on the trip are responsible for carrying the essential items appropriate for a given trip.

Here are some other ways to keep your load as light as possible:

• Hike with a partner who carries the lion's share and keeps you warm at night
• Share tent, stove, cookware, water purifier, etc., and divide the common load evenly
• Travel where there's abundant water and good weather
• Purchase the lightest equipment available
• Ask other wilderness travelers how they trim their pack weight

Sample Equipment List

FOR DAY HIKES

Wear or carry in pockets

- ❐ Long pants
- ❐ Polypropylene shirt
- ❐ Long-sleeve, light- colored shirt
- ❐ Wool sweater
- ❐ Hat with brim
- ❐ Bandana or handkerchief
- ❐ Hiking shoes or boots
- ❐ Socks—liners and wool socks
- ❐ Sunscreen
- ❐ Sun-protective lip balm
- ❐ Sunglasses
- ❐ Water bottle (in a belt bag)
- ❐ Hiking stick
- ❐ Swiss army knife with file and scissors
- ❐ Compass
- ❐ Wallet or plastic bag with driver's license, credit card, health insurance info, emergency phone numbers, money, coins for phone

Carry in your daypack

- ❐ Shorts
- ❐ Hooded rain jacket and pants
- ❐ Wool hat and mittens
- ❐ Large trash bag (for emergency shelter)
- ❐ Lunch and snacks (along with extra food for delays or emergencies)
- ❐ Water or electrolyte replacement drink
- ❐ First-aid kit
- ❐ Nylon cord
- ❐ Closed-cell foam sit pad
- ❐ Maps
- ❐ Pencil and paper
- ❐ Flashlight with extra batteries and spare bulb
- ❐ Whistle
- ❐ Lighter or waterproof matches, and candle
- ❐ Toilet bag to carry toilet paper, trowel, plastic bags
- ❐ Ditty bag for personal items (*e.g.*, comb, hand lotion, hair barrette, tweezers, moleskin, pain-relief tablets, towellettes.

FOR BACKPACK TRIPS

Add the following to the day hike list on the left. Select gear and quantities appropriate for your planned trip:

- ❐ Frame backpack (also take along a daypack if you will be day hiking away from camp)
- ❐ Tent
- ❐ Sleeping bag
- ❐ Sleeping pad
- ❐ Ground cloth
- ❐ Stove
- ❐ Cook pots
- ❐ Cup, bowl, utensils
- ❐ Water bottles
- ❐ Water purification (filter, disinfectant tablets, or extra fuel for boiling water)
- ❐ Food and beverage powders
- ❐ Larger first-aid kit
- ❐ Safety gear (rope, ice axe) as needed
- ❐ Long underwear
- ❐ Parka
- ❐ Gaiters
- ❐ Mitten overshells
- ❐ Lightweight shoes or booties (to wear in camp)
- ❐ Toothbrush
- ❐ Biodegradable soap
- ❐ Glacier glasses (for snow)
- ❐ Insect repellent

> **Note:** *Not all of the items listed here are essential for all trips. Some trips require less equipment and some trips require more.*

PRODUCTS

Dozens of companies, large and small, manufacture high-quality wilderness gear. Some design for light weight and style as well as function. Check with local stores and read outdoor publications to learn about manufacturers' reputations—the quality of their products, the length of time they've been in business, and their warranty and service capabilities. Check the product labels for specifications, care and cleaning, fit, and guarantees. Ask sales people if their store offers any guarantees beyond those offered by the manufacturer. After you've made a purchase, follow directions carefully to keep the gear performing as intended.

Product Sources

Where you buy your equipment may be just as important as who manufactures it. Your best bet is to purchase from a source that
• is reputable
• has been in business a long time
• offers a product satisfaction guarantee
• has knowledgeable sales people
• offers rental equipment (this is most helpful for a person evaluating gear)

Fortunately, sports and adventure outfitters tend to attract sales people who love the outdoors and try out a lot of the equipment they sell. Mail-order outfits may offer considerable savings, but many don't offer personal service. You can also scan Sierra Club publications and other newsletters and newspapers for bargains. Even the trendiest outfitters have periodic sales to clear out excess stock or demo and rental equipment. Not all your equipment needs to be brand new. Swap meets, thrift stores, and military surplus outlets are all good hunting grounds.

Cost Considerations

When outfitting yourself for the sport of wilderness travel, you may want to prioritize your purchases. The list is short for day-hikers—boots (or the appropriate walking shoes), daypack, and miscellaneous essentials. Accumulating backpacking gear, though, involves major purchases. Fortunately, some of the more expensive items needed for backpacking can be easily borrowed or rented. Personal items such as boots and special clothing are probably first priority, then sleeping bag, pad, and backpack. You may be able to share a stove and cookware for some time before deciding what kinds to buy. A tent is a key purchase—you may want to rent or share one for a while before investing in your own.

Making your own equipment was once an economical way to ensure excellent quality in your gear. It still is—for some—but equipment prices are low compared to the amount of time it takes to create a finished piece of gear. It's really more fun to spend weekends out hiking rather than laboring over a sewing machine. But do keep your needle sharp for repairing or modifying equipment and clothing.

MAJOR PURCHASES

Footwear

During a typical hiking day, your feet hit the ground 10,000 to 20,000 times (about 2,000 steps per mile). Your boots better fit well!

Fortunately, running-shoe technology has spread to hiking boots, and many good choices are available. Lightweight boots are relatively inexpensive, comfortable, and provide enough protection for most uses. Choose ankle-high boots with padded ankle collars. Uppers made of nylon or other synthetic material require almost no "break-in," while leather uppers are more rigid. If you're susceptible to ankle twists or if rougher country dictates the need for more protection against rolling rocks, consider the heavier, all-leather models.

Old-fashioned, heavy leather boots are still necessary for most snow travel and for cross-country travel over very rugged terrain. If technical rock climbing is involved, you may need special close-fitting, high-friction climbing shoes (see Chapter 13). Rigid, plastic boots are appropriate for crampon use when climbing hard snow and ice (see Chapter 14). For any use, though, the primary consideration is fit. The latest technology is useless if the boots hurt your feet. Shop very carefully at a store with a knowledgeable staff. Try on several pair, and accept none if you have any doubts. If you are shopping for other items in addition to boots, go to the footwear department first. When you think you have found the right pair, ask if you can wear the boots in the store while doing your other shopping. The extra time will allow you to better evaluate the fit.

Allow about a half inch of extra toe room. You'll need that for steep downhill hiking when your foot slips forward inside the boot. The heel cup should slide up and down no more than a quarter inch with each step. Bring your own thick socks to the fitting (although good stores will have extras for your use). If you normally use orthotics or special pads in your shoes, bring them too.

No boot can be expected to fit perfectly, so consider these possibilities:
• Will the boot stretch as it "breaks in," or will your foot "break down?" (Note: for leather boots you can wet your socks, wring them out, and then wear them inside your boots as you walk. This may help soften the boot and improve the fit.)
• Can the boot be stretched mechanically in the toe or heel cup areas to improve the fit? (Can you locate a cobbler who will do this?)
• Can the heel cup be padded with glue-in pads to reduce heel slippage?
• Can cushioned insoles added to the boot make a thin, hard sole more tolerable? (They may make boots feel narrower, however.)

If nothing works, you can always purchase custom-made boots. Look in outdoor magazines for boot maker ads.

Ask about resoling before you buy. Even the most durable soles will wear out with time, often well before the boot upper is significantly worn. Some boots can live as many as three lives—at a rather modest additional cost. Inexpensive boots, however, may be worth less than the cost of a resoling.

Most leather boot uppers deserve a periodic treatment with a beeswax-based boot seal. First, warm the wax and boots to about 120°F. You can do this in a prewarmed (not hot) oven, or outside in the sun on a hot day, or with the use of a hair dryer. Brush on the melted wax until it no longer soaks in. This treatment will keep the leather supple and enhance the boots' ability to repel snow and water. Don't use silicone or petroleum products on your boots. They can dissolve the glue that bonds the sole.

Any pair of boots will benefit from an optimum combination of socks. Start with lightweight polypropylene (which keeps moisture away from your feet) and use thick wool as your outer layer. Avoid cotton socks—they trap moisture. In general, two thinner socks used together work better than a single thick one. You may need to add an intermediate layer, or use thicker socks, as your boots stretch with age.

Keeping your feet warm in cold conditions is more a measure of how you enclose them than a measure of your boot's weight. You need full circulation to keep your feet warm, so don't pinch your feet by overloading socks or by over-tightening boot laces. In subfreezing conditions, vapor barriers (moisture-impervious layers) worn close to your feet can be very effective. A vapor barrier (which can be as simple as a bread bag) worn outside an inner polypropylene layer keeps foot perspiration from reaching the outer, insulating sock layer. Gaiters, which are designed to keep snow out of boots, also serve to insulate the ankle area. Even when there is no snow, gaiters are useful in keeping sand particles and pebbles out of boots.

Clothing

Your clothes must shelter your body from sun, wind, rain, and cold— sometimes all in the same day! Each clothing article must continue to function, wet or dry. As you travel, body heat and water vapor (perspiration) must be allowed to escape, while wind and rain are repelled.

Almost every year clothing and fabric manufacturers introduce new high-tech gear and claim everything else is obsolete. Sales clerks and colorful ads push you to spend a fortune on fabrics that wick, breathe, repel, vent, warm, cool, and of course flatter.

The sad truth, however, is that even the best garment can perform well only in a limited range of conditions. The well-equipped wilderness traveler must assemble a lightweight, compact outfit that will do the job, rain or shine. This is done most effectively through the "layering system." That is, each item of clothing should work well with any combination of the others, so that you can quickly adapt to the demands of the environment (or your own heat output) by adding and subtracting layers of clothing. Ideally, you need only adjust the outer layer; if needed, though, you can remove an inner layer.

Outer layers require different kinds of materials than inner layers, so let's now examine the various clothing materials available:

Cotton and silk: These are great for comfort, and fine in warm weather, but not recommended for most cold weather conditions. These materials absorb water readily. When wet, cotton is very slow to dry. Combine cold with wet conditions and they can be deadly. Blue jeans seem ideal for outdoor use—and so they are for dealing with bucking horses and brambles. But jeans, and other heavy cotton items like sweat

shirts, become damp and clammy when the weather turns soggy. On warm, dry days though, thin, light-colored cotton shorts, shirts, and bandanas can keep you comfortably cool.

Wool, polypropylene, and polyester pile: Wool and synthetics like polypropylene and polyester fiberpile ("pile") garments can soak up varying amounts of moisture (wool can retain as much as 100% of its dry weight; synthetics around 30%), but they retain much of their insulating ability even when wet. Oiled wool garments are slow to absorb moisture. Synthetics are easier to wring out in case they do get wet. Both wool and synthetics make good insulating garments.

Down: Down, typically the inner feathers of geese, is a very effective insulator when dry, but completely useless if wet. It is a poor choice for cold and wet conditions.

Water- and wind-impervious materials: Water-impervious, but breathable materials such as Gore-tex have revolutionized the construction of outerwear. These materials contain a thin membrane perforated with tiny pores. In theory, the pores allow water vapor (from perspiration) to pass outward, but resist the passage of liquid water inward. Unfortunately the amount of water vapor these materials can handle at one time is about the same as that exuded by a person at rest. With increasing activity, additional venting is needed. Gore-tex costs more, may weigh more, and is bulkier than a cheaper alternative—coated nylon (nylon material coated with a waterproof, nonbreathable substance). Uncoated nylon can be woven very tightly or treated to block the wind, but not heavy rain.

Vapor barrier materials (like thin plastic) worn close to the skin in very cold conditions may prevent your skin from perspiring excessively. Human skin exudes water vapor not only to cool but also to maintain a moist layer of air just above the skin. Without the barrier, this water vapor moves outward to where it may condense on the outer layers of your clothing. With the barrier in place, humid air is kept close to the skin, so the skin no longer needs to keep pumping out moisture (and heat). Vapor barriers that cover a large part of the body are practical only when you're relatively inactive.

When building your layering system for active sports in cold weather, consider the following:

First layer: The purpose of this layer is to move moisture away from the skin. This layer is normally long underwear, preferably made of polypropylene or polyester. Wool, silk, and cotton absorb too much moisture. Polypropylene has proven itself very effective over the years, but it tends to retain body odors. Polyester is more expensive, is less durable, and has the advantage of staying a little fresher (for the nose at least). For most activities, thin underwear is more versatile than medium or expedition weights. If needed for extreme cold, a vapor barrier can be added on top of the long underwear. Ventilation is extremely important for any vapor barrier used when you are physically active.

Middle layer(s): While the inner layer keeps the skin comfortable, the middle layer provides the bulk insulation needed to protect against the cold. On a trip you may have to adjust the ventilation in this layer a lot as the temperature rises and falls and your activity waxes and wanes. Pile pants and jacket together can offer effective insulation at a cost in weight of only three pounds. For lighter duty, expedition-weight long underwear might suffice (about one pound total). Quilted down or synthetic-fill vests or jackets can be used, but quite often these garments include a heavy shell as well—that cuts down on your versatility. Remember that down is ineffective if it gets wet and slow to dry out. Wool sweaters are good, but they can get heavy when wet and are difficult to dry out.

Outer layer: Under adverse weather conditions, this layer is supremely important. The outer shell of your layering system blocks wind, sheds rain, and re-

pels snow. Adequate ventilation (like zippered openings) must be provided so that plenty of air can reach the middle insulating layer when needed. Coated nylon is relatively cheap, very effective in shedding rain, but difficult to ventilate. In addition, some coatings will survive only a few washings. A low-cost outer-shell system could consist of wind-repellent (uncoated) nylon pants and windbreaker, plus a coated nylon shell of some sort (a two-piece rain suit or one-piece raincoat, cagoule, or anorak). Use the coated garments over the uncoated ones only when rain threatens. (Under warmer storm conditions you could use the coated layer alone.) For adequate ventilation, the coated pants should have full-length side zippers, and jackets full front zippers. Underarm zips may help, but you'll find it's your back that perspires the most. A more expensive (but heavier and bulkier) solution, a parka made of Gore-tex or similar materials, may keep you drier and more comfortable, at least in a light rain. When backpacking with a bulky pack, a coated nylon poncho is sometimes the best solution for rain protection. Ponchos can act like sails in a wind, but you can install and fasten snaps along the edge of the poncho so as to run a tighter ship. Rain chaps used with the poncho can keep your legs dry. Shop carefully for your outer garments; some rain and wind shells contain too many pockets, extras, or styling features that simply add to the weight of what should be a lightweight, functional article of clothing. Remember, too, that some outer garments may need to be seam-sealed. Give extra attention to seams around the pockets, zipper, and hood, which usually have no sealant applied at the factory.

In addition to above layers, you'll also need protection for your head and hands:

Headwear: Did you ever hear the maxim "If your feet are cold, cover your head"? It's true; in fact the whole body benefits when you plug the torrent of heat that leaks skyward from the blood-rich vessels of the head. Under very cold conditions, you can use a layer system here as well. A lightweight balaclava with eye slits when folded down will allow you to recycle warm moisture from the lungs. A second hat or knitted cap will add middle-layer insulation. The outer layer is simply the hood of your parka or other shell. It should have enough of a brim to keep rain off your face. Pulling the drawstring narrows the opening to the face, helping to prevent heat loss. Taking off headwear is the fastest way to cool off if the weather warms. You'll want to do that first before shedding other layers. When the sun shines brightly, however, don't forget to put some kind of hat back on to protect from the sun's radiation.

Handwear: Most knitted gloves and mittens suffice for cold, dry conditions (mittens are usually warmer than gloves). Wet conditions, though, are really a test for handwear. When you're active, water can easily be soaked up inside mittens, but not enough body heat is delivered to your hands to evaporate it. Waterproof mitten shells are a first defense (don't forget to seal the seams). Inside that, thick wool or pile mitts provide insulation. You may also want to have a thin pair of liner gloves for tasks that require some dexterity. You can try vapor-barrier protection as well. Plastic bags or disposable rubber gloves work well—you'll be surprised at the difference they can make. Gloves and mittens are items easily lost on trips. The almost negligible weight of a lightweight extra pair is good insurance.

Sleeping Pads

Sleeping pads are the foundation of your wilderness bed. No sleeping bag will keep you warm on a cold night unless you're thermally insulated from the ground. Thick pads have more insulating ability at the cost of greater weight, bulk, and expense. Short pads (48 inches long or so) are fine for summer camping if you don't mind sacrificing a little comfort, while the standard 72-inch ones are best for winter.

Closed-cell foam pads are excellent insulators, do not absorb water, and come in several varieties. Some have contours and forms that help reduce weight while maintaining as much comfort as possible. In general these are good values in terms of providing excellent insulation for low cost and light weight. (Avoid open-cell foam pads like mattress cushions. They're good for car camping, but they're water-absorbent and too bulky for backpacking.)

Self-inflating pad

Closed-cell foam pad

Self-inflating pads are quite comfortable to sleep on, but more expensive and heavier than closed-cell foam pads of the same thickness. They require more care on the trail to prevent punctures and valve failures (repair kits are available). You can make them last for years if you use a ground cloth underneath them and avoid thorn punctures. The "superlight" one-inch-thick models are more comfortable to sleep on than most closed-cell foam pads. The $1^1/2$-inch-thick self-inflatable is positively blissful, allowing you to sleep comfortably on your side.

For additional sleeping comfort, you can put some extra clothing in your sleeping-bag stuff sack and place it under your knees when sleeping on your back, or under your abdomen when sleeping on your stomach. Any number of soft items can be used as a pillow. If you're using a short pad, place some clothing under your lower legs and feet for extra comfort and insulation.

Sleeping Bags

Don't scrimp on this one. Buy a reputable brand with a lifetime guarantee—your bag could last the rest of your life with moderate use and proper care.

The warmth of a bag depends primarily on the amount of "loft"—the thickness of the insulating layer. The more dead (nonmoving) air there is between you and the environment, the warmer the bag seems. Another factor is the style (shape) of the bag. Most efficient are close-fitting bags that don't permit your body heat to bypass the insulation between you and the cold environment.

Different styles of baffles—compartments that hold the insulating fill—are available. Their purpose is to to distribute the fill evenly. From a practical point of view there's not too much difference among them. What matters is that you avoid a quilted bag that is stitched straight through top and bottom layers, because it would let warm air escape (and cold air in).

Mummy bags are the lightest and warmest style. Rectangular bags weigh more but offer more foot room (nice for the warm-blooded). They're also roomier when two bags are zipped together for a twosome. Bags used in this fashion must have mating zippers.

Common sleeping bag features include a contoured hood with drawstring to keep the head warm, a filled "draft collar" that helps keep the shoulders and neck warm, and a "draft tube" over the zipper to prevent leakage of body heat there.

Summer-weight bags are rated (in Fahrenheit) from 40° down to 20°, three-season bags are rated 10° to 0° degrees, and winter bags are rated -5° to as low as -50°. These ratings are of help in comparing bags, but may not guarantee your comfort at those particular temperatures. Outer bags and liner inserts are available to increase the warmth of any bag—not a bad way to go if you want a single bag to cover a broad range of seasonal conditions.

Bags filled with synthetic materials (Polarguard, Quallofil, Hollofil) are heavier, less compressible, and are more reliable than down-filled bags. Stuffing a synthetic-filled bag into a stuff sack, washing it, and exposing it to heat such as in a hot car or in a dryer breaks down the fibers. Damaged fibers keep the bag from regaining its loft, and warmth depends on loft. Advantages of synthetic bags are their ability to retain insulating ability in case they get wet, and lower cost. Synthetic bags are great for extended winter trips, kayaking, and other outings where there's a likelihood of getting the bag damp.

Rectangular   **Semi-Mummy**   **Mummy**

Down bags are lighter and more compressible than synthetic bags. They are serviceable over a wider temperature range, rejuvenate after laundering, and are very cozy and comfortable. They're more durable, but much more expensive. When wet, they're practically useless. Down is slow to dry. Gore-tex shells or outer bags are available to protect them from dew or wind when sleeping without a tent. Down bags don't need to be cleaned very often, but when they do they should be professionally laundered. Check with your local outdoor-equipment outfitter—they may offer this service.

A shell made of Gore-tex or Texolite (a punctured aluminized mylar film) or other similar materials added to the bag's shell can add warmth and wind protection, but may also make it feel clammy in warm weather.

Here are some tips for getting the best performance out of any sleeping bag:

• Always fluff your bag before using it to get the maximum loft.
• A zipper that opens at both top and bottom ends of the bag helps you cool off on warmer nights and helps ventilate perspiration.
• Perspiration often condenses on the fibers of the insulating fill during cold weather. Your bag may need some drying time during the day to keep from getting heavier and colder each succeeding night.
• At home, store your sleeping bag by hanging it in the closet; never keep it wadded up in a stuff sack. Make sure it's fully dry before putting it away in an unventilated place.

Tents

Sleeping under the stars on a clear, bug-free night is a glorious experience. But when there's wind, snow, rain, or annoying insects, a tent can be most welcome. In extreme situations, your survival may depend on a sturdy tent. One that's large enough to hold both people and packs is convenient, but obviously heavier and more expensive. For tents, especially , you'll have to balance the comfort of using a bigger model against the discomfort of carrying it.

Tent costs vary dramatically, and generally you get what you pay for. Cost is based on materials, quality of construction, design, features, and options. When shopping for a tent consider the following features and options:

• Weight and size
• Ease of setup
• Freestanding ability
• Ease of entry and exit
• Ventilation
• Doors, windows, bug screening, storm flaps
• Vestibule for cooking
• Flashlight loops, pockets

Freestanding tents weigh more than tents that need to be staked out, but they can be set up almost anywhere. (Be sure your tent is staked anyway if you intend to leave it. A sudden wind could blow your unstaked tent into a lake or over a cliff.) Dome tents tend to give with the wind and can withstand strong winds, assuming they are anchored properly. A double-wall design with a full-coverage rain fly (waterproof outer shell) repels rain and also helps keep condensation from accumulating on the inner tent walls. Flat tent walls tend to flap in the wind more than curved walls do. Tents with a vestibule or awnings keep raindrops from blowing in through the tent door or windows, and provide a place to cook in bad weather. Almost all tents need to be seam-sealed before use. Don't forget to buy the seam-sealer if it doesn't come with the tent. When comparing manufacturer's specifications, determine if the specified weights include the stakes, stuff sack, and ground cloth.

Always set up your new tent at home before heading out. A missing or broken pole could totally disable a tent, and you won't want to spend half an hour reading the directions in camp anyway. A lightweight ground cloth made of synthetic material will help protect the bottom of the tent from punctures, dirt, and condensation during the night. You should fold or cut the ground cloth to the tent's shape so it doesn't channel rainwater underneath the tent.

Stoves and Cooksets

Please see Chapter 9—Foods and Cooking—for detailed information on stoves and cooksets.

Packs

The last "S" in ESSENTIALS refers to packs (Something to carry gear in). There are numerous options for the wilderness traveler:
• Fanny pack (it's compact, but often too small for even the essentials)
• Small daypack (for short hikes)
• Full daypack (for longer hikes)
• Extra large daypack (sometimes called a "day-and-a-half pack")
• External-frame backpack
• Internal-frame backpack

For the moment we'll restrict our discussion to the latter two on the above list. The backpack you choose will greatly affect how much you enjoy the sport. Fit and style are as personal as with a pair of shoes. What works great for one person may not work for you. Another person's reject may be just what you need, so you decide. Never buy a pack without trying it (or a similar rental) first, preferably on an overnight trip. Select the right size for your body frame, load it up with enough weight of any kind, and walk, climb up and down, tip, turn, and twist. You've found a winner if the pack feels like an extension of your body, moves with you, doesn't poke or gouge, and doesn't make you gasp for joy when you take it off. After prolonged use, you shouldn't have excessively sore spots on the collar, hips, or elsewhere.

When you try out a backpack, realize that the perceived load may vary by as much as ten pounds depending on how you distribute items inside. Place the

External-frame backpack

Internal-frame backpack

heaviest items such as water at shoulder-blade height, close to your back. Don't hang anything out from the back of the pack. Adjust the waist and shoulder straps to distribute weight more or less evenly between shoulders and hips. Test the water-resistant properties of the pack material—if it leaks through the seams or the material itself, then you may want to buy a waterproof pack cover or waterproof stuff sacks to protect your gear. Other desirable features include padded shoulder straps, padded waist or hip belt, and sternum strap (this is tightened across your chest to relieve pressure on your shoulders).

Internal- and *external*-frame backpacks are quite different from each other. Internal-frame packs have vertical stays (curved, rigid structural members) inside the pack sack. Internals are relatively compact and fit snugly against your body. They're designed to hold sleeping bags, and sometimes tents and pads, inside. Adjustable straps compress the load and keep it from shifting. For most people, internal-frame models feel more balanced. When stepping over boulders, traversing ledges, crossing streams, and dodging brush, internal-frame packs move with you, helping you maintain your balance and pace. Drawbacks include generally higher cost, more difficulty in getting at your gear (in top-loading models, particularly), and less air circulation for your back. Internal-frame packs are currently soaring in popularity.

The rigid, exposed frame structure on an external-frame pack keeps the load a few inches away from your body, allowing more air circulation. These packs have fewer adjustments. Sleeping bag, pad, and tent strap onto areas provided for them on the frame, and most other gear fits inside the pack's many pockets. Some have a rigid, metal hip support as part of their suspension system. External-frame packs are easier to load and may handle heavy loads (50 pounds or more) better than most internal-frame packs. Unfortunately, they tend to move where iner-

tia leads them, which may not be the direction you want to go. If heavily loaded they can throw you off balance when you twist, turn, or lift. Gear strapped on the outside tends to snag on branches and rocks. Some models make it impossible for you to tilt your head back and look up. Most external packs are bulky—they can take up a lot of space in the trunk of a car.

As of this writing, manufacturers of both styles are working to blend together the best features of each. Newer internal-frame models have divided compartments for easier loading. They're now handling heavier loads with more comfort. The newer external-frame packs are becoming less boxy and more contoured to enhance stability, while maintaining their carrying volume.

For recreational (as opposed to expeditionary) backpacking, you'll need a pack capacity of 4000 to 6000 cubic inches in an internal frame pack (which holds sleeping bag and possibly tent and pad) and 3000 to 3500 cubic inches in an external frame pack. Don't be tempted to buy a too-large size (what you choose to fill your pack with always seems to exceed the capacity available anyway). Choose the size that would fit your needs most of the time. You can always use add-on pockets for additional space, or you can rent a pack for occasions when you require extra capacity.

If your search turns up more than one suitable model of backpack, then consider individual characteristics or special features like pack weight, color, extra pockets, ice axe loops, tie-on patches, and versatility (some packs, for example, have top pockets that can detach and be used as a day or fanny pack).

Finally, once you've made your choice, ask that your pack be fitted properly. The structural members of both internal- and external-frame packs should be carefully adjusted to fit the contours of your body.

Whether you day-hike exclusively, or want to climb peaks and make side trips on backpack excursions, you'll need a small pack. With regular day-packs, most weight is carried on the shoulders (waist belts and sternum straps are stabilizers); with fanny packs the weight is on the hips. For a summit bid, you may need a pack holding as much as 2000 cubic inches of necessary equipment such as rain gear, extra clothing, food, water, first-aid kit, and other essentials. On any pack, look for good construction, nonmetal zippers and fasteners, padded straps, and reinforcements where the straps are sewn in. Cordura material and leather reinforcement make for a heavier but more durable pack. Compressibility is a very desirable feature if the smaller pack has to fit inside a backpack.

Recommended Reading

The best way to keep current on equipment and manufacturers is to read equipment articles and reviews in magazines such as *Backpacker*, *Outside*, and *Sierra*. These are available on newsstands or by subscription. *Sierra*, the monthy magazine of the Sierra Club, comes with membership. Back issues of these publications may be available at your local library or Sierra Club chapter office.

Resources

For buying equipment locally, check your local telephone directory for backpacking and sports outfitting stores such as A-16 Wilderness Outfitters, Big 5, Oshman's, Pat's Ski and Sport, REI, Sports Chalet, and others.

Mail Order Companies:

Campmor
Box 999 6FB
Paramus, NJ 07653

Indiana Camp Supply, Inc.
P.O. Box 211
Hobart, IN 46342

Frostline (specializes in clothing kits)
2501 Frostline Ave.
Grand Junction, CO 81505

REI (Recreational Equipment, Inc.)
P.O. Box 88125
Seattle, WA 98138-0125

Pack Manufacturers:

(Manufacturers listed below make a variety of styles for both the occasional and the serious wilderness traveler. Their products are not necessarily endorsed by the authors and publishers of this book.)

Bergans of Norway
P.O. Box 699
Enfield, NH 03748

Camp Trails
P.O. Box 966
Binghampton, NY 13902

Dana Designs
P.O. Box 3210
Bozeman, MT 59715

Gregory Mountain Products
100 Calle Cortez
Temecula, CA 92390

JanSport
Paine Field Industrial Park
Everett, WA 98204

Karrimor
3800 Annapolis Lane
Minneapolis, MN 55441

Kelty
P.O. Box 7048-A
St. Louis, MO 63177

Lowe Alpine Systems, Inc.
P.O. Box 189
La Fayette, CO 80026

Mountain Equipment, Inc.
1636 S. Second St.
Fresno, CA 93702

Mountainsmith, Inc.
1100 Simms St.
Golden, CO 80401

The North Face
999 Harrison St.
Berkeley, CA 94708

Chapter 6

Wilderness Navigation

Nelson Copp and Ted Young

*"It's pretty hard to get seriously lost, if there's no place
 you'd rather be."*

—Don and Reanne Douglass

M ore and more Americans are discovering the beauty and tranquillity of our parks and trails, and the fun of wilderness camping and travel. Many of us are seeking out the more remote trails and cross-country routes, yet more people need a good command of the navigation techniques and skills that make such outings safer, more predictable, and more rewarding. As we'll see in this chapter, navigation requires relatively little in the way of equipment. It's primarily a mental effort that keeps one constantly aware of position, direction, and speed of travel. Like the mental effort required in driving an automobile, it requires plenty of practice, but gets easier with time.

As a normal part of living, you're continually faced with challenges of navigating. You're probably quite accustomed to using city-navigation tools and cues such as road maps, street signs, and verbal directions. Wilderness navigation is simply an extension of the same route-finding skills you use in the civilized world. Instead of signposts and road maps, you'll use a topographic map, compass, and the physical features of the land.

Since cues indicating precise location are not always visible in the wilderness and you won't likely be meeting other travelers very often, you'll have to get used to being a little uncertain about your exact position from time to time. This does not mean you'll be "lost." It only means you'll be somewhere in transit between one known position and the next. The more you practice reading the "lay of the land," the more comfortable you'll be in the wilderness.

THE TOOLS OF NAVIGATION

Map

Topographic maps are almost always best for navigation purposes. These are scale maps with a unique feature—contour lines indicating elevations above (or in some cases below) sea level. "Topo" maps also show bodies of water and watercourses, vegetation types, named geographical points of interest such as mountain peaks, and man-made features. A skilled user of a topo map is able to clearly visualize the topography by carefully studying the patterns made by the contour lines.

Topo maps published by the U.S. Geological Survey (U.S.G.S.) can be purchased at backpacking and map stores, or directly from the U.S.G.S. Private publishers often use U.S.G.S. maps as a base and update the man-made features on their maps, like roads and trails.

Other maps, such as road maps or trail maps without contour lines, may be of some use for navigation as long as they are drawn to scale. Also useful to some degree are shaded relief maps, giving some rough indication of the topography.

Compass

Transparent Base

Direction of Travel Arrow

Circular Housing

Orienting Arrow

Compass Needle
(North end often painted red)

The compass has developed over many centuries from a simple direction finder to a sophisticated tool. In most modern versions used for navigation, the compass needle (a small, bar-shaped magnet) turns freely while suspended in a circular housing filled with a transparent liquid. The liquid quickly damps out oscillations in the needle's rotation whenever the compass is moved or adjusted in any way.

For map and compass work in the field, you should use an orienteering compass. In this design the circular housing is transparent and rotates on a transparent plastic base. The perimeter of the housing is inscribed with the cardinal directions (north, east, south, west) and a 360° scale, typically in 2° increments. The north-pointing end of the needle is usually painted red, and there's a prominent arrow on the base which can be used to indicate your direction of travel or the direction to a prominent land feature.

In some compasses the needle's north end is coated with phosphorescent paint, allowing readings to be made at night. Most compass base plates include a small ruler in inch or centimeter units to facilitate measuring distance on maps. More expensive compasses include a built-in mirror that helps you make more accurate sightings.

Altimet'

In ' navi a r ba. (see L. your posi. lines on a top. readings are affec. weather, so it's import. altimeter's reading whene, at a point of known elevation.

We won't discuss the use of a. ters further in this chapter; rather we . concentrate on navigation techniques using map alone, compass alone, and map and compass together. While reading the text that follows, it would be helpful to have a topographic map and orienteering compass handy for reference.

NAVIGATION BY MAP ALONE

First we'll look closely at the kinds of symbols appearing on topo maps. There are four classes of map symbols; point, line, surface, and contour.

Point Symbol Examples:

Building (in black)   ■

Mine (in black)   ✗

Spring (in blue)   ⌂

Line Symbol Examples:

Watercourse— year-round (in blue)

Watercourse— intermittent (in blue)

Modern compass angles are in reference to north (0°) and increase in a clockwise direction.

ad

（ack）

road
（in black）   ++++++++++

Boundary
（in black）

Surface Symbol Examples:

Lake; Ocean
（blue tint）

Glacier
（white）

Forest
（solid green tint）

Scrub Vegetation
（green dot pattern）

Peak:

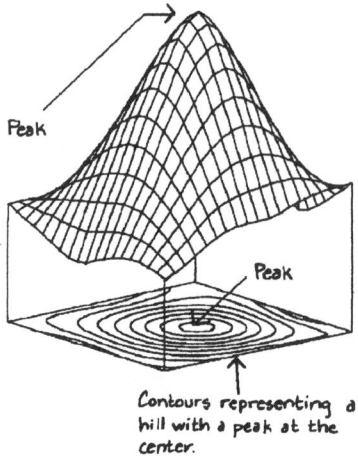

Peak

Peak

Contours representing a
hill with a peak at the
center.

*Canyon, valley, draw or
desert wash:*

Contours representing
the valley, canyon, draw
or desert wash

Contour lines, typically printed in brown ink on topo maps, are imaginary lines of constant elevation. If you could actually see these lines on the earth, they would curve around the terrain, but always remain level. The elevation difference between adjacent contour lines on the map is called the contour interval. Depending on the type of terrain and the scale of the map, the contour interval can vary from 200 to 20 feet or less. A map with a contour interval greater than 80 feet is generally not very useful for critical navigation. Visualizing the terrain represented on a topo map involves understanding the patterns of the contour lines. The following examples show several types of terrain and the corresponding contours.

Ridge line:

Saddle:

Cliff:

Here is a more complex terrain, which is typical of many mountainous areas of the West (except that the vertical scale in this view has been exaggerated):

All topo maps are printed with the direction of *true north* toward the top of the map. From any place on the earth, true north is the direction toward earth's geographic north pole—the north end of its spin axis. *Magnetic north*, on the other hand, is the direction toward the earth's magnetic north pole, which is located some distance away from earth's north pole in northern Canada. For any place on earth, there's a correction, called *magnetic declination*, that expresses the angle from the direction of true north to the direction of magnetic north. For western North America, magnetic declinations range from about 10° east to 20° east. If you aren't using a compass, the magnetic declination is of no use; if you are, then knowing your declination is essential, as you'll see later.

U.S.G.S topo maps come in two types: *15 minutes*, in which one inch on the map equals about one mile; and *7¹/2 minutes*, in which one inch on the map equals about 2000 feet. (The "minutes" refer to minutes of arc in latitude and longitude: 15 minutes covers ¹/4° of latitude and longitude, while 7¹/2 minutes covers ¹/8°.) It takes four 7¹/2-minute maps to cover the same area shown on one 15-minute map. Knowing the map scale, it is possible to calculate the distance between any two points along a line or curve. For example, if the route on a 15-minute map measures 8.3 inches, the distance is 8.3 inches x approximately 1 mile/inch = approximately 8.3 miles.

Quite often a route will span several maps. Each U.S.G.S. topo has the names of adjacent maps (usually eight of them) printed on the sides and corners. (Provisional topo maps indicate all adjoining maps at the bottom.)

Although topo maps reflect a great deal of information about the terrain, it is impossible to show every detail. Certain features too small to be detected in the pattern of contour lines may be insurmountable to the traveler. On a map with a contour interval of 80 feet, for example, a cliff or waterfall 60 feet high may not be shown at all if it happens to fall between contour lines. On a map with 40-foot contours, cross-country travel over a gently sloping hillside may appear simple, but not so if the slope is strewn with 10- or 20-foot-high boulders. Some features on topo maps are necessarily vague. A vegetation pattern indicating forest may represent anything from scattered trees to a dense redwood forest. The pattern indicating scrub vegetation could mean scattered bushes or impenetrable chaparral. A desert wash (a brown stipple pattern on the map) could be filled with anything from sand to boulders. Streams indicated by a thin blue line could be 1 foot wide or 50 feet wide.

Always take note of a map's publication date and the information in fine print at the bottom. The fine print may indicate that the map area was surveyed several years before the map was actually published. Significant changes may have occured since then. Landslides or simple neglect may have obliterated roads and trails, buildings may be reduced to nothing but half-buried foundations, and vegetation may have changed as a result of a fire, logging activity, or urban development. Considering all the information a map contains, it alone may be all you need to determine your location and plot your course. This works particularly well when distinct features such as road and trail junctions, peaks, passes, or uniquely shaped lakes are within view. This map-alone method of navigation, however, is not effective in bad weather or low visibility. In those cases a compass is often necessary as well as a map.

The locating process begins with aligning the map so that it corresponds to the landscape in view, and ends with fixing your exact location on the map. You're ready to begin if you can identify features seen on the land with their printed representations on the map. Rotate the map until the features are in the

same relative position on the map as they are in view around you. For example, if you recognize a peak in front of you and a known river junction just below on your right, the map should be rotated and aligned so that when the map is held between you and the peak on the horizon, the peak on the map lies in front of you, while the river junction on the map appears to the right, but closer than the peak. Then find the spot on the map where the river junction is at the same angle to the right of the peak as is the river junction in your view. That's your approximate location. To further refine your position, look for other nearby distinctive features. Are you standing on top of a ridge, or somewhere along the slope? Is there a meadow or lake in view? Are there any other high points around you that may help to fix your position?

Locating your position by map alone

Once you have located yourself, keep the map within easy reach or carry it in front of you as you travel so that you can periodically relocate yourself. If you're carrying the map, you may want to encase it in a large, transparent plastic envelope to protect it from rain, perspiration, and abrasion.

NAVIGATION BY COMPASS

Basic compass skills involve setting, taking, and following bearings. A compass bearing is simply the angle, as measured by your compass, between the direction of magnetic north (the direction a compass needle points) and the direction of an object or destination. As suggested by the scale on your compass's circular housing, bearing angles increase eastward from north, that is, they increase to your right.

Setting a Bearing

Let's say a friend tells you her favorite fishing hole is on a magnetic bearing (compass bearing) of 60° from a certain parking area. Without a compass you might have only a vague idea of which direction to hike after you park your car. But if you set a bearing of 60° on your compass, you can simply follow the direction-of-travel arrow on the base of the compass to head in the right direction.

To set that 60° bearing, hold the compass flat in the palm of your hand and turn the housing until the 60°-mark lines up with the direction-of-travel arrow on the base plate. On some compasses, the arrow is labelled "Read Bearing Here."

Turn the entire compass until the north end of the needle lines up with the orienting arrow on the bottom of the circular housing (the red end of the needle now points to the "N" on the housing).

Your compass is now "oriented" to magnetic north, the direction-of-travel arrow is pointing toward the fishing hole, and you are facing in the direction you want to go. Soon you'll learn how to successfully follow that bearing.

Be aware that nearby metallic objects, such as mechanical pencils or pens, a pack frame, a metal watch or ring, or a car can affect the pointing accuracy of a compass needle. Always make compass measurements away from these kinds of objects. A compass can also be rendered useless in certain areas where large amounts of iron-bearing rock is present.

Taking a Bearing

"Taking" a bearing is the opposite of setting a bearing. In this case, you can see where you want to go, but you don't yet know what the bearing angle is. For example, let's say your goal is to reach a peak visible in the distance. You can see a good route straight ahead and you realize that much of the time you'll be hiking in a forest where your view of the peak will be obscured. First you need to take a bearing on the peak.

To take a bearing, hold the compass in your hand with the direction-of-travel arrow pointing toward the peak. You may want to hold the compass near eye level to sight more accurately, but remember to keep the compass level. With the direction-of-travel arrow fixed on the peak, turn the housing until the orienting arrow in the housing lines up with the needle. In effect, you are setting up a measurement of the angle between magnetic north (the direction of the needle's north end) and the peak (the direction indicated by the direction-of-travel arrow).

As you walk through the forest, you can refer to your compass often to maintain your course. The degree reading on the compass is not really important, as long as you don't rotate the compass housing along the way. Just keep the needle lined up on the orienting arrow, and the direction-of-travel arrow points your way. Still it's a good idea to memorize or jot down the degree reading in case your compass housing accidentally gets reset.

Following a Bearing

In the previous example, you took a bearing on a peak. You're now ready to start hiking through the forest. Since the bearing is already set on your compass, all you have to do is hike in that direction. But how easily can you follow this bearing? What happens if you must skirt obstacles like dense brush or large boulders? To answer these questions you must learn how to select intermediate points.

Before you start hiking, turn the compass until it is oriented toward north (don't turn the housing). The magnetic needle lines up with the north arrow on the housing and the direction-of-travel arrow on the base plate points in the direction of your hike to the peak.

Now look for an object in the near distance that is between you and the peak, such as a distinctive tree or a pile of rocks. This is your first intermediate point. Walk toward the intermediate point as directly as you can. Moving a little to the left or right to avoid obstacles will not make you lose your original direction. Just keep heading, on average, toward the intermediate point. You should not have to check your compass again until you reach it.

Let's assume that at the first intermediate point you can't see the peak anymore. No problem, just orient your compass to north again, and look along the direction-of-travel arrow. Then pick out a second intermediate point in that direction of travel you can hike to without losing your way. You can continue leapfrogging in this manner until you reach your goal.

Distinct tree

Rocks

Point on pond

Back-sighting

Now and then you may lose sight of your next intermediate point. To make sure you are still on the right course, use the technique of back-sighting to find the previous point.

Turn around and reorient your compass by lining the *south* end of the needle with the north end of the orienting arrow (since you are looking 180° back). Now the direction-of-travel arrow will point back toward the previous intermediate point. If it does not, move in a direction either left or right until it does. Now you are on the correct bearing again. It's good practice to backsight often to make sure you stay on course. It will also help you recognize the terrain for the trip back if you plan to return using the same route.

Back-bearings

Let's say you've spent an enjoyable hour on the summit, and now you want to return to your car. You never took a bearing on the car, in fact you can't even see the car. How do you get back? Easy. Your car is just 180° from your original bearing. Here are two techniques you can use to get back.

In the first method you find the angle that is 180° from your original bearing (if your original bearing is less than 180°, then add 180° to it; if your original bearing is more than 180°, then subtract 180° from it). Reset the housing to this new bearing, orient your compass, and start the journey back.

In the second method, you leave the original bearing set, but orient your compass by aligning the south end of the needle with the orienting arrow (which indicates north).

To mountain   To car

**Back bearings: In the diagrams above, 180°
was added to the original bearing of 40° to
produce a back-bearing of 220°**

AN EXERCISE IN COMPASS NAVIGATION:
FOLLOWING A CIRCUIT

This circuit exercise will give you and your friends some practical experience in taking and following bearings. First find a rather large, open outdoor area with at least a few obstacles. Pick out five or ten points on the landscape that can be linked together in a more-or-less circular course. It's more interesting if some of the points can't be seen from the starting point.

Number and describe the points on a sketch map and give everyone a copy. The object is to take bearings on each successive point, and to navigate to each successive point using compass techniques. Each participant should record the measured bearing on each leg of the circuit. After completing the circuit, the participants can compare their bearings and discuss any problems.

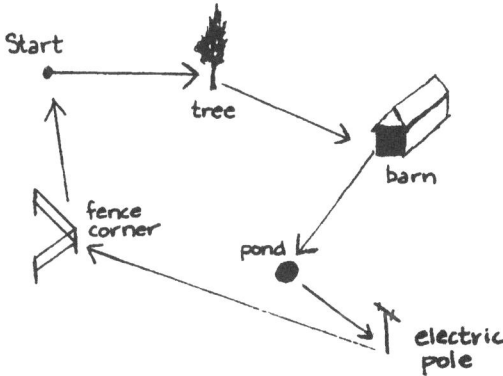

Navigating Around Obstacles

Using intermediate points to reach a goal is nice, but sometimes there are obstacles you can't easily sidestep. You might encounter some obstacle you'd rather not try to climb over that also blocks your view of the next intermediate point. You could walk around it, but you're afraid that would throw you off course.

One fairly exact solution to this dilemma is to navigate on a right-angle course. First determine whether going to the left or the right will be easier. Orient the compass, and face your original bearing. Notice that the near and far ends of the base plate are perpendicular to your original bearing; this will be your new direction. Start walking in this new perpendicular direction, either left or right, as far as you need to, counting your paces as you walk.

Let's say you had to walk 100 paces to the right to get a clear shot past the hill. Orient the compass again and walk in your original direction to a point beyond the hill. Then turn left (in this case) and follow a course 100 paces back to your originally projected course. Reorient your compass and continue toward your next intermediate point.

NAVIGATION BY MAP AND COMPASS

As we've seen, the needle of a compass points toward the earth's magnetic north pole. From most places on earth (including the western states) this is not quite the same direction as the earth's true north pole. Since maps are drawn with true north up, this means that the magnetic bearings you've been setting and taking will be skewed a little, relative to directions on the map. The difference in degrees between the true north and magnetic north directions as measured from any given location on earth is the magnetic declination.

If you are just using a compass merely as a direction finder independent of a map, then declination is unimportant. When using a map and compass together, however, you'll have to take declination into account.

On topographic maps magnetic declination is usually indicated at the bottom left. The symbol includes a vertical line pointing toward a star representing true north, and an arrow labelled "MN" indicating magnetic declination (assumed to be 15°, as shown here).

Once you know the declination for your map, you may apply either of two methods for orienting your map correctly:

Compass-oriented map method:

First place your map on a flat spot. Roughly orient it by looking at the features around you and comparing them to the map. Then rotate the compass's circular housing to line up the orienting arrow with the direction-of-travel arrow on the base plate. Place the long edge of the base plate along the left or right border of the map, with north pointing to the top of the map (don't use any vertical lines drawn inside the map area since they can represent roads or boundaries that may not really go precisely north and south).

For east declinations (everywhere in the western U.S.), turn the map and compass together (as illustrated below) until the needle points to the number on the housing that matches your declination. Your map now has its vertical dimension oriented to true north, and its orientation is also correct relative to the landscape around you (diagram below).

Parallel declination lines method:

Adding parallel declination lines to a map simplifies navigation technique when using that map in the field. It's much easier if you draw the lines on your map at home before your trip. In addition to your compass, you'll need a sharp pencil and a long ruler or straight-edge.

Turn the compass housing until the scale reads the same value your declination (this assumes your declination is east). Place your map on a flat, hard surface and rotate the entire compass until the direction arrow on the housing lines up with the border of the map. The long edge of the base plate and the direction-of-travel arrow are now lined up with the correct declination. (You can double check this by making sure they are angled in the same direction as the

declination arrow on the bottom of your map.) Place the straight-edge along the long edge of the base plate and draw a straight line the entire length of the map. Starting from this line, mark one-inch increments along the top and bottom edges of the map. Then use the straight-edge to connect each pair of these marks until your map—or at least the area you'll be hiking in on the map—is covered with parallel declination lines (see diagram below).

Map orientation is very simple using this method. Rotate your map so that the parallel declination lines are also parallel to the direction of your compass needle. Make sure the north end of the compass needle points toward the top of the map, not the bottom.

Navigation Steps

Let's assume you want to hike to a small lake you can see on the map. You'll need to take a bearing on the lake from your present position and then follow that bearing.

If you are using the compass-oriented map method, lay the map on a flat spot and orient it to true north as described earlier. Place one of the back corners of your compass base plate on your current (known) location on the map. This point will act as a pivot. Hold this corner down with your thumb and rotate the entire compass until the front corner on the same side of the base plate is in line with your destination. The long edge of the base plate should now be making a line between the two points. Holding the base plate in this position, rotate the housing until the orienting arrow on the housing lines up with the north end of the needle. You have now set your compass to the correct bearing from your location to the lake. The number of degrees is not important. As in the illustration below, just follow the direction-of-travel arrow on your oriented compass to navigate to the lake.

For the parallel declination lines method, follow the first few steps described above, but rotate the housing until the orienting arrow on the housing lines up with the declination lines drawn on your map. When using this method, always ignore the magnetic needle when you're working on the map. In this case the declination lines you have drawn represent magnetic north. The direction of the needle is not important. (In the following illustration, a magnetic declination of 20° is assumed.)

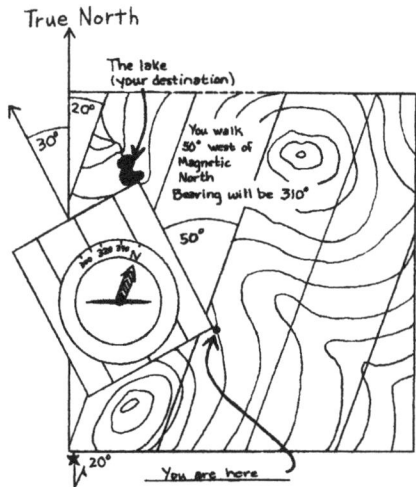

Following a Bearing

Now that you have successfully set the bearing to the lake, you are almost ready to start hiking. First you must choose the best route to your destination. If you start hiking without checking the route you may end up having to climb steep hills or hike through dense vegetation. So take a few minutes to plan your route, using that wonderful tool—a map.

Take note of any obstacles you may detect on the map and mark them. Then plot your course, which may or may not be a direct route. To avoid tough spots, you can pick out intermediate points, take their bearings from the map, and plot a crooked course, with bearings noted for each leg.

Aiming Off

If a destination is not large, like a small lake hidden in the trees, you could walk right past it. To reduce that possibility, try to find on the map a prominent stream or an obvious road or trail touching or passing near the lake. If you can find some feature like that, aim slightly off the target lake so that you will cross the obvious feature sooner or later. When you get there, you'll know which way to turn to find the lake.

Checking Your Location

A good way to keep track of your position, especially during critical navigation, is to frequently recheck your position relative to nearby landmarks and "update" your position on your map. You can do that by keeping your thumb on your current position on the map at all times, or by making a series of pencil marks on the map.

If, for whatever reason, you do lose track of your position on the map, you can use the "triangle of error" technique to rediscover your location. First you must recognize three identifiable points both in the surrounding terrain and on the map. The closer the points are to you, the better. Take a bearing on the first point and leave it set on the compass. Transfer it as a line on the map by placing one of the front corners of the compass on the point, holding it with your finger, and pivoting the entire compass until the direction arrow either lines up with the needle, if you are using the compass-oriented method, or lines up with the parallel declination lines if you drew them on your map.

Draw a line from the first point back along the long edge of the base plate and extend it beyond where you think you are. Repeat these steps for the next two points. The three lines should converge to a small triangle. You should be somewhere inside the triangle!

Lake

Stream

Ridges blocking view

Aim left of the lake, then follow the stream to the lake.

Your position

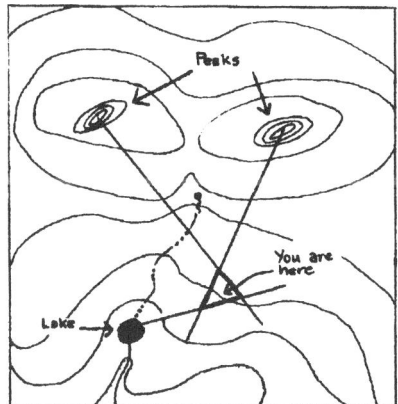

Peaks

You are here

Lake

If the triangle seems inordinately big, then you've erred in taking or plotting a bearing, or you may have mis-identified one of your points, either on the map or on the landscape. If this happens, check your bearings and try it again.

After getting at least a general fix on where you are, it may be useful to do a second triangulation on closer landmarks (if you can identify any) to determine your location more precisely. Once you have a better fix, you may be able to determine your location to a precision of just a few yards by examining the contour lines on your map, and recognizing around you the features they represent.

Taking Cross Bearings

Suppose you want to hike to a hidden spot, say a desert mine you noticed on the map, which is some distance away from an easily traveled linear feature like a straight wash. Let's further suppose there are no distinguishing fea-

tures along the wash to indicate the best place to turn off. But the map shows the mine lying between a distant hill and the wash.

Draw a line connecting the mine and the hill and extend it backward to where it intersects the wash. Using your compass, take a bearing of this line on the map. This is the bearing you will want to follow when you reach the right spot in the wash. Set this bearing on your compass.

Then as you walk down the wash, stop often and point the direction-of-travel arrow on the base plate toward the hill, as if you were going to take a bearing (do not rotate the housing). See if the needle lines up with the orienting arrow. If not, keep walking. As you continue, a place will be reached where the needle will line up with the orienting arrow. You're now on the bearing line you drew on the map. Turn and head toward the mine by following the direction-of-travel arrow.

SPECIAL TECHNIQUES

The techniques we've discussed so far are basic ones you will use again and again. There are several other techniques to be aware of for special situations.

Using Baselines

Aiming off, which we discussed earlier, involves intersecting a baseline, like a road or stream, and then following this baseline to the destination. In the last example (of cross bearings), you were hiking down a wash looking for a bearing line to a distant hill. When you reached the bearing line you simply had to walk in that direction to reach the mine. There were really two baselines in that example—the wash itself and the imaginary bearing line connecting the wash, the mine, and the hill.

Imagine you've found the spot where the bearing intersects the wash and you're heading toward the mine. But after an hour you haven't found the mine and you want to head back to the wash. No problem. There are actually two baselines you can rely on. Recheck the bearing on the hill, which is one of your baselines. Move either left or right until you line up with that bearing and are on that baseline. Now simply walk in the reverse direction, picking intermediate points along the way if needed, until you hit the wash.

The other baseline, the wash, is even easier to find. You know it's behind you when you're facing the hill, so turn around and walk away from the hill. You will soon find the wash and can then return to your starting point (if you know which way to turn when you reach the wash).

Always be aware of the location of at least one baseline—a stream, a road, or some other fairly linear feature—before you start your excursion.

Finding a Favorite Spot Again

We have already covered the triangle-of-error technique that is useful in pinpointing a location. There are other applications for this technique. Imagine you are hiking in the desert and come across a beautiful Indian-made *olla* (clay vessel). You don't want to disturb it but would like to inform a ranger of its exact whereabouts. There are no distinguishing landmarks nearby, only some nearby hills. So how can you find this spot again? You guessed it—take bearings of at least three of the hills and mark the location on your map using the triangle of error technique.

Dead Reckoning

When visibility is poor, it is often wiser to stay put until conditions improve. However there may be circumstances in which it is essential to keep moving. You may not have the opportunity ahead to confirm your position very often because of darkness or fog. In this situation, you may use the technique of dead reckoning. While you are still certain of your position, find your destination on the map and mark a number of easily distinguishable points along the way. Draw lines between each of these points, take their bearings, and write them next to each point.

Set the first bearing on your compass and start walking using intermediate points. If conditions are really bad, you may have to count your paces to determine how far you have gone. Continue doing this from point to point. This technique is risky since you can easily loose the thread of your course. If you do, you can try to retrace your footprints back to the last known location.

Navigating by Sun, Moon, and Stars

Carrying a compass is a necessity on any trip in the wilderness. There are, however, a few tricks you can use that will make you feel like an explorer.

The path of the sun can be used as a general direction indicator. At middle latitudes in the Northern Hemisphere, the sun always lies toward the south at midday. Therefore your shadow points north at approximately 12 noon standard time, or 1 p.m. daylight time. On the summer solstice (late June) the sun rises roughly in the northeast, passes high overhead in the south at noon, and sets in the northwest. On the winter solstice (late December), the sun rises roughly southeast, passes low in the south at noon, and sets roughly southwest. During the equinoxes (late March and late September) the sun rises due east and sets due west.

A good technique, if you're patient, is to put a stick in the ground and mark the end of its shadow. Do this several more times at intervals of 10 or 15 minutes. A line connecting these points will be generally east-west; a line perpendicular will be generally north-south.

Stick →

W ⊕─⊕─⊕─⊕ → E

⊕ Ends of shadow at different times

Shadow

If you have a watch with sweep hands, you can use it to find rough directions. Make sure the watch is set for standard time (not daylight savings) and face the sun. Move your body so as to point the hour hand to the horizon below the sun. South will be roughly halfway between the hour hand and twelve o'clock. This works because the sun moves only 15° in an hour while the hour hand moves 30°. During the months near summer solstice this does not work well near the middle of the day.

During late afternoon, another interesting feat is to use your hand to estimate the time before sunset. Hold your hand at arms length with fingers parallel to the horizon, and count the number of fingers between the horizon and the sun. Each finger represents about 10-12 minutes. You can also determine how long the sun has been up in the morning using the same method. Since this technique depends upon your latitude, you may want to experiment first; check how long it takes the sun to traverse one finger-width.

Time until sunset is 10-12 minutes for each finger above the horizon.

Like shipboard navigators, you can also use the stars to indicate directions. The stars move across the sky in the same direction as the sun, east to west. So stars that climb in the sky are somewhere near east, and stars that sink are somewhere near west. Polaris (the North Star), however, hovers in the northern sky all the time.

You can find Polaris by first looking for the Big Dipper. A line extended through the two outermost stars of the Big Dipper's bowl points to Polaris. When the Big Dipper is not visible, Cassiopeia usually is. The top of Cassiopeia's W-shaped form points toward Polaris. A further hint is that Polaris' altitude, or angle above the horizon, very nearly matches an observer's north latitude. An observer at Yellowstone National Park (latitude 45°N), for example, would locate Polaris halfway up in the sky.

We've explored the basics of map and compass navigation in this chapter. From simple day hikes to longer wilderness trips, it's important to keep your sense of direction and maintain an awareness of where you are. Carry a map and a compass when you travel in unfamiliar areas, and refer to your map often. With practice, navigational skills become everyday habits.

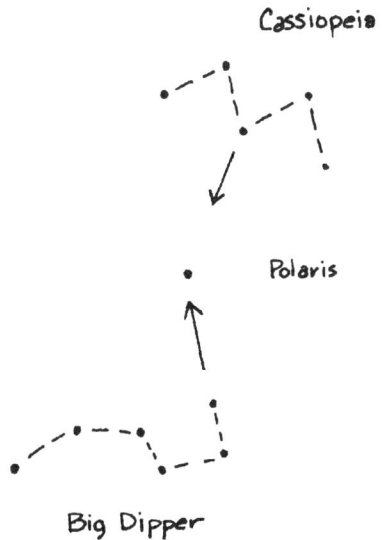

Cassiopeia

Polaris

Big Dipper

Recommended Reading:

Be Expert with Map and Compass
Bjorn Kjellstrom
Charles Scribner's Sons
(A valuable reference for information on all aspects of map and compass navigation, including competitive orienteering.)

Staying Found
June Fleming
Random House, 1982
(An easy-to-understand book covering the basics of map and compass navigation. Lots of helpful illustrations and drawings.)

Resources:

U.S.G.S. topographic maps, and many other maps useful for hikers can be purchased at outdoor equipment stores and map stores in every metropolitan area in the West. For large orders of U.S.G.S. maps, you may want to contact the Branch of Distribution, U.S.Geological Survey, Box 25286, Federal Center, Denver, CO 80225.

Chapter 7

The Weather

Keith Gordon

"You don't need a weatherman to know which way the wind blows."

—Bob Dylan

I t's true. Although they are often helpful, you don't always need a weatherman. You can be your own! In fact, making educated guesses about the weather is a valuable skill for anyone on a trip in the wilderness. Later on we'll discuss some of the many sources of current weather information that will help you in that effort, but for now let's cover some ground rules of meteorology.

First, let's remember that when discussing the weather we're dealing with events and outcomes that are never absolutely predictable. Scientists now consider meteorological systems, as well as many other natural systems, to be inherently chaotic. However even chaotic phenomena can have probable, if not strictly predictable, outcomes over the short term. That gives us some confidence in our daily weather forecast, even though it seems imprecise and occasionally turns out dead wrong.

All weather phenomena involve air, water, and the transfer of heat energy from place to place. For this discussion we should recall that air consists of various gases plus water vapor. The water vapor content can be highly variable, ranging from almost nothing up to about four percent. Within clouds, water is also present in the form of liquid droplets, or ice crystals, or both. The sun's radiant energy is both the source of most of the heat on the earth and the motivating agent of forces that transfer heat from one place to another.

We should also recall that air tends to expand and rise when warmed, that warm air can hold more water vapor than cooler air, and that (generally) temperatures within the lower atmosphere decrease with increasing elevation. If a humid mass of air is cooled sufficiently, the water vapor in it condenses to myriads of tiny, freely floating water droplets. These water droplets are big enough to reflect light, so we see an opaque white mass—a cloud. If a great deal of cooling takes place, heavier droplets or ice crystals may form and

drizzle, rain, sleet, hail or snow may result.

The so-called *lapse rate*, the rate at which temperature decreases with increasing elevation, averages about $3^{1}/_{2}°F$ per 1000 feet elevation ($6^{1}/_{2}°C$ per 1000 meters elevation). If a mass of warmish air holding nearly its capacity of invisible water vapor rises, it cools, more or less at the lapse rate. If the temperature inside falls to less than the *dew point* for that mass of air, condensation occurs and a cloud forms. The opposite process, exemplified by a cool cloud moving to a lower, warmer elevation, may result in the cloud disappearing.

Solar heating of the earth's surface and oceans and the rotation of the earth are the driving force behind the weather machine. As sun rays warm the surface and lower atmosphere, "bubbles" of air expand and begin rising. As long as a bubble is warmer than the air that surrounds it, it will continue to rise. On a larger scale, these bubbles are equivalent to *air masses* that can move both vertically and horizontally. Whether or not a rising bubble or air mass is destined to become a cloud, the air surrounding it moves in more or less horizontally to take the place it vacated. The process of air moving about, redistributing heat in the atmosphere, is known as *convection*. The horizontal movement is what we know as wind.

Local topography can influence the course of the winds and affect other factors such as precipitation. Mountains, for example, tend to create updrafts, resulting in greater precipitation on the high windward slopes. The drier air that continues flowing down the lee slopes compresses and becomes warmer. (Think of how hot a bicycle pump gets from compressing air and you'll appreciate this process.) Thus many arid lands, including most of North America's deserts, lie in the so-called "rain shadow" (usually east) of major mountain ranges.

Of course there's more to the weather than convection on a local or regional scale. A global view takes into account the dynamics of very large air masses, some big enough to cover a good portion of a continent.

GRACE UNDER PRESSURE

The *Highs* and *Lows* pictured on weather maps are representations of huge high-pressure (relatively compressed) and low-pressure (relatively uncompressed) air masses covering the earth. A typical scale, used in barometers, for measuring atmospheric, or *barometric* pressure is "inches of mercury" (the amount of pressure needed to raise a column of mercury metal one inch). A barometer at sea level, for example, should measure close to the standard sea level pressure of 29.92 inches of mercury. In the metric system, the sea-level pressure can be expressed as approximately 1 bar or 1000 millibars.

Significantly higher or lower readings indicate the dominance of either a High or a Low nearby. Remember, though, that pressure readings will go down if you climb a mountain. This happens at a rate of about 1 inch of mercury per thousand feet (100 millibars per 1000 meters) of elevation change. If you're carrying an altimeter with you, you're really carrying a barometer. Both instruments measure barometric pressure, but are scaled differently. Altimeters measure altitude above sea level,

Figure 7-1: Cloud types

Stratus (layered) clouds are formed by gentle lifting of warm, moist air.

Cumulus (lumpy, billowy) clouds are formed by vertical air currents. Rain, hail or snow can fall from these in heavy showers.

Cirrus (wispy) clouds are the high (20,000+ feet), gossamer-like formations of tiny ice crystals that often precede the passage of a storm front.

Cumulonimbus are huge, towering clouds formed by strong updrafts. The friction from air movements within these clouds builds up the electrical charges that are released as lightning. These clouds can unleash great torrents of rain or hail, but are short-lived.

but must be corrected for the local influence of Highs or Lows. Barometers, if not read at sea level, must be corrected for altitude. Climb 500 feet and your barometer should show about 1/2 inch less pressure.

If a High dominates your area after initial calibration, your altimeter will indicate lower than your actual altitude. A Low, on the other hand, will cause your altimeter to show a higher reading. If you go to sleep with your pocket altimeter indicating 6000 feet elevation, and a Low moves in, you'll awaken at a "higher" elevation. No, you didn't sleep-hike; the weather's changing!

Highs and Lows are distributed across the earth's surface and move about in ways that are only partially predictable. In addition, because nature abhors a vacuum (even a partial vacuum), air tends to move from a High toward a Low. But the air does not usually move on a direct path. The rotation of the earth causes an apparent force (Coriolis effect) that induces a clockwise flow of air around a High and a counterclockwise flow around a Low in the Northern Hemisphere. (In the Southern Hemisphere the directions are reversed.) Clouds outlining the spinning vortices surrounding the more intense Lows create the elegant, graceful spiral patterns shown in satellite images of our planet.

Figure 7-2: Facsimilie of a weather map.

Think of this map as a kind of topo map in which the contour lines (isobars) denote equal pressures across the surface of the earth. Generally air moves from Highs (H) to Lows (L), across the isobars, but the earth's rotation induces a clockwise circulation around a High, and a counter-clockwise circulation around a Low. Just as on a topo map, the closer the contour lines, the "steeper" the pressure gradient. The steeper the gradient, the faster the winds.

Around Highs the air is usually stable or even stagnant. Cloudless skies are typical, but dust, smoke, and smog can collect due to the lack of vertical mixing in the air.

Within a Low, the air is unstable and has a potential for rapid vertical movement. Cumuloform (billowing, towering) clouds [see Figure 7-1] can form, with a likelihood of precipitation or even violent weather.

If you have an idea of where Highs and Lows are located, and which way they're moving, you might be able to make short-term predictions about the weather in the area you plan to visit. If a High is moving over Mexico, for instance, you might expect warm, tropical air to invade much of the western U.S. A High over the Gulf of Mexico or the Sea of Cortez can sling moist air up into the Rocky Mountains and the Southwest desert, triggering thunderstorms and flash floods. A High sitting in the Gulf of Alaska can send a rush of cold, unstable air down the spine of the Cascades and the Sierra Nevada, generating the kind of stormy weather climbers dread.

During much of the year the usual "Pacific High" west of California produces clear weather and a steady flow of air inland over the West Coast and mountains. Occasionally, however, a High over an interior state like Nevada and a Low in the Pacific offshore from California results in a reverse flow of air from east to west, especially over southern California. During these episodes, dry, often hot winds called "Santa Anas" howl through the mountain passes. If you're camping in the mountains east of Los Angeles, you risk having your unstaked tent delivered to Santa Monica via air mail.

In general, approaching Lows feature increasingly lower clouds and the possibility of precipitation, while receding Lows feature clearing skies. But Lows, which can be squeezed between Highs, sometimes travel in series like water in a pipeline, so always beware of the next squirt that might lie just over the horizon.

Start watching the weather on a daily basis, and keep informed of the Highs and Lows around you. It's part of understanding and enjoying the rhythms of our planet.

BEING UP-FRONT ABOUT THE WEATHER

A *front* in meteorological parlance is the contact between one air mass and another. There are several types:

A *warm front* means that the leading edge of a moving air mass is warmer than the air mass it is overtaking and replacing. Stratiform (flat, layered) clouds are associated with this type of front. Figure 7-3 shows the usual sequence of clouds seen during the approach of a warm front:

The wispy, high-level cirrus clouds can appear as far as 1000 miles ahead of the surface position of the front, giving up to two days advance warning of its arrival. Near the front itself, the nimbostratus clouds are very low. If anything actually falls out of the hazy, gray sky, it is usually steady precipitation in the form of drizzle or light snow.

A *cold front* (see Figure 7-4), in which cold air wedges under and replaces warmer air, produces a different scenario. With the passage of a cold front, the temperature decreases, the wind shifts to a southerly direction, and (if the lifting of warm air is rapid enough) cumulonimbus (billowy, rain-laden) clouds unleash rain or snow. A fast-moving cold front can be preceded by a squall line, a line of thunderstorms.

There's not much warning of the approach of a cold front, though a careful observer would note increasing cumulus clouds and a falling barometer. Some cold fronts can sweep in with only a few minutes warning, much to the chagrin of big-wall climbers pinned to the likes of Yosemite's sheer walls. Cold-front precipitation, however, is relatively brief and the aftermath is usually serene, with crisp, clear air and scattered cumulus clouds in the sky for a while. Of concern to the wilderness trekker is

Figure 7-3: Approaching warm front

the sudden drop in the freezing level, which may leave unprepared campers or hikers stranded in hypothermic conditions.

An *occluded front* is where two or more fronts converge. This can happen when a faster-moving cold front overtakes a warm front. Often described as a zipper being pulled across the sky uniting the two fronts, occlusion may yield the worst characteristics of both fronts.

Stationary fronts develop when opposing fronts balance each other so that no movement occurs. The clouds and

weather associated with stationary fronts are often similar to those associated with warm fronts.

In Figure 7-5, A cold front, (identified by the icicle-shaped barbs of its symbol) is moving southeast across California. A warm front (with rounded barbs like rain drops) extends across Nevada and Idaho. South of the California-Oregon border, the two fronts have joined to form an occluded front. A stationary front (symbolized by sharp and rounded barbs on opposite sides), lies across New Mexico.

Figure 7-4: Approaching cold front

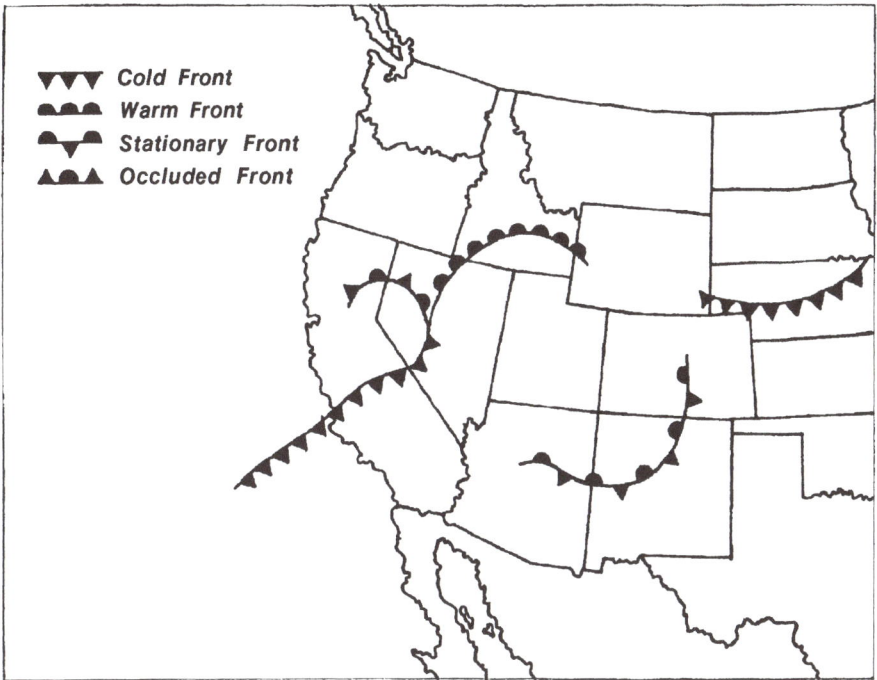

Figure 7-5: Weather fronts

Fronts can, and do, pass without any significant weather being created at all. The air behind a warm front can be only one degree warmer than the air it overtakes. So don't expect a heat wave to follow a snow siege just because a warm front is approaching!

Frontal passage can usually be detected by a shift in the wind. If you're enduring a typical cold-front storm, for example, you'll know the front has passed when winds from the south change to winds from the north. This doesn't mean the show is over, but the end is near.

MICROCLIMATES: WEATHER OR NOT SIZE COUNTS

As we've seen, mountains and other topographical irregularities on the earth's surface can affect the weather. In addition, the presence of a nearby large body of water, like the ocean, can profoundly alter local conditions. Relatively small areas that experience weather patterns substantially different than those around them are said to have distinct microclimates.

In the mountains, the astute traveler will consider the effect of microclimate when choosing a camping spot. At night, canyons frequently become conduits for cold, dense air flowing down from higher elevations. On calm nights, this chilled air tends to pool in low-lying valleys, often the same spots where inviting lakes beckon the inexperienced camper. The result is a *temperature inversion*—warmer air overlying cooler air. During the colder months you may want to avoid canyon bottoms and valleys and take advantage of warmer temperatures higher up on the slopes.

Another local phenomenon associated with mountains is the compressional heating of dry air flowing rapidly downslope. In the Rocky Mountains this is called a Chinook wind ("snow eater") since it can rapidly melt accumulations of winter snow. Chinooks occur when strong winds bearing moisture from the Pacific Ocean give up most of their precipitation over the mountain peaks and blast down the lee (east) sides.

Sometimes moving air aloft holds moisture as vapor until it collides with or flows over a high peak. The air compresses on the windward side of the peak, rises along the slope, and then experiences a drop in pressure (and therefore temperature) as it goes past the barrier. A long "banner cloud" streams from the apex of the peak, or the peak may be hidden in a "cloud cap." This is why climbers may encounter white-out conditions when approaching the summits of Mount Rainier and other major summits of the Cascade Range.

When a long chain of high mountains, such as the Sierra Nevada, interrupts the flow of moist, clear air from the west, spectacular lenticular (lens-shaped) clouds can appear downwind of the crest-line, like a phalanx of hovering flying saucers.

Mountains are notorious producers of thunderstorms. Thunderstorms can be dealt with or avoided if you understand their origin and development. Some thunderstorms are initiated by the heating of a broad area of the earth's surface. Others, called *orographic* thunderstorms are those triggered by moisture-laden air moving rapidly up mountain slopes (see Figure 7-6). In many of the Western mountain ranges during the summer months, you can almost set your watch to the daily replay of orographic thunderstorms. Heating by the morning sun causes updrafts, the uplifted air chills over the mountain peaks, billowy cumulus clouds build into monster cumulonimbus (thunderheads), and by afternoon the whole show of lightning, gusty winds, rain, and perhaps hail proceeds. Luckily, mountain thunderstorms are born, live, and die in a rather short time, literally drowning themselves out of existence. The unique hazards of lightning associated with these storms will be dealt with in Chapter 11—Mountain Travel. Lightning mishaps will be covered in Chapter 17—Wilderness First Aid.

Figure 7-6: Orographic lift

Along the Pacific coast, unique conditions give rise to forms of weather distinct from those of the rest of the continent. The coastal strip often experiences a daily cycle of winds that is purely local in origin. During the day, a *sea breeze* occurs when cool air over the ocean is pulled inland to replace air rising over the sun-warmed interior land mass. This wind falters, or even reverses, as the inland temperature plummets at night.

If moist air drawn in by the sea breeze flows uphill along a coastal slope and gets chilled to the dew point, low stratus clouds or *convective fog*, results. Another common phenomenon is *advective* fog along the coast. Here the incoming moist marine air is chilled by cool coastal waters or adjacent land masses and the condensation takes place at surface level, or not far above it. Often a widespread temperature inversion exists under such conditions, with cool, foggy or muggy air (often called the "marine layer") underlying warmer, drier air.

Another kind of fog occurs in valleys both close to and far from the ocean. The circumstances ideal for the formation of *radiation fog* (tule fog) are dominant high pressure; clear, cold, cloudless nights; and almost no wind. As the earth's surface radiates its heat into the atmosphere overnight and cools, water vapor condenses into a fog that hovers just a few feet above the ground. If a temperature inversion is present and there is little mixing of air, this kind of fog can persist for days, as it occasionally does in California's Central Valley.

WHITHER THE WEATHER

Where can you find the best, up-to-date information about the weather? Try the newspaper first. The weather maps, statistics, and forecasts are fairly exhaustive, if not completely timely. Nowadays, however, there is more current and dynamic information available to you.

Television weather reports may range anywhere from entertaining to frustrating. If you subscribe to cable TV that offers a continuous weather channel, try that as well. Most PBS-affiliated television stations broadcast a program called "A.M. Weather," which airs around 6 or 7 a.m. weekdays. A.M. Weather is produced by professional meteorologists for pilots. Although a bit technical, it should be one of your most trusted sources of information. Consider that pilots and wilderness trekkers have some of the same concerns and traverse some of the same rarefied heights, and you will readily appreciate this short, but valuable broadcast.

With a computer and access to a major commercial database network, you can obtain on-line information from the National Weather Service. CompuServe, for one, offers this feature with various levels of detail, ranging from high/low temperatures for selected cities to high-resolution graphic displays of weather charts.

Once you've gathered the available information, it will be up to you to make your own predictions for the specific area you intend to visit. One clue is the terrain. Most of the mountain ranges of the West are oriented along a north-south or northwest-southeast axis. That means that if a Pacific storm is predicted, the west flanks of mountain ranges are likely to receive the brunt of the precipitation; they face the approaching storm clouds. On the lee slopes you would expect less precipitation but powerful downdrafts and gusty winds. A warm air mass from the south bearing tropical moisture, on the other hand, might be expected to collide with large obstacles in its path and unleash the heaviest precipitation on south-facing slopes.

In the field you may have to use your sensory skills to gauge the weather, and perhaps a barometer or altimeter to detect pressure changes. One important clue indicating possible bad weather in the mountains is the appearance of lenticular clouds. If layers of lenticulars develop, followed by lowering overcast, watch out—precipitation is probably on its way.

In general the weather will probably remain clear if the barometer stays steady or rises. Bad weather is likely on its way if the barometer drops. Barometers, however, are of limited use in the Southwest, where changes in pressure span a relatively small range.

Another way to keep tabs on regional weather is to carry a small Weather Band radio along on the trip.

Be prepared for every type of weather and you'll be able to journey with confidence, and appreciate—even enjoy—nature's multifaceted moods. As Mark Twain said, "There is only one thing we can be sure of about the weather ... there will be plenty of it."

Recommended Reading:

A Field Guide to the Atmosphere
Vincent J. Schaefer and John A. Day
Houghton Mifflin Co., 1983

The Weather Companion
Gary Lockhart
Wiley Press, 1988
  (One of the more interesting books on weather legends and lore.
  Explores the scientific basis for old wives' tales about the weather.)

Clouds of the World
(An Encyclopedia of Clouds)
Richard Scorer
  (A beautiful catalog of clouds, with detailed explanations of the
  hows and whys of clouds and how they affect the atmosphere.)

Resources:

Weather Forecaster or Weather Cube.
  These National Weather Service broadcast receivers are available from
  the Nature Company or Radio Shack (approx. $40).

Pocket Weather Trends
  A laminated, full-color slide chart that matches sky conditions and
  wind patterns for a 12- to 36-hour forecast. $4.95 from Sporty's Pilot Shop,
  (800) 543-8633, catalog #1612A.

Pocket barometers.
  These range in price from about $30 to $300, depending on their precision
  and altitude range. Check at your favorite outdoor or mountain shop.

Chapter 8

Wilderness Travel

Don Stouder and Nelson Copp

"Unless someone like you cares a whole awful lot, nothing is going to get better. It's not."

—*The Lorax*, by Dr. Seuss

This chapter focuses on how to travel and camp in the wilderness, with the emphasis on doing it safely and gently. The qualities of wilderness areas are preserved when travelers leave no trace of their passage, and degraded when abused in any of dozens of ways, some of them not too obvious. We can only justify our use of a wilderness area for recreation when we strive to "leave no trace."

TRAILHEAD TIPS

Automobiles are by far the most commonly used mode of transportation to and from wilderness trailheads or entry points. Although criminal activity within the wilderness itself is rare, theft and vandalism can be quite common in places where people leave cars unattended for long periods. Try to park in designated areas and let a ranger know how long your car will be parked. Don't forget to lock your car and remove all valuables. For further protection you can disable your car's ignition, or install an anti-theft device on the steering wheel. If you need to use a trailhead that is known to be troublesome, you can have someone drop you off and return to pick you up.

In some areas you may have to contend with theft and vandalism of a different kind. Bears have been known to force their way into cars to get at food they can smell. Marmots, porcupines, and other animals may chew on rubber hoses under the hood.

If your car has recently been prone to mechanical problems, park near a telephone so you can call for help if your car won't start when you return.

Some of the more remote "non-official" wilderness areas that don't enjoy a ban on motorized travel have dirt roads and jeep trails penetrating deep into their interiors. It is tempting for those who arrive in 4-wheel-drive rigs to maneuver as far as possible into these areas on wheels. This can be environmentally damaging, and it's quite often self-defeating. Trying to save a mile or two of walking can result in getting stuck. You may be faced with no easy way to turn around, or hours of tedious digging to free your vehicle from mud, soft sand, or snow.

TRAIL WALKING

We rarely, if ever, think about the act of walking in our everyday lives. When setting off on a long journey through uneven or hilly terrain, however, we must carefully consider pacing, rhythm, rest stops, foot care, and maintaining our energy.

Efficient hiking requires a steady, rhythmic pace. When going uphill, you should shorten your stride yet try to maintain a steady rhythm. Try not to lift your feet higher than you have to, except to swing them around obstacles like rocks and tree roots. It's better to expend your energy evenly throughout a day-long hike, rather than moving too fast in the first hour when you're feeling unbridled and strong.

Some hikers, especially those who are physically well trained, experience a "second wind"—a surge of energy that follows an initial period in which the body accustoms itself to the demands of hard exercise. With a second wind you may feel more comfortable going faster, but again, resist the temptation to do so if you intend to be walking all day.

After about 20 to 40 minutes on the trail, you may want to stop to remove extra clothing and adjust pack straps or shoe laces. Some trip leaders make this first stop a "divided halt," suggesting that men go in one direction and women another to take care of any unmet needs.

Throughout the day, you should stop at regular intervals of a half hour or hour to rest, relieve the pack weight, stretch, or grab a snack. Make these rests brief—five minutes is good—so that you don't cool down too much or become stiff. In unfamiliar areas, you should be keeping track of your position, so rest periods are excellent times to update or confirm your location on a map.

For longer rest stops, such as lunch, put on extra clothing immediately if the weather is cool or cold. The sensation of warmth you get from hiking uphill is from your body's shedding of heat while it expends extra energy. Warm, sweaty skin can turn cold within minutes after you stop.

Don't eat too heavily at any one sitting, or you'll feel like a freight train when you try to move again. Rather, spread some of your lunch over the numerous other breaks.

When walking up very steep slopes, you won't want to become so winded that you can't continue. One solution is to use the "rest step." In this technique you pause briefly every time you begin a new step:

1. Lift your left leg, move it forward, and place it (unweighted).
2. Pause, keeping all of your weight on the right foot.
3. Shift your weight to the left leg and move the right leg forward.
4. Pause, and then continue with step 1.

The rest step is easier to do on a slope than on flat ground, so practice it there to gain a sense of rhythm.

Some hikers swear by a hiking staff; others could care less about one. A staff can be advantageous in areas where balance is precarious (such as at stream crossings), but awkward when you need both hands for climbing or where dense vegetation renders it useless.

Foot blisters simply can't be ignored. Heed the first signs of friction ("hot spots"): adjust your socks, put on moleskin, or do whatever it takes to relieve the pain and prevent damage to the skin.

When extra energy is needed, your body usually tells you so—you get hungry and feel fatigued. Dehydration is more insidious. When strenuously exercising, your body usually needs more fluids than thirst dictates. In hot weather, it's difficult for the body to absorb moisture fast enough. In dry, cold weather, a surprising amount of moisture can be lost from hard breathing and

from "insensible perspiration" (perspiration evaporating so fast that you don't sense its presence). Sip water or other fluids at frequent intervals, even though you may not feel thirst. If you don't feel the need to urinate every couple of hours or so, your body will not be working at its peak performance.

If you are hiking with a group, ideally your natural pace should match the pace of other members of a group. If you know you're significantly slower than others on a trip, it's essential you communicate about it. If it's a formal or club-sponsored trip, let the leader know. Usually an assistant leader stays behind to keep track of the slower members, but if not, and you or others get spread out or separated, you'll want to know where you're going. Normally the leader keeps the group together, but that's not always realized in practice. Go over a trail map with the leader and discuss any points where there might be confusion about the route for slower hikers who may lose sight of those ahead.

Slower hikers often need as much or more time for breaks than faster hikers. It can be most frustrating when a slower hiker catches up to others taking a break, only to have them take off moments later. Feeling pressured to stick with the group, the slower hiker may not have enough time to rest and recover, thus increasing fatigue even more. In the case of a trip designed on a tight schedule, this may be unavoidable. If there's discretionary time on the hike, though, the slower persons should be assertive enough to make their needs and desires known.

Hikers in groups can get spread apart just as readily when "hot shots" insist on forging ahead. Courtesy dictates that on organized hikes, anyone wishing to go ahead of the leader asks permission first.

Hiking etiquette also requires that you yield the right-of-way to horses and other pack animals. If equestrians approach, move off the trail and stand quietly by the side until they pass.

CROSS-COUNTRY TRAVEL

Cross-country, or off-trail travel, can be more challenging and more fun, but often more dangerous and environmentally harmful than sticking to established routes. (By cross-country, we don't mean short-cutting switchback trails—a harmful practice that promotes erosion.) Cross-country travel can take a hiker to remote peaks and other secluded destinations, but it's usually slower and more difficult than trail travel. Navigational difficulties often increase as well. In a few well-traveled wilderness areas, off-trail travel is prohibited because the impact is too harmful.

Make sure your equipment and clothing are up to the task. Wear long pants to protect against rocks, ticks, and low-lying vegetation; and wear a long-sleeve top if scratchy vegetation is likely to be at least waist-high. Sturdy boots will help protect against ankle twists and stone bruises caused by rolling rocks. Gaiters (normally used in deep snow) fastened around your ankles and boots can keep all kinds of debris from entering your boots.

Cross-country travel is more appropriate for smaller groups than hordes of people. In areas choked by dense brush or vegetation, single-file travel is usually most efficient. Don't let tree and shrub limbs that you have pushed aside snap back into the face of the person who follows you.

Groups should stay close together in order to remain within earshot of each other. When traversing delicate ground or vegetation, too many hikers in a column can cut a deep furrow and hasten erosion. To minimize this effect, members of a party can walk side by side to spread out the impact. When possible, try to skirt delicate areas like wet meadows.

Plotting a cross-country route, either at home (with maps on the table) or in the wilderness itself, is intriguing and challenging. In most cases, you should try to follow the same route that a trail-builder would. Trails are often indirectly routed so as to avoid steep ascents, steep terrain, and obstacles such as rock outcrops—even though that means hikers using them will have to walk farther to get from point A to point B. When planning or choosing a cross-country route, you would weigh the advantages of ascending or descending a steep hill against the advantages of a longer but more gradual route around the hill. You would take into account the nature of the terrain along each alternate route. You would try to avoid crossing steep gullies that could contain dropoffs or harbor snow late into the season. You would take into account the types of vegetation—thick brush, open forest, or perhaps a lack of vegetation (as on scree)—that might be present on any of the alternate routes.

Whether it is more efficient to travel along canyon bottoms or streams as opposed to parallel ridges depends on the nature of the local geography. Does the canyon bottom or stream meander excessively? Will frequent stream crossings slow you down? Are the ridgelines spiked by rock outcrops, or are they smooth and relatively free of impeding vegetation?

In practice, route-finding over rough terrain is an exercise in improvisation. Despite your initial planning, you will find it will be necessary to change your intended course many times. Just keep your eyes open and your mind focused on the important milestones or destinations ahead on your intended route.

When traveling cross-country, keep safety uppermost in your mind at all times. Short-cuts over difficult terrain may be tempting, but often they're a waste of time and effort if not outright dangerous. Cross-country travel is a mind game involving elements of intuition as well as standard navigational skills. Improvements in skill will only come by experience.

WILDERNESS CAMPING

When you choose a campsite, do so not only with your comfort in mind, but also the care of the environment. Strive not only to observe the "no trace" principle, but also to clean up or restore camping areas that have been abused by others. If not done properly, camping can affect the wilderness far more seriously than any kind of travel through it. Even when not required to do so, try to use designated or previously used campsites. If possible your site should be a minimum of 200 feet from lakes, streams, and trails. Avoid camping in areas subject to runoff or rockfall, or below rotten trees. Never camp in delicate areas such as alpine meadows. Sandy areas are preferred over those covered by vegetation. Since cold air often flows downward at night and collects in low lying spots, a higher campsite may be warmer. Flying insects are often much less abundant in the higher and drier areas as well. Consider also the effects of wind and the position of the sun as it rises the next morning. Camping on an east-facing slope sheltered from a west wind will make it easier for you to get up the next morning.

When camping in popular areas, be a considerate neighbor. Don't crowd other campers. Leave sound equipment, pets, and other reminders of the civilized world at home. Peace and quiet are two of the earth's most valuable resources. Listen to the soft music of the wilderness: the wind, water, and bird song.

When selecting a site for your tent or sleeping bag, remove small rocks and twigs, but avoid wholesale "grading." The century-old practice of cutting branches for bedding is environmentally harmful, and unnecessary today now that lightweight sleeping pads provide us with all the cushioning we need. During mild weather, sleeping under the stars can be carefree and enjoyable. Cold, rain, or mosquitoes, however, may dictate the need for a tent or a tent substitute like a bivvy sack, tube tent, or a tarp rigged overhead. In harsh conditions, there's no substitute for a sturdy tent.

Being cold at night is a common complaint. Aside from improvements in equipment, here are a few things you can try to make yourself more comfortable in cold conditions:

- Put on warm clothes before you feel cold.
- Find a wind-sheltered spot or orient yourself so that your head is downwind.
- Eat some protein and fats before or after going to bed (this speeds up your metabolism during the night).
- Exercise before going to bed or do isometric exercises inside your bag.
- Wear plenty of dry clothing, especially the insulating variety, inside your bag.
- Wear a wool cap or down hood to prevent heat from leaving your body through your head.
- Place a bottle of hot water (make sure it doesn't leak) near your feet.
- In an emergency, situation, you can sleep close to others to benefit from their body heat.

You can help eliminate the annoyance of mosquitoes and other biting insects by applying insect repellent, using netting in a tent, wearing a head net, or moving to a breezy spot where the insects can be blown away.

Another problem you will deal with at the campsite is sanitation. Urination is not a big issue, since urine is normally biologically sterile, although it causes odor problems too close to camp (try to keep your toilet downwind from camp). Wherever existing facilities are not available, travel a good distance away from camp and any source of water (usually 200 feet or more) to deposit solid body waste. Dig a small "cat-hole" 6-10 inches deep, and when finished fill in the hole with soil and then tamp it down. It's best to pack out all toilet paper or burn it in a safe manner. Be careful if you do any burning—fires have been started by campers leaving smoldering paper buried in dry leaves or pine needles.

While there used to be many options regarding getting rid of garbage, now there are only two: use trash cans where available, and pack out all garbage from areas where garbage cans are not available.

Many hikers look forward to the pleasure of a crackling campfire. Remember, though, that in many wilderness areas in the Southwest they're prohibited, or regulated by fire permit. Actually, you rarely need a fire. Cooking needs can be easily be met by your camping stove alone (see Chapter 9). A candle lantern, used as a substitute for a fire, can add a nice warm touch. Your high-tech clothing should keep you reasonably warm.

If you do have a fire, make it a small one. Bonfires are "out" these days. Besides, you'll enjoy the closer companionship of your friends as you crowd around the glowing embers of a small fire. Whenever possible, use the stove units found at some designated campsites, or use existing rock rings at other sites where fires are permitted.

CLOSE ENCOUNTERS OF THE ANIMAL KIND

Encountering wild animals in their natural habitat during wilderness travel enhances everyone's enjoyment of the wilderness. If you're quiet and observant, you'll increase your chances of spotting wildlife and observing their interesting behavior. Animal encounters may involve bears, bighorn sheep, mountain goats, bobcats, mountain lions and snakes, as well as the more common deer, birds, coyotes, marmots, rabbits, and squirrels. Unexpected encounters with wild animals can be so surprising and so exhilarating that you may forget the wilderness is really their home and that you are an intruder. As a considerate intruder, you have a special obligation to the animals as summarized by the oft-repeated credo, "Take only

pictures, leave only footprints." In other words, do not disturb wild animals or their habitats. This means you must not feed, harass, or handle wild animals (even if they're injured), or disturb the nest or den of a wild animal.

No matter how cute or how tame a wild animal appears, you should never feed it. When animals develop a taste for human food, such as the goodies in your pack, they can easily come to depend on it. Reliance on unnatural and unpredictable food sources may reduce the animal's chances for survival in the wild. By accepting food handouts, wild animals quickly lose their fear of man, their natural predator. This process, called habituation, can become destructive. A classic example of habituated animals are the black bears of Yosemite National Park who raid trash cans and campgrounds for food, undeterred by human presence. These animals have become pests to humans, which requires either their evacuation to remote areas or their destruction. The very act of feeding a wild animal can be dangerous. Some animals do "bite the hand that feeds." If bitten, you risk rabies, serious injury, and even death.

Never harass wild animals, even if it seems the animal would suffer no harm. Harassment includes throwing rocks at them, chasing them, and invading their habitats, except where such actions are necessary for self-defense. Photographers are often guilty of unwittingly harassing animals to get better shots. In doing so, they risk retaliation. A harassed mother bear can charge and even kill a person if she feels her young are under attack. It's better to remain quiet and silent and simply observe or photograph these animals from afar.

The practice of handling wild animals, even if they appear tame and friendly, carries some risk as well. Handling can promote harmful habituation of the animal and also increases your risk of being bitten. It may lead to injuring the animal as well. Handling young animals (especially birds and eggs in nests), could result in parental abandonment.

In the wild, you'll occasionally come upon an injured or abandoned animal. Being compassionate, you'll want to intervene and assist the animal. According to many naturalists, however, human intervention is not the best course of action. Animals have natural defensive abilities that may be thwarted by our actions, leaving them even more defenseless later on. A doe, for instance, will deliberately abandon a young fawn to lure a would-be attacker toward her and away from the fawn. In such situations, the fawn (which has no odor) simply lies down and waits motionless for the doe to return. Human intervention can destroy this natural defensive strategy and cause the doe to forsake the fawn. Injured animals in the wilderness should be left alone to nature's course. This can be a heart-rending decision but it's best in the long run.

OTHER FORMS OF WILDERNESS TRAVEL

In addition to hiking and backpacking, there are several other non-motorized ways to propel yourself across the land: mountain bicycling, mountain running, skiing, and snowshoeing.

Mountain Bicycling

The new all-terrain bicycles, or "mountain bikes," are becoming popular as a means of travel over backcountry terrain. Mountain bikes allow you to cover greater distances than you can normally cover on foot, while providing similar sensations of fun and accomplishment. Mountain bikes, however, are not welcome everywhere. In fact they are banned outright from all federally designated wilderness areas and many park lands. In some areas mountain bikes are allowed on all dirt roads, but no trails. In other areas, particularly on most national-forest lands, mountain bikes can be used almost without restrictions. They are not allowed on any part of the West's most significant

trail—the Pacific Crest Trail. Still, the possibilities of mountain-bike travel are almost endless. There are hundreds of thousands of miles of dirt roads and trails open to mountain biking throughout the western states.

There are many styles and models of mountain bikes to choose from. If you plan to ride mostly off-road, consider a sturdy bike with fat tires. If you're going to spend some of the time on paved roads as well, then get a bike that incorporates some of the features of a road bike. Some hybrid touring/mountain bikes have rims that can accommodate narrow tires for road riding, as well as 2-inch-wide knobby tires.

For years, trails were the sole territory of hikers and horseback riders. The established etiquette involving hikers and equestrians now has been modified to include mountain bikers as well. Here are some guidelines, written from the mountain biker's point of view:

1. Always ride on established roads and trails. Whenever possible ride on roads rather than narrow trails. Don't ride trails that cannot withstand erosion caused by tire tracks (especially avoid muddy trails). Never follow a route whose use by mountain bikes is expressly forbidden. Never create your own trail. Never cut switchbacks on existing trails.

2. Always yield the right-of-way to hikers and horseback riders even though this may require stopping and dismounting.

3. Approach other users slowly. Let others know of your presence well in advance by verbal signals. Pass with care.

4. Control your speed at all times. Most parks have a 15-mph speed limit. Approach switchbacks and turns in anticipation of meeting someone around the bend. (Most conflicts between mountain bikers and other trail users occur because of excess speed around blind curves.)

When venturing into the backcountry on a mountain bike, check the regulations before you go! Remember to take all of the essentials you would take on a hike: extra water, food, clothing, sunscreen, first aid kit, map, and a compass. You'll also need some simple repair tools, tire irons and patches. A helmet is just as essential for safety on dirt roads and trails as when you ride on paved roads.

You'll be covering ground considerably faster on a bike, so don't forget to check your position on a map often. You may need a map that covers a larger area than the ones you are accustomed to using while hiking.

As with any kind of travel in remote areas, travel with friends; there's safety in numbers. The skills and techniques of mountain biking over rough terrain require considerable practice.

Mountain Running

Mountain running, or "adventure running," in wilderness areas is popular among a dedicated group of hard-core athletes. A trained runner carrying minimal gear can easily cover two or three times as much distance over trails than a lightly burdened day-hiker can. A good technique used by some is to mix running and walking. The easier stretches of trail (the smoother, flatter, or slightly downhill parts) are run, while the rougher, steeper stretches are walked.

Running a trail allows you to get to and from remote areas quickly, but it also exposes you to danger if you are not aware of your limitations or careless about preparation. As on any wilderness outing, you need to carry enough survival gear to cover emergencies. Small backpacks that strap on tightly and hip hugging fanny packs that don't bounce can be used to stow minimal gear such as extra clothes and food. You can carry water bottles in your hands or in a special carrier secured to the back of a belt. Water can also be carried in a plastic tube or sack worn around the waist or on the lower back. Some water storage systems have a plastic tube you can drink from while "on the run."

Traveling with companions is especially important when on running excursions. Usually the amount of survival gear you can carry is quite meager, and you may need outside help fairly quickly if you run into a serious problem.

Snow Travel

Cross-country skiing and snowshoeing have become popular, as people want to explore and enjoy the backcountry in winter as well as during the other three seasons. Winter in the mountains offers a special kind of quiet and solitude, and the chance to explore a totally different world.

When you choose a pair of cross-country skis, you'll need to consider what kind of snow conditions and terrain you'll most likely be involved with. Will you be racing around on groomed trails, breaking your own trail, or perhaps even backpacking on skis? Will you put up with the inconvenience of waxable skis for better performance on specific types of snow, or would you rather sacrifice a little performance for the convenience and greater flexibility of waxless skis?

For lighter uses, you should get a performance or sport ski along with lightweight boots. If you'll be skiing steeper, more rugged terrain you'll probably need metal-edged skis and heavier boots.

Waxable-ski bottoms are designed to be coated with a wax that provides both grip for holding the ski in place when the ski is stationary, and lubrication for gliding when the ski is moving across the surface of the snow. The appropriate grade of wax must be applied to match the particular snow temperature and conditions. Waxless skis have some kind of relief pattern on the bottom to provide grip in one direction and glide in the other, and are useable under most snow conditions. For climbing steep pitches, or when negotiating crusty snow, attachments called "climbing skins" may be needed.

Snowshoes, which help you stay on top of soft or powdery snow, range from older wood-frame models to newer metal-frame designs. Most newer models can be strapped to your feet more securely and provide better traction. For both skis and snowshoes, it's a good idea to rent equipment before you buy. More information about skis and snowshoes can be found in Chapter 14.

Overdressing is a common mistake when preparing for activities in the snow. Skiing and snowshoeing are self-warming activities. If you start out slightly chilly, you'll warm up to a toasty temperature rather quickly. (Remember, of course, that you may need to put on plenty of clothing when you stop.) Use the layer system so you can add or remove clothing as needed. Instead of one heavy layer of clothing, use several lighter layers. Gaiters, which cover the tops of your boots and usually extend to mid-calf, help to keep snow from getting into your boots.

Before starting your trip, check the snow conditions. If there's less than a foot of snow on the ground, you can simply hike with waterproofed boots. In that case you may spend much of your time "post holing," a sometimes very tedious way of traveling. On more than a foot of snow, consider snowshoes or skis. If the snow is especially hard or icy, then crampons and an ice axe may be needed for safety (again, see Chapter 14).

Even if you are embarking on a short trip, be sure to carry the essential items you would take on a hike or backpack: extra water, food, clothing, sunscreen, first-aid kit, map, and compass. You'll need extra wax and a scraper if you're using waxable skis. Again, there's safety in numbers, so double up with others on your snow excursions.

TRAVELING AT NIGHT— A SPECIAL SKILL

Generally, wilderness travelers should always try to arrive at camp or at the car before nightfall. If lost at night, it is almost always better to spend a night out and resume hiking in daylight. For a properly equipped hiker with emergency shelter, extra clothing and extra food (the ESSENTIALS, Chapter 5), an overnight bivouac should present no problems.

Under certain circumstances, it may be preferable to press on at night, assuming one is not lost. Also, experienced persons may elect to travel over familiar trails or terrain at night in order to gain a unique, nocturnal perspective of nature.

Travel at night requires that you see as well as possible. If there's a full or nearly full moon in the sky, you're in luck. When traveling by moonlight, try to preserve your night vision. Generally a trail is more visible to a dark-adapted eye than to one dazzled by a glaring flashlight beam. If you do use a flashlight, hold it low so that you can pick out the shadows of obstacles on the route ahead. Lamps worn on the head are of limited value for hiking because shadows cast by the light are in the same direction as the hiker's line of sight and therefore can't be seen. Two flashlights—one a broad-beam headlamp on the head, the other a regular flashlight in the hand—work best.

You'll discover that if you can retain your dark adaption, your peripheral vision is quite good. This is because the periphery of your retina is rich in the "rod" cells that come into play under low light levels. In order to preserve this advantage while using some artificial light at the same time, some hikers use a red filter over their flashlight (a single or double layer of red cellophane over the flashlight lens or around the bulb works well). This eliminates other colors present in white light that tend to spoil one's night vision.

Recommended Reading:

The Complete Walker III
Colin Fletcher
Alfred A. Knopf, 1984

The Nature Observer's Handbook
John W. Brainerd
Globe Pequot, 1986.

Complete Book to All-Terrain Bicycles
Eugene A. Sloane
Simon & Schuster, 1985
    (Helpful guide to all aspects of mountain bikes.)

The Mountain Bike Book
Rob Van der Plas
Bicycle Books, 1990
    (Helpful information about choosing, riding and maintaining off-road bicycles.)

Cross-Country Skiing
Ned Gillette and John Dostal
The Mountaineers, 1988
    (Includes how-to and instructional photos on all aspects of cross-country skiing.)

Snowshoeing
Gene Prater
The Mountaineers, 1988
    (Helpful information about all aspects of snowshoeing.)

Chapter 9

Foods and Cooking

Scott and Priscilla Anderson

"The proof of the pudding is in the eating."

—Miguel de Cervantes

Old photographs of Sierra Club outings show large groups cooking great quantities of food in cauldrons, with wooden tables lined up beneath the giant redwoods, piled high with freshly baked bread.

John Muir, founder of the Sierra Club, wrote, "My meals were easily made, for they were all alike and simple, only a cup of tea and bread."

The choices of what you eat in the wilderness and how you prepare it have never been broader. You can emulate John Muir and yet subsist quite comfortably on a variety of uncooked foods. Or you can bring along a small camp stove, some lightweight cookware, and all the necessary ingredients to whip up a great feast at the end of each day.

NUTRITION BASICS

The number of calories you need depends on a variety of factors such as your physical size, your metabolism, the length of the trip, and the activities planned. For a short, leisurely trip you may only need to raise your caloric intake over the normal amount by 10-20 percent. For long, strenuous trips with a heavy pack, you may need 50-75 percent more calories.

Some people think backpacking is a good way to lose weight, or they may try fasting in the wilderness for health or spiritual benefits. If by traveling your body is demanding more calories, then the wilderness is not the place to cut back on food intake. This is especially true if you're far from civilization. If an accident or delay occurs, lack of food or energy reserves could prove disastrous. Don't use the wilderness for weight loss—do it at home.

When out in the wilderness, it helps to be conscious of how carbohydrates, proteins, fats, and other nutrition components keep your body fortified.

Carbohydrates are the staple of a hiker's diet. They're easily digested and easily converted into muscle energy. They also keep well and are relatively inexpensive. The majority of your daily calories should come in the form of carbohydrates. They should be consumed frequently during the day to keep your energy level up.

Simple carbohydrates include sugar, honey, jams, candy, and refined flour products. Since they are metabolized quickly, they're most beneficial when consumed immediately before or during strenuous exercise, a small amount at a time. During larger meals you can combine them with other foods.

Complex carbohydrates include whole-grain products, starchy vegetables, and beans. They keep the muscles working smoothly, give you energy, and provide bulk and fiber. They don't burn as fast as simple carbohydrates.

Proteins provide sustained energy, keep your muscles in good repair, and help keep you warm when you're not exercising. They are digested more slowly than carbohydrates but faster than fats. Common foods high in protein include meat, fish, beans, peas, cheese, milk, eggs, and nuts. Two to three ounces of protein are all you need each day.

Fats metabolize slowly, but yield more energy than either carbohydrates or proteins. When eaten at dinner, fats keep you from becoming hungry during the night and help you stay warm. In very cold weather or at times when food sources are at a minimum, your body relies on stored fat to survive. Increasing your fat consumption is desirable if you have to deal with very cold conditions. However, fats eaten in large quantities at high altitudes may cause indigestion. Good sources of fat include butter, margarine, nuts, cheese, meat fat, and oil. Under normal conditions, less than 25 percent of your daily calories should be from fats.

Vitamins and minerals enable your body to make the best use of the food you eat. By eating a variety of foods you should get all the vitamins and minerals your body requires. If you are uncertain, you may want to take vitamin and mineral supplements.

Certain minerals (particularly sodium

and potassium) are lost through perspiration during strenuous exercise. You can replenish them through your food or by drinking beverages designed to meet this need (see below). Foods high in sodium include salt, soy sauce, cottage cheese, tomato juice, and cheddar cheese. Foods high in potassium include beans, spinach, raisins, potatoes, oranges, bananas, and milk.

Fiber in foods is important because it helps keep your bodily functions regular. Fiber is found in whole grains, fruits, and vegetables.

Fluid intake can become critically important while engaged in strenuous exercise. Most of us have experienced the discomforts of "cotton-mouth," dizziness, weakness, and headaches when exercising heavily on hot days. These conditions are symptoms of dehydration—the loss of water and minerals from our body, mostly through perspiration. It is very important that lost body fluids be replaced by drinking water or other fluids and by eating sodium-rich and potassium-rich foods. Sport or activity drink mixes (Gatorade, ERG, and other brands) containing simple forms of sugar and minerals (also called electrolytes) can be used. They can be purchased at camp supply stores and grocery stores. Be sure to check the labels to be sure you're getting what you need rather than just flavorings.

Before you start your hike, be sure to "fill up" with fluids and keep drinking throughout the day. Drinking smaller amounts frequently is better than one long gulping session. In general, you should consume one gallon of water or other fluids per day. In the desert you may need much more, and in cool or wet conditions you may need less. With experience, you'll learn what your own body requires.

Alcohol is a fluid, but the effects of alcohol should be considered before consuming it on an outing. Taken in excess, it generates a feeling of warmth for a short time, but it actually promotes a net loss of heat in cold conditions. Alcohol impairs your judgement, balance, coordination and awareness. It also dehydrates the body and decreases your appetite. These effects are multiplied at high altitude. Simply put, excessive alcohol consumption puts you at risk in an environment that magnifies mistakes and misjudgments.

When exercising strenuously for long periods of time, your muscles can only work effectively when your glycogen (internal energy) reserves are high. The best way to achieve this is with a steady intake of carbohydrates throughout the day. Three ounces of carbohydrates every two hours is sufficient for moderate exercise. Sport drinks can help provide additional glucose as well as water and electrolytes. When you're on the move, it's better to avoid high-fat snacks such as cheese, nuts, and chocolates. The energy required to digest them is too great, especially at high altitudes.

Even with frequent meals and snacks, your glycogen reserves can be somewhat depleted after a hard day. You can replenish them by eating plenty of carbohydrates during your evening meal. Foods like pasta fit the bill nicely. If you forget to eat frequently, or skip some meals, exhaustion may come within only a few hours. Recovery is slow. It usually takes more than 24 hours to restore your glycogen reserves if they get depleted.

TYPES OF FOOD

Deciding whether you should take fresh, frozen, dehydrated, and/or canned foods depends on how many days you plan to travel and how much weight you want to carry. Your meals will be more appetizing if you incorporate all three types of food.

Fresh and frozen foods are the healthiest foods you can bring, but most of them spoil easily and weigh a lot. They are great for weekend trips, but less practical for longer trips.

Some homemade breads, energy bars, and cereal mixes will keep for days or weeks and also have high energy-to-weight ratios. By making your own foods in advance you can control the ingredients, thus eliminating or reducing additives such as preservatives. Canned foods expand your choices because they do not spoil. However, the weight of the packaging is a consideration on longer journeys (remember that you'll have to pack out the empty cans). Certain flavorful items that will enhance your versatility in meal planning are available in small cans.

Dehydrated and freeze-dried foods offer good alternatives for longer trips. They are widely available through grocery stores, camp supply stores, and by mail order. Some of these foods are laced with chemical additives, but some companies offer healthier alternatives. Dehydrated foods, especially specialty items, tend to be quite expensive.

Dehydrated food can be bought as pre-packaged meals (turkey tettrazini, beef almondine, etc.) or as individual-item packages. As long as any dehydrated food is properly rehydrated, you can follow recipes as you normally would at home. A disadvantage of dehydrated foods is that some are slow to rehydrate. Pre-soaking helps, and aids digestibility. You can start the soaking process several hours before making camp by mixing the dehydrated food with cold water in a carefully sealed container or water bottle.

If you have the inclination, you can dehydrate your own food at home. The process is fairly simple and can be done in an oven, but better results are obtained from a food dehydrator. Commercial freeze-drying processes remove about 96 percent of the moisture, whereas home dehydration removes about 90 percent. That's not bad considering the money you will save for the little time invested and the control you have over what goes into the food. Almost any kind of food can be dehydrated.

In some cases, foraging for wild foods can supplement your diet. However this requires specialized knowledge of plants and their uses. Learning about

non-poisonous and edible plants and gathering them in the right areas can add a new appreciation of nature's bounty and beauty. Foraging can be time-intensive, and you may not locate what you want when you want it. Always check with the local rangers first to see if harvesting wild plants is legal in the area you plan to visit. In many parks, cutting or picking any plant is illegal.

MENU PLANNING

Planning your meals can be time consuming until you develop a repertoire of recipes. It is important to create a menu and then to check off each item as you purchase it and pack it. When formulating menus, you need to consider both nutritional value and weight. In addition to food for the regular meals and trail-side snack breaks, plan to purchase some extra food for use during emergency situations.

When trying to decide which foods to take, consider the length of your trip, the expected climate, the size of your cooking group, meal preparation time, food variety and taste, and the cost.

For weekend trips you can eat almost anything. Nutrition is not a major concern, except that you must take in enough calories to cover your energy expenditures. Trips longer than three days require more planning regarding nutrition and weight. One and a half pounds of dry weight per person per day should be enough.

Be sure to study a map of the area where you intend to camp. Know where water supplies are located. Determine whether you'll have to make do with one or more "dry camps." An important factor affecting your selection of food is the amount of water you'll have to carry. One gallon of water weighs 8.3 pounds.

Heat reduces your appetite but increases your water needs. Cold increases your body's need for more calories. Hot foods and liquids are more appetizing in cold conditions, and help you stay warm. Never underestimate your needs for food and water. Carrying a few extra pounds is far better than suffering dehydration or hypothermia.

Forming a cook group of people who share the same menu cuts down on the amount of weight carried. There's less duplication of cooking equipment, and the weight of the food and equipment is distributed among those who carry it. Cook groups of three or four people work quite well, as many pre-packaged meals are designed for four servings. With a large group you should consider arranging a group commissary ("central commissary") in which two stoves and two large pots serve up to about 15 people, and cooking and clean-up chores are rotated among the members of the group. Central commissary is commonly used on longer Sierra Club outings.

If you need to get an early start on a given day, keep some breakfast flakes or instant cereal and powdered milk handy in a plastic bag while you start your hike. During your first break, add water to the cereal and powder and have a quick meal before continuing. High-carbohydrate snacks every hour should keep the furnace burning. If you return to camp late in the day, hot soup and a dehydrated meal are quick and easy.

If your plans are more leisurely, you could enjoy a more elaborate breakfast such as eggs, pancakes, sausage and biscuits, which take time to prepare and to clean up. A day hike could start in the mid-morning and you could return by mid-afternoon. Dinner could be a multi-course meal with salad or soup, a main course of fresh fish and vegetables, and dessert, with time to clean up and relax before going to bed.

Neither type of trip, or variations in between, is better than the other—it's a matter of choice, and you can do both on the same trip. Remember that advance preparation at home can save hours out in the wilderness where you will lack the convenience of a modern kitchen.

Striving for well-balanced meals should give you plenty of variety. Longer trips require more variety to meet your taste desires and to ensure that your nutritional needs are met. Failure to meet these needs could result in a loss of appetite and possibly a debilitating weakening of the body.

Keeping costs down is another consideration when preparing a trip menu. Perhaps you would put this high on your importance list, but food cost should never be the primary factor in choosing what is right for a trip. If a trip requires a great expense, you should consider whether or not you should go, not how little you can bring to survive.

To simplify your menu planning, you can create a chart, such as the one below, which includes the trip days, the meals required for each day, and a list of foods for each meal in the gridboxes.

Day	Breakfast	Lunch	Dinner	Snacks/Misc
Friday	(Home)			
Saturday				
Sunday				
Monday				
Tuesday		(Home)		

SAMPLE MENUS:

	Day 1	Day 2
Breakfast	Oatmeal with fruit Milk Coffee	Western omelet Fruit juice Hot cocoa
Lunch	Jerky Crackers with honey Dried fruit	Bagel Low-fat cream cheese Granola bar
Dinner	Tomato soup Chicken a la king Roll Chocolate pudding	Beef stew Crackers Fruit cobbler

A substantial breakfast is important. It gives you much of the energy you'll need for the first half of your day's activity. Generally, this meal should consist of carbohydrates (both simple and complex) to get you going and some protein or fat to help sustain you for several hours.

Because time may be limited in the middle of the day, you may decide to base your midday meal on whole-grain breads or crackers with spreads such as jam, honey, and peanut butter. Lunch may not be a "square meal," but instead intermittent snacking on high-carbohydrate, low-protein, low-fat foods that digest quickly. A common trail snack is GORP, which stands for "good ol' raisins and peanuts." Today, GORP (or trail mix) comes in a variety of combinations of nuts, seeds, small crackers, dried fruits, and candies. Most prepackaged trail mixes are loaded with fats. You may wish to create your own combinations.

Dinner should include carbohydrates, protein and fats. There's ample time for your body to properly digest all of them. This is also the time to replenish the salts and liquids you have lost during the day. Start your dinner with a hot beverage or soup (unless it's a warm evening, in which case something cool might be more refreshing). To conserve fuel and save time, try "one-pot" meals. The use of spices and seasonings can enhance the flavor of many prepackaged meals. A shake of curry livens up a rice dish. Add onion flakes to your stew. Sprinkle a little sage and basil in the butter or oil before cooking your freshly caught trout. Last, but not least, top the meal off with a satisfying dessert and enjoy a social gathering around the campfire.

Your menu should also include extra foods that could see you through an emergency situation. Take foods that will keep well and need little or no cooking in case you run out of fuel. Your emergency supplies might include jerky, granola bars, trail mixes, dried fruits, and additional dehydrated, prepackaged meals. Don't pack foods that are too tasty, or you may be tempted to dig into them unnecessarily. Wrap the food up tightly, store it in the bottom of your bag, and forget about it. You can use the same batch of emergency food for multiple trips, as long as it remains fresh enough.

SHOPPING AND PACKAGING

Once you have planned your meals, create a shopping list of needed foods. Check each item off as you find it, and again as you pack it for the trip. There are a variety of places you can shop: supermarkets, natural food stores, camping stores, ethnic food stores, mail order catalogs. Camping stores and mail order catalogs are a good source for dehydrated foods and meals.

Packing foods takes time. You can't start randomly stuffing food items into your pack wherever you have a little room, or you'll find that you'll still be searching for ingredients while others are enjoying their hot meal. Repackaging and grouping your food supply takes some time at home, but will save weight, shorten preparation time in camp, and make it almost impossible to run out of food on the last day of a trip. Before doing that, decide how much weight you can handle, what containers will work best, and how you will organize your foodstuffs to make them easily accessible.

To keep weight to a minimum, remove all unnecessary store packaging. (Some crackers travel best in their boxes; canned meats, of course, are best left in their cans.) Measure and pack ingredients for individual meals together in a labeled plastic bag, and don't forget to include instructions. If the whole of your food supply ends up too heavy, then examine the heaviest items and ask yourself if there is something lighter that could be substituted.

Most of the containers you'll need are probably around the house already:

• *Bags.* Most food items can be repackaged in plastic or cloth bags. Bags are economical, convenient, light, and reusable, but they don't meet every backpacking need. For example, freeze-dried products are often packaged in foil packets. Don't repackage them. These pouches are moisture tight and also serve as good containers for rehydrating the food.

• *Plastic bottles and jars.* Dry seasonings can be packaged in film cans or pill bottles. These are light in weight and have tight-fitting caps. Use wide-mouth plastic jars and other plastic storage containers when necessary, but keep these to a minimum as they are bulky. Plastics can absorb odors, flavors, and oils from the contents, which may foster bacteria. Be sure you thoroughly clean these containers between trips. If the contents are a liquid or powder, be sure to enclose the plastic container in a self-sealing plastic bag to contain any possible leakage.

• *Squeeze tubes:* Reusable squeeze tubes (as opposed to squeeze bottles) are great for foods such as honey, peanut butter, jam, and mustard. Squeeze tubes are filled from an open end that is later sealed tight by a plastic clip. They can be obtained at camp supply stores and by mail order.

• *Egg cartons.* Plastic egg cartons come in sizes to hold as little as two and as many as a dozen eggs. You can use one to carry fresh eggs as long as you place it in a self-sealing plastic bag—just in case. (If you plan to use fresh eggs very early on the trip, you can break them into a plastic bottle at home, and then simply pour them out when it's time to use them.) Egg cartons can also be used to transport delicate items such as chocolate truffles, if it's worth the trouble.

For the final organization of your foodstuffs, you can employ either of these two methods:

• *Package by common meals.* Select a different colored stuff sack for each type of meal—breakfast, lunch/snack, dinner—and another sack for coffee, tea, sugar, and condiments and seasonings that could be used during any meal.

• *Package by day.* Group all breakfast, lunch and dinner foods for a given day in the same sack. You'll still want to keep a separate bag for items that could be used during any meal.

COOKING EQUIPMENT

The simplest source of energy for cooking is, of course, a campfire. Even in areas where such fires are permitted, however, you will in most cases have a much easier time using a camp or backpacking stove. If you do plan to use a campfire, you can find many cookbooks that discuss the use of grills and dutch ovens, and various open-fire cooking techniques.

A good selection of lightweight stoves and cookware can be found at most camp supply stores. When planning meals, you'll need to consider equipment as well. You can't prepare 3 quarts of one-pot meal in a $2^1/2$ quart pot! You won't want to place a massive kettle with a meal for a large group on a tiny Svea stove.

When choosing a stove, consider first its performance under the conditions—temperature, wind, and elevation—you'll likely encounter during your trip. Also consider the stove's weight, ease of fueling and operation, reliability, and the availability of the fuel it uses. To help you choose the right stove, talk to people who use them and to sales people at camp supply stores. Several outdoor magazines have published comparative information about stoves and reviews of new models.

Stoves can be classified by the types of fuel they burn:

Liquid fuel: These stoves burn kerosene, white gas (Coleman fuel), unleaded gasoline, and alcohol. In most cases, the fuel reservoir must be pressurized (with a small air pump) and the liquid fuel must be heated in the vicinity of the burner so it can be vaporized for combustion. The start-up procedure, known as "priming the stove," can be quite a ritual for some models.

Liquid fuel stoves are economical to operate and have a high heat output. Most are designed to run on white gas, but a few stoves utilize two or three different types of fuel (white gas, kerosene, unleaded gasoline). That is a good feature if you're traveling to a foreign country where kerosene is available but white gas is not. White gas is very flammable (which is why it's a good stove fuel), burns cleanly, and evaporates quickly when spilled. Kerosene is less volatile than white gas, and slower to ignite and evaporate, but has more heat per volume of fuel. It has a greasy feel, a lasting odor, and a tendency to give off smoke and soot when burning. Alcohol is safe to use as a stove fuel and is usually contained in a cup under the stove. When the alcohol is ignited, the surface layer burns and the heat is regulated by a lever that allows more or less air into the cup. Alcohol burns clean, but has the lowest heat output, and the highest cost, of all the liquid fuels. Cooking a meal seems to take forever. Stoves that burn alcohol appear to be on the decline.

Canister-type stove

Liquid fuel stove

Extra fuel outside of any liquid fuel stove tank should be carried in special fuel bottles with tight fitting caps and special seals. For some models of liquid fuel stoves, the tank is an integral part of the stove, while for others the stove has no tank but is designed to be connected to a fuel bottle. Some stoves have small tanks (you hope you can finish cooking dinner before running out of gas), while others will run full blast for over three hours. Some operate nicely over the entire range from simmer to full heat, while others perform best when operating like (and sounding like) a hissing blowtorch.

Canister Fuel: These stoves burn propane, butane, a propane/butane mix, or isobutane, all of which are gases at normal temperatures and pressures. Before use, the burner of the stove is attached to a non-reusable metal canister that holds the fuel. The fuel inside the canister is pressurized, which keeps the gas in a liquid state. It is hard to tell how much fuel is left in a canister (especially from one trip to the next), so you must carry one or more spare cans, depending on the length of your trip. Propane canisters are heavier than butane canisters. Some canisters have a built-in valve which allows for detachment from the burner between uses, while other types are punctured upon installation and must remain attached to the burner until empty. (Spent canisters, of course, must be packed out as trash.) Canister stove use is quite simple—just light a match and open the single valve. To simmer, close down the valve part of the way. These stoves have less heat output than white gas or kerosene stoves and cost more to operate, but are always easy to use. Butane, however, must be warmed to operate at cold temperatures.

Solid fuel: Solid fuels include jellied alcohol (Sterno), heat tablets, and charcoal. These fuels are very safe to handle, but all have a low heat output. Stoves using these fuels are of limited use in the wilderness.

Stove stability varies quite a bit among models. The bottom of the stove or the breadth of its tripod legs (its "footprint") determines how stable the stove will be on the ground. Generally the larger the footprint, the more stable the stove. It is also important to pay attention to the method by which cookware is supported on top of the stove.

Many stoves feature a windscreen that is either part of the stove or an accessory. Some pot sets are designed to seat into certain windscreens to improve stability and performance. A windscreen, however, should never allow the fuel tank to overheat. Because all stoves are very sensitive to winds, a windscreen should be considered a mandatory piece of stove equipment.

Stoves that disassemble for transport (such as the MSR brand liquid fuel stove) must be protected from dirt. Any dirt that enters the pump body or fuel tube will clog the small orifice that helps vaporize the fuel. The use of a cleaning needle may just push dirt particles around. A dirt-clogged burner must be carefully disassembled to clean it well. To avoid complications, always keep the pump body in a clean plastic bag. Never leave it unprotected on your fuel bottle. The end of the fuel tube should be capped securely with a rubber eye-dropper bulb.

One-piece stoves with built-in cleaning needles (such as the Coleman Peak 1) are heavier, but often more reliable.

All stoves must be considered dangerous, but with a little knowledge and common sense it is possible to minimize this danger. The most important thing to do is understand how your stove works—read the instruction manual. Some models have instructions printed on the stove itself. Test the stove's operation at home (outside) to see that it works properly before taking it on a trip.

The following are some precautions and tips for fueling a stove:
• Never refuel a liquid fuel stove when the stove is hot.
• Use care when pouring liquid fuel into

the stove. Use a small funnel or a pouring cap and add fuel slowly. Check the level in the tank and don't overfill. A filter funnel may help keep the fuel inside your stove clean.
, Leave a little air space on top of the fuel for stoves that need pumping.
. Refuel away from flame sources.
. Don't pour fuel inside a tent.
, Check the fuel level before starting to cook a meal to ensure that the stove doesn't run out of gas while you're cooking.
, Replace the cap on both the fuel bottle and stove before lighting the stove.
. When attaching a canister to a canister-type stove, be careful. The screw threads should be easy to turn (don't cross-thread the fittings) and the gasket surfaces must be clean.
• After the canister is attached, make sure it doesn't leak (listen for a hissing noise). Make sure the on-off valve is closed and the canister is tightly attached.
• Puncture-type canisters must not be removed unless empty.
• Never throw an "empty" canister into a fire. It might not be empty!

Operating a stove can be simple and easy, but hazardous if not done properly. By observing these guidelines, you can prevent accidents and end up with a warm meal:
• Avoid cooking inside a tent. A burning stove consumes oxygen and gives off deadly carbon monoxide gas. If you are forced to cook inside, open the door flap and vents to let plenty of fresh air inside. Some tents have a covered vestibule that can be used when cooking. If possible, prime and light the stove outside and carefully bring it in after the stove is operating properly.
• Make sure that the stove is in a safe place and is on a stable, level surface.
• Place a pan on the stove to make sure everything is stable enough before lighting the stove.
• For canister stoves, light the match and hold it next to the burner before turning on the gas.

• Do not leave a stove unattended while it is burning.
• When cooking on snow, insulate the stove from the snow with a piece of cardboard, wood, foam, or a pan lid.
• If the stove has a removable key that operates the flame adjustment, remove it during stove operation.
• Carry spare parts, tools, cleaning needles, and instructions on how to repair your stove. Clean orifice holes regularly.

Economize, but don't skimp on your cookware and utensils. One pot and perhaps a small water kettle may suffice for one or two people, but fancier meals may require the use of two pots. Most backpacking pots are made of aluminum or stainless steel, and some now come with a non-stick surface.

Some cook sets consist of two pots nestled together with handles that fold down, or no handles at all (a pan grip is used), and a lid that also serves as a fry pan. You can also modify ordinary pans by removing or shortening the pan's handle.

It is very helpful to have your cookware marked with common intervals of volume measurement (1 cup, 2 cups, 3 cups, etc.). If your pots are not already so marked, you can do it yourself with a hammer and screwdriver.

If you're cooking alone, one spoon can serve for both cooking and eating. In a group, you'll need separate utensils. Be careful when cooking with a metal spoon—don't leave it in the pot when you're cooking or you may burn your fingers. Other common cooking utensils include a spatula and knife (a pocket knife often suffices).

The stainless steel "Sierra Cup" has been popular with backpackers for years. It is easy to clean; however it can burn your lips when you drink freshly poured hot liquids, and it allows liquids to cool down too quickly in cold temperatures. An insulated plastic cup, with or without a lid, is easier to use for drinking and keeps your beverage or soup hot for a longer period of time. Some plastic cups with volume markings can double as measuring cups.

If you're cooking only for yourself, you can simply eat from the pot or pan. Otherwise, each person will need a bowl or plate to eat from. A divided plate works well if your menu calls for more than a one-pot meal. As a minimum, use a pocket knife for cutting food and a spoon for eating. A fork is nice, but not necessary.

Here are a few other useful items: Wide-mouth plastic bottles marked at $1/4$ cup intervals are handy for mixing beverages, pancake batter, and pudding. A small wire whip takes the place of your mixer back home for dry ingredients combined with liquids. Don't forget a small can opener (if you have cans), a measuring cup (if nothing else you have measures volume), aluminum foil (for a variety of uses), and a wooden spoon. A bandana can serve as a mini-tablecloth, dish towel, hot pad and more. For cleaning up, you'll need biodegradable soap and a pot scrubber.

WILDERNESS COOKING

Once you're out in the wilderness, your thorough planning and preparation will pay off. Make sure you have plenty of water, and allow the right amount of time to prepare your meals.

Unfortunately, the days of blithely filling your canteen and drinking from untested or untreated sources of water are gone. Even in the most remote areas water may be contaminated with a small protozoan, *Giardia lamblia*. Giardia is transmitted from an infected animal (including humans) whose body waste is deposited or seeps into a water supply which is then consumed by another animal or person. It may cause severe diarrhea, cramps, nausea, and vomiting. Many physicians haven't had enough experience with the disease to correctly diagnose it. If untreated, the disease may go on for years. Incubation time is one to two weeks, though some people have gone as long as two months before getting sick. Not everyone ingesting Giardia shows symptoms of the disease. Some may simply be carriers.

In addition to Giardia, there may be other contaminants in the water supply. You should always assume that the water found in the wilderness is contaminated and you should use one of the three basic methods to purify the water:

Boiling: This is the most reliable and preferred method of treating drinking water. Most organisms are killed instantly when water reaches the boiling point. Another five minutes ensures the purity of your drinking water even at high altitudes. With this method, you need to make sure you have plenty of extra fuel.

Chemical treatment: Iodine tablets ("emergency drinking water germicidal tablets") are a convenient way to purify water. There is a slight iodine taste in the water, but it can be camouflaged with flavored beverage crystals. The tablets lose their strength over time. Make sure the date is marked clearly on the bottle and replace them every other year. Be aware that some people are allergic to iodine.

Filtering. Water filters are expensive, but filtering can be done almost as fast as chemical treatment and it does not introduce a bad taste. Make sure the filtering apparatus you buy can either be easily cleaned or has a replaceable filter cartridge or element. Filter pores must be 0.4 microns or less in size to be effective against Giardia.

When you establish your campsite, take time to pick out a cooking area nearby that is at least 100 feet away from any water source. You don't want your garbage and waste water to contaminate rivers and lakes. Look for a flat, wind-protected spot to put your stove on. A large, flat rock or rock ledge, or a low area next to a large fallen tree works well for setting up your kitchen. If the soil is sandy or soft, or if you're camping on snow, you may need to put some support under your stove to steady it.

Your first step in preparing any hot meal is to start up the stove and heat some water. Hot water is always need-

Boiling Point of Water:	
Elevation	*Temperature*
Sea level	212°F
5,000 feet	203°F
10,000 feet	194°F
14,000 feet	187°F

ed—for preliminary hot drinks or soup, and for your main course or courses. After cooking the main course you may want to keep your stove busy heating hot water for more hot drinks, dessert, and dishwashing.

For freeze-dried and dehydrated foods, read the instructions carefully. These foods can be quite inedible if not properly rehydrated. Presoaking of some foods may take 15-60 minutes, so allow enough time for it. Food that has been shredded, grated, or powdered usually takes a short time; whole pieces take longer. The higher the water temperature, the shorter the time it takes to rehydrate it.

High-altitude cooking is always slower because the higher the elevation, the lower the boiling temperature of water (see the table above). Some packaged-food instructions give cooking-time adjustments for various altitudes. Cooking time for most boiled or simmered food doubles at about 10,000 feet. You may want to keep notes on the cooking time of your favorite foods for reference on future trips. Remember to take extra fuel if you'll be cooking a lot

Cleaning up after a meal is quite simple, and should be done immediately so as not to attract animals into your camp. For some foods, a thorough cleaning in plain hot water is sufficient. For meats or greasy foods or those that stick to cookware, the use of biodegradable soap is recommended. This is especially important for groups to help prevent the spread of germs. Water used for washing (dishes or self) should be dumped well away from camp, among stones or by a bush, and at least 100 feet from any body of water.

Disposing of garbage is a simple matter—pack it out. If you have a campfire, you can burn paper products; but plastics, aluminum, orange peels, apple cores, egg shells, and the like should be packed out. Garbage in or near a camp is unsightly and trains animals to become camp thieves. Most non-food garbage degrades very slowly, and even some food garbage can take months or years to rot away in a cold and/or dry environment.

It may be impossible to stop hungry critters from visiting your campsite at night To accommodate them in a way that is best for both you and them (some human foods may be tasty but harmful to animals), remove all food from your backpack and leave all the pockets unzipped. Usually, if an animal can't get access to the contents of a pocket that smells of food, he simply chews or tears into it. Move all food away from your pack to a safe place. Hanging your food in bags several feet above the ground may be effective against the usual bandits such as rodents and raccoons. In bear country, use "bear boxes" if they're provided. Otherwise, certain hanging techniques work best (see Chapter 11). In any case, never keep food in your tent in bear country. To discourage any visitation at all, keep your camp clean and free of garbage scraps.

Bon appetit!

Recommended Reading:

Backpacker's Cookbook
Margaret Cross and Jean Fiske
Ten Speed Press, 1974
(A good beginning book on the basics of backpack cooking. Includes instructions on how to sew stuff sacks and a pot bag. Recipes included.)

Simple Foods for the Pack
Vikki Kinmont and Claudia Axcell
Sierra Club Books, 1976.
(Includes 175 trail-tested recipes using natural, inexpensive ingredients.)

The Back-Packer's Food Book
Hasse Bunnelle and the editors of Backpacker Magazine
Backpacker, Inc., 1981
(Includes information on seasonings for foods, a chart of food values for commonly used camp and trail food items, food additives and chemicals, 300 recipes, provisioning for short to long trips, and more.)

The On and Off Road Cookbook
Carl Franz and Lorena Havens
John Muir Publications, 1982.
(A book for hikers, boaters, campers, and travelers of all kinds. Humorously written. Includes planning, economizing, equipment, a food values chart, packing and storage, recipes, and more.)

Camping Secrets
Cliff Jacobson
ICS Books, Inc., 1987
("A lexicon of camping tips only the experts know." Topics are organized alphabetically and range from Anchor to Yard Goods.)

Chapter 10

Coastal Travel

Don Stouder and Emily Troxell

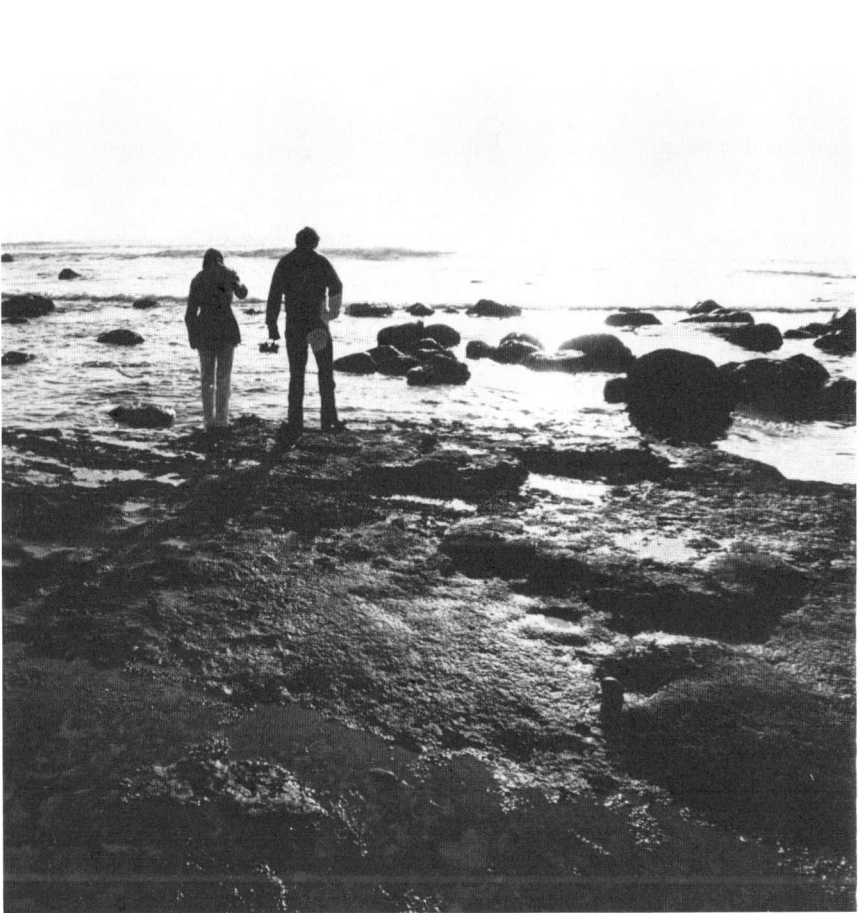

"Go west, young man."

—John Soule (popularized by Horace Greeley)

"Go west" was heeded by hundreds of thousands of nineteenth-Century Americans. Their descendants, plus millions of recent immigrants, populate much of the land in the U.S. within 20 miles of the Pacific Ocean. Today, visiting a crowded beach is as "wild" an experience as many citizens ever get. But that's no reason to sell our coastline short—it's still one of the world's most magnificent meetings of land and sea. For every overcrowded beach there's a quiet lagoon or a rocky shoreline where nature reigns.

Let's look at the natural history of the coast, some travel techniques, and how we can minimize our impact on this unique part of our world.

THE DYNAMIC COAST

No matter if the beholder is a biologist, geologist, artist, surfer, or beachcomber, the thin edge of our continent has much to offer. For biologists, the coastline is interesting as an *ecotone*, a boundary where diverse biological habitats converge (this particular boundary is the *intertidal zone*). Geologists look at the wave-battered cliffs and see the structure of the earth laid bare. Artists, surfers, or anyone for that matter, can appreciate the power and dynamism of the waves.

The slowest kind of dynamic change on the coast is geological in nature. America's west coast is young and restless. During the past few million years, the edge of the continent has experienced repeated episodes of uplift (not to mention lots of horizontal movements), while ocean levels have risen and fallen many times. The most common kind of rock found along the coastline is sedimentary—sandstone, shale, conglomerate—the product of river silt and sand deposited in low lying areas on land and offshore long ago. This type of rock, which is inherently weak, is constantly exposed to severe erosion by wave action. Other types of rock, volcanic among them, resist the battering of the waves somewhat better but eventually

succumb and crumble like all the rest.

More rapid changes, still in the geologic realm, involve the movements of sand particles. These particles are tiny bits of hard minerals eroded from rocks that lie inland. Carried coastward by rivers, they bide their time along the shoreline before being dragged offshore by wave action or perhaps being blown inland. Unfortunately, the sources of our beach sands are being choked off as the natural course of rivers are blocked upstream with dams. Would-be beach sand simply accumulates behind the dams. This problem is particularly severe in Southern California, where some communities have had to import vast quantities of river sand and dredging spoils to maintain their beaches.

The ebbs and flows of the tides cause rapid and repetitive changes in the environment of the intertidal zone. In the past, some cultures attributed the rise and fall of the ocean waters to the breathing of a gigantic sea monster. Today the explanation is, in a way, even more romantic: tides are a consequence of the moon's attraction for the earth. The basic fact is that the moon's gravitational pull produces two watery "bulges" on the earth—one on the side facing the moon, the other on the side facing away from the moon. As the earth turns on its axis once per day, we pass through the bulges twice a day, and that gives us two high tides and two low tides. Because the moon keeps moving around the earth (taking roughly one month to complete one orbit) the double high-low cycle repeats over a period of not exactly 24 hours, but roughly 24 hours and 50 minutes.

The rise and fall of tides are actually very complex. The sun's gravitational pull has some affect: During new and full moons the solar influence adds to that of the moon, and we have higher high tides and lower low tides (*spring* tides). During first- and third-quarter moons the solar influence diminishes, but does overcome the moon's pull, so we have less extreme highs and lows (*neap* tides).

Despite these general rules, tidal periods and heights cannot be accurately predicted without sophisticated mathematical modeling. The results of these calculations are found in tide tables. Newspapers carry daily or monthly tidal predictions. Most bait-and-tackle shops and marine outlets offer a yearly tidetable booklet. Tide information is essential for hikers who plan to explore coastlines hemmed in by cliffs.

In a very immediate sense, the coastline environment is dominated by the ocean waves. Waves are born in the high winds of storms, and can travel to distant shores. On the open ocean, waves may differ in speed, in height, and in spacing. The time interval between successive waves (the period) is controlled by both the spacing (the wavelength) and the speed. The typical period is 10-15 seconds. If waves of diverse character travel a great distance together, they tend to coalesce in the form of swells. And when a swell encounters the increasingly shallow water close to shore, it curls over as a breaker. A multitude of breakers is surf. Surfers are aware that the waves seem to come in "sets." There's no magic formula for predicting sets; in fact there's always a lot of natural variation in the sizes of waves. Hikers on the shoreline should always be wary of the rogue wave that may sweep in unexpectedly.

When water in a breaking wave runs up along the shoreline, it must return to sea again. Frequently it does so as a narrow outgoing stream called rip current, riptide, or undertow (actually this type of water action has nothing to do with the tides). Rip currents can be dangerous to those unfamiliar with them. If caught in one, don't try to swim against it—it will wear you out. Instead swim parallel to shore, even if that action takes you away from shore temporarily. You'll eventually come to a place where the current goes toward the shore.

THE INTERTIDAL ZONE

The intertidal zone—the narrow strip of coastline between the reach of highest and lowest tides—contains one of the world's most fascinating environments. It's a bit subtle though. You won't notice the churning life underfoot unless you pause and take a very close look.

The animals living here have had to adapt to many different environmental forces. Most live both in and out of the water. Food is usually brought to them. Each animal's territory is quite small and most of them don't move around much—not a very exciting life story. But in accelerated time, these creatures are actually very active. Let's take a look at the four basic intertidal zones and explore the life styles of some of the creatures found in each.

The *splash zone* lies above the reach of high tide, but not the momentary surge or splash of a breaker. Some parts are never covered by water, other parts can be inundated for short periods of time. Animals living here must move about and hunt for food without the aid or cover of water. Certain kinds of limpets, crabs and lice are found here.

The next lower zone, the *high tide zone*, is squeezed between the "mean high-tide" level and the "mean higher high-tide" level. This area experiences the pounding of the waves almost every day. Animals here must withstand the great crush of water as well as alternating wet-dry conditions. Limpets, chitons, aggregate anemones, certain crabs, and periwinkles are found here. Most interesting are the aggregate anemones. These beautiful flower-like mollusks are far from beautiful in their behavior. Their tentacles shoot poison barbs at invading creatures and at prey (interestingly, humans are not affected by the barbs). When the tide is low, aggregate anemones look like a mass of broken shells and sea trash in the cracks of the rocks found in the tidal pools.

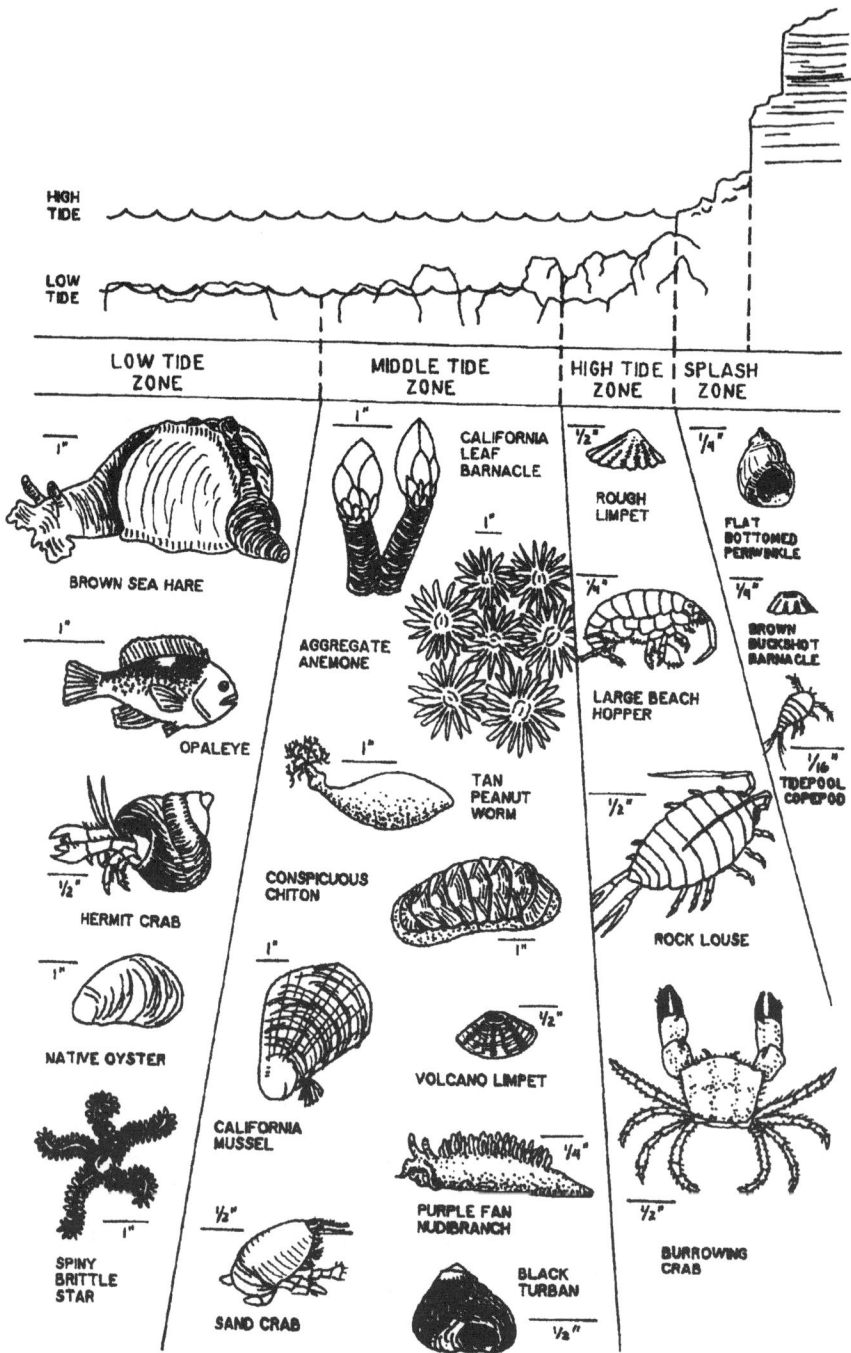

| HIGH TIDE | | | |
| LOW TIDE | | | |

| LOW TIDE ZONE | MIDDLE TIDE ZONE | HIGH TIDE ZONE | SPLASH ZONE |

1"
BROWN SEA HARE

1"
CALIFORNIA LEAF BARNACLE

½"
ROUGH LIMPET

¼"
FLAT BOTTOMED PERIWINKLE

1"
OPALEYE

AGGREGATE ANEMONE

1"

¼"
LARGE BEACH HOPPER

¼"
BROWN BUCKSHOT BARNACLE

½"
HERMIT CRAB

1"
TAN PEANUT WORM

½"

1/16"
TIDEPOOL COPEPOD

1"
NATIVE OYSTER

CONSPICUOUS CHITON

1"

ROCK LOUSE

1"
SPINY BRITTLE STAR

1"
CALIFORNIA MUSSEL

½"
VOLCANO LIMPET

½"
SAND CRAB

¼"
PURPLE FAN NUDIBRANCH

BLACK TURBAN
½"

½"
BURROWING CRAB

The most diverse of the four zones is the *middle tide zone*, where creatures spend about as much time in the water as out. Mussels, barnacles, sand-castle worms, turban snails, green anemones, and sea hares make their homes there. Sea hares are giant slug-like creatures that live on algae. They're slimy—and so distasteful that no other creature will eat them.

Some of the most mobile intertidal creatures are found in the *low tide zone*. This area is seldom free from water, and seldom accessible to beach walkers. Sea hares, sea stars, urchins, keyhole limpets, sea cucumbers, and nudibranchs are found here.

The name of the game in tidepool exploring is timing. Scan the tide tables in search of the lowest tide levels, and plan to arrive at the coast a little in advance of the predicted extreme low tide. On the Pacific coast, tides of lower than minus 1.5 feet (tides are measured relative to a reference level of "mean lower low tide") are needed for you to gain access to the lowest of the four intertidal zones without getting soaked. These extreme low tides occur on one or two afternoons (on or near the days of new and/ or full moon) each month from October through March.

TRAVELING THE COAST

Although only a fraction of the Pacific coastline actually lies within parks or preserves, public access to shoreline areas is generally guaranteed. In California, for example, all areas seaward of the "mean high-tide line" are publicly owned. This is interpreted to mean that visitors have the right to walk on the wet sand. Access to the shore from the nearest street or coastal highway can be somewhat problematic, however. In some areas, public-access roads, paths, and stairways are clearly marked. In other areas you may see nothing but fences and NO TRESPASSING signs. Guidebooks and visitor centers are good sources of local information.

The Pacific coast almost always has a cooler, windier, and more humid environment than areas even a short distance inland. The sun's rays are more intense due to reflection from sand and water. You're quite likely to get your feet wet, and the salt-laden water or spray may be damaging to the gear you carry. Keep these things in mind when you plan a coastal trip.

You can leave the mountaineering boots at home. Light hiking shoes (properly treated to repel water), sneakers, sandals, and even bare feet all work fine on the easier terrain. Rocky shorelines require something more substantial. For very wet areas, mud boots with rubber lug soles are ideal. Be sure to wear thick socks with these boots for extra cushioning.

In terms of clothing, remember that you must protect yourself against both the wind and the ultraviolet radiation from the sun. Keep most of your body covered, wear a hat and sunglasses, apply sunscreen to exposed skin, and remember that even the most innocent of overcast days can pack a bad burn (especially in spring and summer). Dress in clothing that will give you many temperature-regulating possibilities. A layering system works best (as described earlier in this book). You can wear shorts on warm days, and any comfortable, loose slacks that would dry quickly work well the rest of the time. Top quality rain gear is essential for wet or misty conditions. Storms on the coastline often bring wind-driven torrents of rain, and there's no easy way to dry out your inner clothing if it gets soaked. If you're well prepared for rain, though, there's no better time to be on the beach. Only then can you fully appreciate the savage beauty of the coast and the awesome power of the breakers (from a safe viewing distance, of course).

Be sure to include an ace bandage in your first-aid kit. A twisted knee or sprained ankle is a very real possibility when traveling over slippery or jagged rocks. There's water everywhere, but not a drop to drink—so don't forget to take plenty of drinking water. Topographic maps are a must for unfamiliar coastlines. They indicate the precise shape of the coastline and the height of the bluffs, and they show sandy beaches and shoals. They're important for plotting escape routes if an emergency occurs. Tide tables are just as important for routes that involve tight passages between the cliffs and surf. Finally, if you want to take along non-essential items like a camera and binoculars, consider the potential effects of exposure to salt water or salt spray.

Whether you're day hiking or backpacking, you'll need a sturdy pack to carry everything in. Good pack features would include tough, waterproof material, padded shoulder and hip belts, and non-metallic zippers, buckles, and closures.

Some coastlines (such as those in Olympic National Park in Washington and in parts of Northern California) are true wilderness areas. Here, and in other areas where remote camping is allowed, you may have a whole beach or cove to yourself. Observe the following common-sense practices: Consider the prevailing direction of the wind when seeking a sheltered spot. Use heavy rocks to secure tent stakes driven in sand. Camp well above the next high tide or tides (remember that tidal differences are greater during spring tides, less during neap tides).

The hazards of coastal travel are many and varied, and sometimes unexpected. For example, both poison oak and rattlesnakes may be found in the ravines or on the bluffs just behind the beach. The coastal bluffs themselves are often very unstable—don't camp or spend a lot of time beneath steep cliffs. The seemingly solid brink of a cliff can crumble in the blink of an eye if you walk too close to the edge.

You'll want to minimize your chances of encountering unfriendly marine life. Stingrays, batrays, and jellyfish like to hang around in the surf and shallows, especially when the water is warm. Sea urchins, found in the rocky intertidal zones, are equipped with brittle purple spines that can break off if stepped upon. If severe pain results from any of these encounters, seek medical attention.

THE FRAGILE COAST

Because much of the life found along the coast is fragile and inconspicuous, you must exercise great care during your visit. Footprints left on the intertidal zone "wash" away eventually, but not so the effects of a heavy-footed traveler. Here are some basic guidelines:

1. A large group of people should spread out when crossing a tidepool or wetland area. Each person should try to step on the ledges and rocks that do not have creatures attached to or living on them.

2. Look at the creatures, but let them live their lives undisturbed. It's more interesting to watch a keyhole limpet move from one rock to another than to pick it up and look at its bright yellow foot. Observe the contortions of a sea star as it envelops its prey. Watch an octopus slink between the rocks and change color to blend with its environment. Watch the shorebirds as they fish or forage for marine creatures. As always, patience yields great dividends.

3. Many of the tidepool creatures are nocturnal. They will hide under rocks by day. It's OK to turn over rocks to find these animals, but don't allow the animals to remain out of the water for long periods. Return the rocks to their original location, so that the animals' habitat is unchanged.

4. Take nothing that belongs there out of an intertidal zone or wetland, and bring nothing (permanently) into these environments. Each natural object plays a role in the healthy functioning of the ecosystem there. Even small shells and shell fragments have a use: shells are

used by hermit crabs as homes, and anemones use the fragments to coat their bodies when exposed to the air.

WHY

There's a sense of peace and serenity on the shore. Perhaps you've had the experience of sitting on the beach, sand between your toes, sun-warmed rock against your back, watching and feeling the ocean ebb and flow with every wave. There's a sense of comfort and serenity—a sense of coming home. At day's end the sun bathes the bluffs and dunes in a golden radiance and then disappears under a glistening horizon. Your world, at least for the moment, is at peace.

Recommended Reading:

Seashore Life of Southern California
Sam Hinton
University of California Press, 1987
(This popular guide to intertidal life in Southern California also includes a "Selected References" list of books about other areas along the Pacific coast.)

Seashore Discoveries
Wesley M. Farmer, 1984
(Descriptions of intertidal creatures found in the San Diego area. Includes 240 line drawings.)

California Coastal Access Guide
California Coastal Commission
Univeristy of California Press, 1983
(Information on all the scenic and recreational facilities of the California coast, including descriptions of several hundred public accessways.)

Chapter 11

Mountain Travel

Mike Fry and Bob Feuge

"Mountain clouds on bronze skies
 Give us great memories"

—Carl Sandburg

The restless wanderings of the earth's crustal plates exert forces—up, down, and sideways—that create the three-dimensional landscapes known as mountains. Most of our Western mountains (especially the Sierra Nevada range, the Rocky Mountains, and much that lies in between) have been thrust upward along faults and folds. Others, like the Cascade mountain range, are evolving through repeated violent episodes of volcanism.

The titanic forces of colliding and grinding plates are just the opening salvo. Mountains collect extra rain and snow, and the erosive forces of running water and creeping ice tear at their flanks, opening up ravines, widening canyons, and creating jagged crests.

When mountains are formed, every aspect of the regional environment is altered. Weather patterns can be affected hundreds of miles away. On the Pacific coast, for example, moist air moves inland over the coastal mountain ranges, dropping most of its moisture on the west-facing slopes. Once over the mountain crests, the air blasts down the east-facing slopes, warming and drying as it approaches the relatively arid lands beyond.

Mountains make possible a great diversity of habitats that support a wide variety of plant and animal life. Timberline and alpine zones occur at high altitudes where the short summer growing season is not long enough to allow trees to repair the damage caused by severe winter storms. A lone, dead snag high on a ridge may indicate that a milder climate existed there in the past, but mostly the plants and animals of these airy retreats keep a low profile. At lower elevations, biological richness and diversity increases. Here, the lush forests and cascading rivers are prized for commercial as well as recreational use. Wilderness areas containing old-growth forest are increasingly restricted to the national parks and designated wilderness areas. Unfortunately, much of the West's forested lands (including many national forests) have been sacrificed to commercial logging and massive water projects. Alpine and timberline wilderness areas have fared better because of their more limited resources.

VISITING THE MOUNTAINS

Most backpackers will want to visit mountain areas in the spring through early fall. In the alpine and timberline zones these "warm" seasons may be compressed into a period of just a few weeks, so you may have to time your visit carefully. A severe winter may have left high passes blocked by snow even into August, and swollen streams at a lower elevation may have knocked out bridges, or rendered certain streams impassable. Be sure to inquire with the local agency (park service or other authority) before your visit.

In the Sierra Nevada, which is fairly typical of the big mountain ranges of the West, early summer is the best time for flowers, but the worst for mosquitoes. Midsummer through early fall usually brings fine weather—notwithstanding the occasional thunderstorm—to the Sierra Nevada and the Cascades. This is not the case for the Rocky Mountains. Violent thunderstorms, typically occurring in the afternoon, are common there. Usually, sunny weather prevails each morning, but cloud buildups over the higher peaks by noon signal that all prudent hikers seek refuge from the rain, wind, and lightning by early afternoon.

Early autumn—anytime from late September through October—is the best time to enjoy the fall colors of the aspens, cottonwoods, and deciduous shrubs. Mountain weather in the early fall is usually calm and stable, but this is also the period when the season's first heavy snowstorm is likely to arrive.

Deer hunting season in the national forests and other public lands usually runs from late September into October. Since there's a lot of space for hunters to wander throughout the West, this is not necessarily a serious conflict for hikers and backpackers. However, you should be extra careful to wear bright colors and make your presence known if you decide to visit areas frequented by hunters. Better yet, you can stick to state and national parks, which usually prohibit any kind of hunting.

MOUNTAIN TRAVEL CONCERNS

Altitude Effects

Air at higher altitudes tends to be both thinner and drier. Both of these characteristics affect the local climate. Temperatures tend to be much cooler than in the lowlands, and they also can swing from warm daytime highs to bone-chilling night-time lows.

While trying to keep cool in the midday sunshine, you may be tempted to shed as much clothing as possible. Don't. When the sun stands very high in the sky, as in a clear summer sky, the ultraviolet radiation is intense. The bombardment comes from all directions, as UV readily reflects off of snow, rocks and water. It also scatters in thin clouds, so a cloud cover is no guarantee of protection.

Unprotected skin at high altitudes burns very quickly. Areas of the body that normally receive a lot of sunlight, like the nose, the tops of the forearms, the backs of the hands, are affected the most. Often and liberally, apply one of the more powerful sunscreen lotions, and cover up with a long-sleeve shirt and a brimmed hat. To protect your hands, you can wear lightweight cotton gloves.

In the mountains especially, don't neglect the health of your eyesight. Use sunglasses or goggles with 100% UV-absorption characteristics. Exposure to high-intensity sunshine and excess UV can cause such temporary distresses as snow blindness or sun blindness, while repeated episodes of UV overexposure may trigger serious vision problems later in one's life.

The thin mountain air is refreshing once you get used to it. During the first couple of days on the trail, though, you may be gasping for breath when working hard, so plan easier days on the early part of a trip. When exercising heavily, be sure to exhale completely so that you effectively remove carbon dioxide from your respiratory system and leave plenty of room for incoming oxygen. By concentrating on your exhale, you will naturally breathe in enough air on the inhale.

Some people who cannot acclimate properly to high altitudes (sometimes as little as 8000 feet) develop altitude sickness. The surefire antidote is to remove the victim to a lower altitude (for more details see Chapter 17).

During altitude acclimation, many people tend to fall into an alternating cycle of rapid breathing and very slow breathing while at rest or asleep. This is nothing to be alarmed about; it is a normal part of the respiratory system's adjustment to a new balance between oxygen intake and carbon-dioxide output.

Crossing Streams

Fording fast-moving streams can be deceptively dangerous. First you'll need to choose the best spot to cross. Where water flows through a constricted area, as between boulders, you may be able to hop over safely if the gap is narrow enough. However, the water flows fastest there, so these areas are most dangerous if you fall in. Wider stretches of the stream may contain either deep pools with slow-moving water; or fast-moving, shallow water with riffles.

Take the time to thoroughly investigate the stream well above and below where you want to cross. Make certain there are no waterfalls or swift rapids below your intended crossing spot, in case you stumble. If the water is more than knee depth and very swift at the most favorable spots, consider turning back, outflanking the stream via a long detour, or waiting until the water flow decreases. The latter alternative is often practical for streams fed by snowmelt. In the early morning such streams may be running at a far lower level than during the heat of the afternoon.

When fording fast-moving streams, keep your boots on, snugly attached to your feet, with or without socks. Before wading in, try to estimate the stream's depth and toss a twig in to gauge the speed of the flow. Loosen your pack straps and unhook the hip belt in case you fall in (your pack is expendable, you're not). Use a hiking staff or a sturdy branch as a "third leg" downstream of you while crossing. Cross facing downstream so your three points of support form a triangle. If the current is swift, choose a path that takes you diagonally across and downstream. That way you won't have to fight the force of the water quite as much as you lift each foot.

More sophisticated methods of stream crossing involve rigging a rope across the stream to assist passage. Never tie yourself to the rope, because if you fall the rushing water may hold you under. Cross on the downstream side of the rope, holding on as you walk across.

You must be especially careful about waterfalls. Every year, people are killed in the mountains by foolishly trying to scale slippery waterfalls or by being swept over the lips of waterfalls.

If you're going to be wading through water quite often, try wearing lightweight boots with uncoated fabric panels and polypropylene socks. The water will quickly drain from the boots, and the socks will wick away excess moisture, preventing a clammy feeling. Applying a lubricant such as Vaseline or Bagbalm[1] may keep your feet a little warmer and more comfortable. If the crossings are sandy or muddy, gaiters will help keep debris out of your boots.

Snowfields and Ice

In the mountains, the north sides of high passes may be choked with snow all year round. In the morning, and again late in the day, these slopes may be icy on the surface. A slip and a fall on such a slope could result in a long slide. With an ice axe and crampons (see Chapter 14) safe passage across such icy slopes may be possible; otherwise you must bide your time and wait for the snow to soften in the afternoon.

Ice-covered lakes pose another obvious, but insidious hazard. It can be all too tempting for an inexperienced person to venture out on what may appear to be thick ice. If the ice breaks and you tumble into icy water, it's almost impossible to haul yourself out. Without a rope to toss or special equipment, a would-be rescuer can easily fall into the same trap and face the same consequences—death by hypothermia in a matter of minutes. By simply staying on the shore, you'll won't have to worry about these possibilities.

Sometimes snow can be advantageous for travel on cross-country routes if deep, consolidated snow covers brush, boulders, or downed logs on the less-steep terrain. There are potential hazards, though, especially when the snow cover is too soft, thereby allowing a hiker's leg to plunge into holes. Be especially careful when you cross "snow bridges" across streams, as these could collapse if the temperature is too warm and the snow too soft.

When trails are obscured by snow, you may have to follow blazes (indentations chipped into trees) or other markers, if they're available. Where snow is present, a trail hike can often turn into a cross-country ramble, so keep your map handy and be prepared to use your navigational skills.

Lightning

In many mountain areas, the pattern of crystal-clear mornings, afternoon thunderstorms, and evening clearings repeats like clockwork for days on end.

If you're planning to climb a peak in a thunderstorm-prone area, the obvious

---

[1] Bagbalm is a veterinary product (for cows) with a small, but loyal following among hikers.

thing to do is get an early start, and get off the peak well before the storm moves in.

If you care to know the distance between yourself and a bolt of lightning, use the rule of thumb that every five-second interval between a visible streak of lightning and the audible thunder means a mile of distance. Sometimes there's not much advance warning though. First there's a billowing cloud above, then hail, then the first lightning strike somewhere nearby. Your hair may stand on end, and sparks (corona discharge) may jump from eyeglasses, pack frames, or other metallic objects. If this happens, you're clearly in trouble—a lightning strike is imminent. Immediately assume a position as low as you can. Sit or crouch low on your pack or other insulating object to avoid ground currents. After the strike, move quickly downhill. If you feel the charge building again, get into a low position, as before.

Any tall object, reaching above its surroundings, is a highly probable target for a lightning strike. Obviously you do not want to be that object. Sharp-edged objects also have a tendency to attract lightning discharges. A good strategy, then, is to find a safe haven in a low spot close to, but not directly under an object such as a tree that would bear the brunt of a strike. A 30-foot-tall tree would probably protect you if you're 20 or 30 feet away from it.

When seeking a low spot, don't position yourself in a soggy basin, along a creek, along the base of a cliff, close to cracks in the rock, or at the entrance of a cave (the center of a spacious cave, if dry, is OK). These places are likely to conduct ground currents traveling along the paths of least resistance on the surface of or through the earth.

Pack Stock

Horses and mules have been tramping the mountains, serving the needs of prospectors, cattle and sheep herders, and more recently tourists and hikers, for well over a century. Remember that trail courtesy dictates that hikers yield the right of way. The pack-train leader, who knows his animals well, may ask you to move to a position where the animals can pass safely. This can be a tense moment; stand quietly by the side of the trail (the uphill side is better if there's room) and don't do anything that may play upon the animals' skittish tendencies. Talking in quiet tones to the animals may help put them in a state of ease.

Fragile Ecosystems

The short growing season of the alpine and timberline zones poses severe challenges to the survival of the unique plants and animals existing there. Most park agencies rightfully prohibit campfires in these areas. Leave that dead wood to build soil, or for someone to use in an emergency. Those sticks lying on the ground could be hundreds of years old, and they cannot be replaced tomorrow.

When below timberline, restrict your campsites to forest duff (pine needles, no shrubs or grasses), bare soil, or sandy areas free of vegetation. Never build a campfire on duff, however, since duff can smolder for a long time, possibly triggering a wildfire. Mountain meadows, especially just below timberline, are attractive looking as campsites, but most assuredly *not* appropriate for that use. Many of the mountain parks prohibit camping in meadows, or 100 feet (sometimes 200 feet) from sources of water or trails. Take along a filled two-gallon water bag to a campsite high on a sandy ridge or along the timberline, and you'll have all you need for a comfortable night at a dry campsite. With dramatic views at sunrise and sunset, this can be as good as wilderness camping gets.

FOOTHILL TRAVEL CONCERNS

Between the lowlands and the wild mountains there are often areas covered by either forests or blankets of chaparral that could broadly be termed foothills. Many of the newer officially declared wilderness areas in the national forests of California encompass these mid-elevation environments. Here are some of the special concerns associated with these areas:

Poison Oak

Poison oak thrives in moist ravines and canyons, as well as on hillsides and even hilltops (if protected from intense sunshine), below about 5000 feet elevation. The maxim "leaves of three, let it be" is a good one. Learn to recognize poison oak, and to distinguish it from other three-leaved plants (wild blackberries, for example) that are harmless.

By wearing long pants and a long-sleeved shirt you can keep skin contact to a minimum. In winter, and sometimes in very dry conditions, poison oak loses its leaves yet still retains some of its irritating resin. It's a good idea to learn to recognize the stem color and structure of the plant before you do any cross-country hiking among the leafless plants.

If you know you've been exposed, any effort at washing the resin off will probably help—the sooner the better. Hot, soapy water works best. Keep any clothes that have brushed against poison oak separate from your other gear (and you) and don't forget to launder them at the earliest opportunity.

Rattlesnakes

Rattlesnakes of various kinds thrive in a broad range of environments, though not at high elevations where the long winters are too harsh. In the foothills they will often be found in rocky areas, or near canyon bottoms where the small creatures they prey upon are abundant. You're most likely to see them out and about when temperatures are in the 75-90° range.

Normally not aggressive, rattlesnakes will usually buzz unmistakably if you approach too closely. When in rattlesnake country, scan the path ahead, and never put your feet or hands in places you cannot see without probing ahead with a stick. It may also help to walk with heavy footfalls so that any snakes will be warned of your presence through ground vibrations.

Remember that snakes may enjoy sunning themselves or relaxing where you might also choose. Be especially careful in these areas.

Ticks

When hiking along overgrown trails or "bushwhacking" (traveling cross-country in brushy terrain), check yourself for ticks frequently. These small, blood-sucking parasites feed on wild animals such as deer and domestic animals such as horses, dogs, and cattle. They lie in wait on tips of shrub branches along hiking or game trails waiting for a warm-blooded creature to come along.

If a tick successfully hitches a ride on a human host, it usually crawls upward to some protected spot underneath clothing before choosing a spot to attach itself to. By visually checking yourself often, and by being aware of the slightest irritations on your body, you can intercept the tick before it decides to bite. If it does bite, you will almost certainly be aware of an itchy irritation.

Ticks can be difficult to remove when attached. You can try to put some vegetable oil on the tick's body to block its breathing ventricles. Applying heat (holding a match nearby or other method) may work as well, but you must be careful not to kill the tick in the process. You can also try grasping the tick and gently pulling it out.

BEARS—A SPECIAL CONCERN OF MOUNTAIN TRAVELERS

A sudden encounter with a bear in the wilderness is both exciting and potentially dangerous. In the western U.S. there are two types: the grizzly bear and the black bear. Encounters with each type must be handled differently to minimize the chance of injury.

Within the contiguous United States, the modern range of bears has shrunk to encompass the larger mountain ranges of the West and a few areas in the East (Figure 11-1). The black bear is found in almost all mountainous regions of the western U.S. and beyond, while the grizzly is limited to regions in and around Yellowstone and Glacier national parks.

| Black bear range | Grizzly bear range |

Figure 11-1: Present ranges of bears

Bears are omnivorous—they'll eat almost anything including nuts, berries, bark, insects, fish, and small animals. A bear's diet changes with the seasons and the climate. Bears spend much of their waking hours foraging far and wide for food, moving mainly along established trails, stream banks, or through "wildlife tunnels" in dense vegetation. In dry seasons, bears will readily invade populated areas to find food.

Much of the human-bear conflict stems from our underestimation of a bear's mental and physical prowess. Bears are not far behind primates in the order of intelligence. They're not dumb animals. Instead they're extremely curious animals who tend to investigate whatever piques their curiosity. While humans rely primarily on their visual sense, bears rely on their very keen sense of smell. Bears will readily investigate unusual smells, not necessarily those related to food. They'll check out sunscreen lotion, toothpaste, and lipstick, to name a few.

Relative to man, bears are superior in strength, probably poorer in vision, and probably equally endowed in hearing. Despite their ponderous appearance, they're quite capable of outrunning humans, climbing trees, and swimming.

Figure 11-2 shows some anatomical differences between black bears and grizzly bears. The black bear is shy, preferring to avoid humans unless it is habituated, protecting its young, or desperate for food. Compared to the grizzly, the black bear is much less prone to violent, deliberate attacks on humans.

A grizzly bear must always be regarded as a potential threat. Grizzlies may interpret a sudden encounter with a human as a threat, and charge, maul, and kill with little warning. What seems threatening to a grizzly may not coincide with your idea of a threat.

No shoulder hump

Pronounced shoulder hump

Straight facial profile

Concave facial profile

BLACK BEAR

Long claws

GRIZZLY BEAR

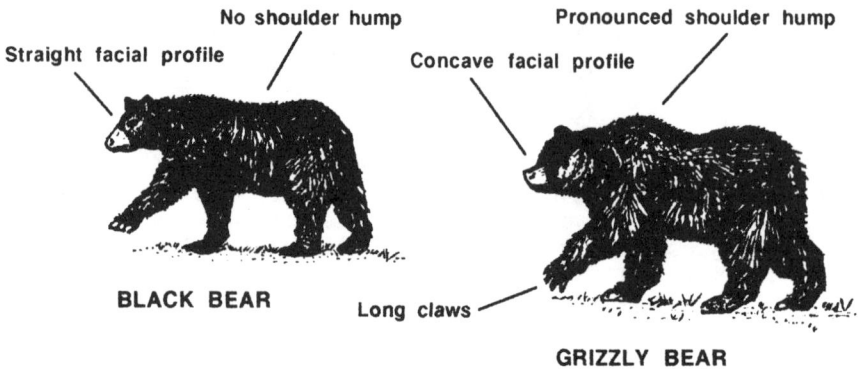

Figure 11-2: Black bears, despite their name, range in color from black to brown to cinnamon. Grizzlies are generally brown in color and larger than black bears.

The best way of preventing a bear attack is to avoid surprising or threatening the bear. In grizzly country, it's wise to make noise (sing, talk loudly, ring bells) on the trail. Look for signs of grizzly presence like claw marks on trees, bear scat (feces), and bear prints. If you do spot a grizzly, it's best to circle about widely (staying downwind of the bear), or simply abort the hike if you have to.

Black bears are not prone to attack. But, if that happens, don't be passive! Defend yourself—kick, yell, throw rocks, swat it with a branch. The bear will usually back down.

If a grizzly attacks, you have only two alternatives: You can quickly climb a nearby tree to a height of about 30 feet, or "play dead" (see Figure 11-3). Playing dead removes the perception that you are a threat. Never charge a grizzly or run from it. The passive response may result in some mauling but generally the bear will not continue the attack once it has asserted its dominance. If the bear continues to be aggressive, then you must change tactics and do whatever is possible to save your life. Your best strategy, of course, is early detection and avoidance.

When selecting a campsite in bear country, it's best not to camp immediately alongside a trail or a stream because bears will travel in these areas searching for food. Bears also like to investigate regularly used campsites, usually at night. If you detect tracks, scat, or other signs of a bear in the vicinity of your selected campsite, then move to a safer place.

Figure 11-3: Play-dead positions.

Hands behind neck, with arms protecting the face and side of the head (top).

Fetal postion, lying on one's side (bottom).

Bear box with double
latch and chain

It's safer to sleep inside a tent in bear country, because the tent wall provides some separation should the bear decide to claw at smells emanating from the tent. All food and smelly items should be placed in stuff sacks and stored downwind at least 100 feet from the campsite. In certain campgrounds, you can store your food supplies in bear-proof boxes, or on cables or poles (see Figure 11-4). If these are not available (in most designated wilderness areas they are not), you can use the "counter-balance method" of hanging food from trees, recommended by the National Park Service (see Figure 11-5).

Regular Counterbalance method: Find a tree with a sturdy limb, not close to other limbs, that stands about 20 feet high and extends at least 10 feet from the trunk. Next, place no more than 10 pounds of food in a sturdy stuff sack and attach a strong rope at least 50 feet long to the stuff sack. To the opposite end of the rope, tie a rock that is light enough to toss over the limb but heavy enough to fall to the ground after it has crossed the limb. Before tossing, ensure that the rope isn't snarled. Toss the rock over a point on the limb at least eight feet away from the trunk of the tree. Pull the rope to elevate the stuff sack and remove the small rock from the other end of the rope and replace it with a rock (or another food sack) that weighs the same as the food in the first stuff sack. Make sure the rock is tied securely so that the rock does not drop on someone's head. The rock (or sack) should be tied at a point on the end of the rope that allows both weighted ends to be suspended about 12 feet from the ground. Stuff excess rope into either or both stuff sacks. Find a long stick (or use a ski pole or hiking staff) to shove the rock or the second sack upward and also to retrieve the stuff sack later.

Alternate counterbalance method: An alternative to the stick is a second rope, looped through the strings of the first stuff sack before it is hoisted. The sec-

Bear pole

Bear
cable

Figure 11-4: "Bear-proof" systems for storing food

ond rope can be used to pull the first bag down to a counterbalanced position with the rock. To prevent a bear from using this rope to pull the food bag down, separate the two ends of the second rope and leave them dangling well apart. When you want to retrieve the food, simply pull the two ends of the second rope together and pull them both downward. This action will lower the first stuff sack while raising the rock or second stuff sack. Once the stuff sack is released, the counterbalanced rock or second stuff sack should come down easily. But watch your head!

If there are no trees in the area, you can try wrapping all odorous materials in two or more plastic bags, taking care to seal them tightly. Stuff the bags into a

Figure 11-5: Counterbalance method, illustrating retrieval with second rope (diagrams ④ through ⑦ not to scale)

deep crevice in rocks, well away from camp. This may or may not work, but it may be the best you can do. Never simply give up and sleep with the food—this practice may invite a midnight bear encounter!

At the campsite itself, try to eliminate food odors. All cooking should be done downwind and away from the main campsite. Food residue should be buried deeply or burned completely. Fish remains should be buried well away from camp, fish odors should be washed from hands and clothing. Dishwashing water also should be buried downwind, well away from camp.

It's thrilling to see bears in the wild, and even more pleasing not to have an unpleasant encounter or loss of your food. By understanding bear behaviors and being prepared to act accordingly, you can ensure that the only bear victories will be in Chicago!

Figure 11-6: An ideal campsite in grizzly bear country. "Escape tree" can be useful in grizzly country, as grizzlies are not good climbers.

Recommended Reading:

Bear Attacks: Their Causes and Avoidance
Stephen Herrero
Nick Lyons Books, 1985
    (A good blend of anecdotal and research information. Highly recommended for those who plan a backcountry trip in the grizzly territories of the U.S. and Canada.)

Desert Travel

Hal Brody

"To me the desert is stimulating, exciting, exacting; I feel no temptation to sleep or to relax into occult dreams but rather an opposite effect
which sharpens and heightens vision, touch, hearing, taste and smell.
Each stone, each plant, each grain of sand exists in and for itself with
a clarity that is undimmed by any suggestion of a different realm...
the desert reveals itself nakedly and cruelly, with no meaning but its
own existence."

—**Edward Abbey,** *Desert Solitaire*

F ew love the desert to the extent that I do. Before sharing a lot of "technical" information about this elusive wilderness, let me highlight some of the reasons I have fallen in love with it.

The desert has a certain spiritual quality I've not found on the seashore, in the mountains, or along the rivers. There's an overwhelming sense of stillness, solitude, and space. The isolation and quiet is restful, and I never have to put up with the hordes of people I used to meet on the mountain trails. With its meager vegetation and clear, dry air, the desert is full of mind-expanding perspectives.

Going cross-country in the desert is relatively easy—there's usually no bushwhacking involved. There's not much to screen the view either, so even a slight elevation gain yields tremendously broad vistas. When camping, I'm not concerned about bears or other varmints getting into my possessions and food. And I sure don't miss those clouds of mosquitoes found in the mountains.

When you travel through the desert you can see its geologic structure laid bare, revealing a kaleidoscope of shapes and colors. But the desert is full of other surprises as well. It's a real thrill to come upon a rare cactus, a trickling spring, or a hidden palm oasis.

To help you understand the desert and desert travel in the West, let's first look at the anatomy of the North American deserts:

NORTH AMERICAN DESERTS

The desert regions of North America have little (about 10 inches or less) and irregular rainfall. Other common features are high summer daytime temperatures; low humidity; wide swings in temperature from day to night; frequent sunshine and clear, blue skies; soil that is low in humus and high in minerals; and a ground surface that gets easily eroded by wind and water. Under these severe conditions, plants and animals have had to employ unique—and sometimes bizarre—strategies in order to survive.

The North American desert can be divided into four regions based on distinct kinds of vegetation. The Great Basin desert (dominated by the grayish Great Basin sagebrush—or "purple sage") is the largest and most northern of these divisions. It comprises most of Nevada, southeastern Oregon, southern Idaho, western Utah, and a small amount of northern Arizona.

Second largest and most southern is the Chihuahuan desert, indicated by a particular type of agave (spiny, succulent plant). This desert lies mostly in Mexico, but occupies a small area of southern New Mexico and western Texas.

The Sonoran desert is the third largest, covering southeastern California, most of southern Arizona, and much of Baja California and the adjacent Mexican state of Sonora. More complicated assemblages of vegetation, including the ocotillo (a spindly, spiny plant), the giant saguaro cactus, and fan palms represent the many subregions of the Sonoran desert.

Smallest of our deserts is the Mojave (also spelled Mohave), which extends through parts of southeastern and eastern California into southern Nevada and western Arizona. The Joshua tree, a type of giant yucca, dominates the higher elevations of the Mojave Desert.

In general, the most interesting places to explore in any of the four deserts are the mountains that rise from the desert floor, the storm-carved canyons and dry river courses (washes) that infrequently carry runoff from these mountains, and the enigmatic, salt-encrusted sinks that collect the runoff. Wherever water has forced its way through soft earth (often old seabed sediment), fascinating "badlands" are formed.

You can find plants almost everywhere in the desert—animals too, but their activities are usually secretive and nocturnal. Generally, you'll encounter many more varieties and quantities of spiny plants in the southern deserts than in the northern (Great Basin) desert.

CLOTHING AND EQUIPMENT

The desert can be extremely tough on the feet. The stiff and spiny vegetation, the rocky terrain, and even soft sand will present unaccustomed challenges. Boots with leather uppers will provide excellent protection from cactus as well as good support. When walking over rocks of all shapes and sizes, your feet and ankles need as much support as possible, especially if you're carrying the weight of a full backpack. Before wearing boots made of more flimsy material, consider that a cactus spine can penetrate nylon boot material with almost the same ease as a sewing needle passes through nylon fabric.

To avoid bruises and scrapes from climbing over rocks and scratches from cactus, I wear loose-fitting or stretchy long pants. They don't hinder my stride, and they help protect my (beautiful) legs from the ravages of the sun as well.

Shade is hard to come by in the desert. A sun hat is a necessity to keep from "frying your brain." Gray matter is very sensitive to heat. It will be the first part of your body to malfunction when overheated. Without a hat you risk sunburn, headache, nausea, and dizziness.

When the sun's up, your eyes should be shielded by ultraviolet-blocking sunglasses, and your skin should be covered by long-sleeved and long-legged garments—especially if you're fairskinned. These precautions will become more urgent as the earth's ultravioletblocking ozone layer continues to be attacked by certain gases—byproducts of modern industry—that have migrated into the upper atmosphere.

DESERT SURVIVAL

As in all wilderness travel, water is critical. In the desert, water's availability and abundance is subject to the whims of nature. Although many natural water sources exist in the desert, you cannot necessarily trust maps that show springs and permanent streams. Springs dry up, seasonally or permanently, and cartographers have a tough time keeping up with such changes.

As you survey the desert landscape for possible water sources, look for a line of trees or bushes that may indicate water at or near the surface. A clump of grass or sedges is a good indicator as well. Another likely place would be the base of a steep canyon wall. Flocks of birds can sometimes be seen circling over waterholes, especially during the morning and evening. Take note of the type of vegetation around a source of water. If perennial grasses or cattails aren't present, then the source probably dries up during the summer. When you find water, mark it on your map with the date. That way you can build a valuable history of water sources in your favorite areas.

Tanks or tinajas (naturally formed, water-filled depressions in rock) often serve the needs of desert animals. If the water supply is especially low, don't draw water from them unless you have to. Large tanks holding thousands of gallons are good sources, though the water will probably need filtration or chemical purification. Spring-fed pools should be used only for drinking. Water in running streams, however, can be used for limited washing. Never do any washing in a natural water source; always carry the water far from the stream, and wash with a small amount of biodegradable soap. Swimming in pools of the larger streams is a real treat in hot weather!

A few areas of the desert contain springs with unpalatable (salty or alkaline) or even poisonous water. Beware of water sources close to mine tailings (spoils). If the water has a normal amount of algae and crawling or wiggling critters, it's probably not poisonous. Beware of stagnant water with nothing alive in it! Tracks of animals coming and going to drink are another positive sign—unless there are a lot of skeletal remains in the area. If in doubt about the water quality, check first with local authorities or rangers.

More often than not, you'll be unsure of the availability of water, and you'll have to plan on carrying all you'll need for both drinking and cooking. A rough rule of thumb is one gallon per day (per person), but this refers to sunny, mild weather. Actual requirements could range from as little as two quarts on an overcast winter day in the high desert to more than two gallons on a 100°-day in the low desert. Since water weighs 8.3 pounds per gallon, your mobility may be severely limited if you're forced to carry all the water you'll need. Carry your water in leak-proof containers (such as sturdy plastic bottles). If you're planning an out-and-back trip, consider stashing some of your water on the way in. Unless you trust your memory absolutely, make a written note of where you placed the water on your map, so you can find it on the way out.

Because it's possible to hike in almost any direction in the desert, it's very tempting to do so. If you're accustomed to staying on marked and maintained trails in the mountains, you may not realize how easy it is to become lost or disoriented out in the open. Navigational skills are important in the desert, as is a constant awareness of major landmarks around you. Don't allow yourself or others to become separated from the group. The desert's corrugated surface can conceal a separated person as surely as a dense forest.

The desert harbors a wonderful variety of beautiful, yet potentially distressful cacti and shrubs. These plants survive heat and drought, and hungry and thirsty animals, through various strategies. Being sharp is one. If you can't be watchful and careful of their sharpness, then you deserve what you get! Cholla-cactus balls, which fall from the parent plant to become new plants, sometimes end up attached to your arms or legs. If you do get snagged, slide a comb between your skin and the ball and then pull outward. In a pinch, a rock in each hand will usually do the trick. Small pliers or hefty tweezers can usually grip individual spines well enough for removal.

When traveling over steep, rocky slopes, climb or descend diagonally, rather than straight up or down. Any rocks kicked loose will then pass to the side of your comrades rather than collide with them. If a rock is set in motion, yell "rock!" to warn those below.

Some people are quite anxious about rattlesnakes in the desert. (Actually, there are more of them in the mountains.) Between late fall and early winter, most desert-dwelling snakes are in hibernation. When they're out and about at other times, they're usually not aggressive unless provoked. Most will retreat if given the opportunity. Still, you should always avoid placing your hands and feet in places you can't see clearly.

Desert washes are particularly prone to flash flooding. Runoff can be funneled into places far from where the rain falls, resulting in a wall of water packing enormous momentum. There's usually some forewarning in the form of a low roar, but often not enough time to get to higher ground. Unless you're absolutely certain no rain will fall either locally or upstream, don't sleep in a wash.

In all seasons except summer, the weather in the desert is often quite gentle. Expect daytime highs in the 60s-80s. Winter nights however, can get downright frigid—low 30s in the lower deserts, 20s in the Mojave, even less in the higher elevations of the Great Basin. Even the driest parts of the desert can get occasional heavy rainfall, while snow dusts the upper-elevation Mojave and Great Basin deserts regularly. You must be prepared with the appropriate clothing and sleeping bag. Hypothermia can be an unexpected threat. Have lightweight rain gear with you, and a tent as well if you'll be camping away from the car.

Springtime weather in the desert can be quite fickle, ranging from high winds with mild temperatures to oven-like heat. If the weather service says a warming trend is building with predicted temperatures in the 90s or higher, you should consider either cancelling your trip or scaling back the miles you expect to cover.

The time from late May through September is usually too hot for strenuous activity in the desert. You should also be wary of early May, however, as the daylight hours are long, and the sun's high angle at midday steals away the shade.

If you do find yourself in the grip of a heat wave and low on water, start thinking and planning immediately. Rest in the shade during the hottest part of the day, and make haste to get back to your car (or other point of safety) in the cool of the evening and early morning. Drink your remaining water as your thirst dictates. Saving your water is not the best solution if you're slipping into dehydration. Don't waste time on schemes to extract water from cactus—you'll sweat out more water than you extract from the plant. Avoid eating too—digestion uses water.

PRESERVING THE DESERT

The toughness of the desert is, in a way, just a façade. The desert ecosystem is actually quite fragile. Desert plants grow very slowly and are always struggling for survival. Any damage we inflict can remain like scars on the land for decades. In some areas of the desert you can still see tank tracks left by our military training efforts during World War II. In other areas, grazing cattle have displaced the native wildlife and pulverized the vegetation. One insensitive person with an off-road vehicle can do a tremendous amount of destruction in only a few minutes. Even hikers can do damage.

One little-known life form that needs our protection is cryptogamic soil, a brittle crust made up of lichens, mosses, algae, and fungi. It appears as a lumpy ground cover about one inch thick, black, green or white depending on the organisms it contains.

Cryptogamic soil is an important link in the desert ecosystem because it stabi-lizes and builds fertile soil by preventing erosion and fixing nitrogen. Spongy and resilient when wet, it becomes vulnerable when dry, which is most of the time. Crunched to a powder when stepped on, it can blow away with the next breeze. Hikers needing to cross areas covered by cryptogamic soil can minimize the impact by using a single set of footprints while walking single file.

When you break camp in the desert, return the site to its natural appearance. Scatter or remove campfire rings or blackened rocks and sand. A "buddy burner" is all you really need at night. Here's how to make one: Cut a strip of cardboard as wide as the height of a small can, line the inside of the can with the cardboard, and fill it to the top with melted paraffin. A cat-food-size can will burn for about two hours, even in a strong wind, and have a flame sufficient for a group of fifteen—not much heat but enough warm light to chat by. A larger diameter can yields a larger flame, and a deeper one burns longer.

I think it's immoral to take anything out of the desert. If you find something of interest out there, I believe my grandchildren and their grandchildren (as well as your own) will probably find it fascinating, too. Artifacts of past human habitation are an especially sensitive issue. Indians lived in many of our deserts up until very recent times, so things like pottery shards are still in relative abundance. In the desert they provide an almost magical reminder of a past civilization and spiritual heritage. On the mantel at home they're just old pieces of clay. In many desert areas it's illegal to remove anything at all. So should it be for all our wilderness areas.

More so in the desert than almost any other place, it's important to pack out paper items like toilet tissue and sanitary supplies. Paper, like everything else, decomposes very slowly in the absence of water. If buried around a campsite, paper can be unearthed by the winds, by animals, or by an unfortunate hiker, thereby announcing the earlier presence of careless humans.

ON THE ROAD

Automobiles are essential tools for reaching the edge of the desert wilderness, but when broken down they can leave you miserably stranded. The following suggestions are meant to help you with the reliability of your transportation. Since overheating is a common problem in the desert, we'll focus mostly on that.

First, it's better to travel in two or more cars rather than one. If one breaks down, someone can take another car to go for help.

Any car used in the desert must be in good mechanical condition. Before going, have your cooling system pressure-tested. Your radiator should be filled with a mixture consisting of water and a coolant designed to withstand higher-than-normal temperatures. Check the condition and tightness of the fan belts, but also carry spares and the necessary tools to install and tighten them. It's wise to carry an extra five gallons of water in case you lose your radiator water through a ruptured hose. This should be clean water just in case you need to drink some of it.

As you're driving, you should monitor your temperature gauge or warning light. If overheating is indicated, stop your car and engine as soon as it's safe to do so. Check your fan belt; if too loose it will slip and reduce the effectiveness of your water pump. Check the coolant level at the overflow tank—determine if and where you are losing coolant. Do repairs if necessary and, once the engine has cooled down, add water back into the system if needed. (Never remove the radiator cap while the engine is hot!)

If the problem is due to a ruptured hose and you don't happen to have the right hose to replace it, radiator-hose repair tape can get you moving again. Wrap, as tightly as possible, the ruptured section of hose, and don't forget to loosen or remove the radiator cap so as to greatly reduce pressure in the system. By doing so, the tape will prevent the coolant from escaping, but the coolant will slowly boil off. On the road again, you must check the coolant level every half hour or so and add as required. The repair tape is, of course, a very temporary quick-fix.

A less likely cause of overheating is a stuck thermostat, preventing coolant from reaching your radiator. This can be cured by simply removing the thermostat once the engine has cooled (learn how to do this ahead of time).

If, after stopping with a hot engine, everything looks OK, then all you can do is proceed at a slower speed (with air-conditioner off) as soon as the engine has cooled. Slower speeds mean less power output and less heat production. By turning on your car's heater (uncomfortable as it may be), you can draw off some additional heat from your engine. Watch your temperature gauge and take it easy, especially on the uphills.

Extra motor oil, jumper cables, and a gas-tank patch kit should be carried. It's easy to puncture your gas tank while bouncing over rocky roads, especially if you yield to the temptation to cover those endless desert miles too quickly. If you need to carry extra gasoline, do so in an approved container. These containers are more safely (and legally) carried if securely attached to the outside of a vehicle, rather than packed inside.

Have a tow rope and shovel stashed in the car and know how to use them. Getting stuck in the sand happens to almost every desert adventurer sooner or later. A one-foot-square piece of plywood will allow your jack to lift more efficiently in soft sand. Strips of old carpet placed under the tires can help you escape problem spots. Soft-sand roads can be more easily negotiated by deflating your tires to about 15 psi pressure, but the process of pumping them back up to recommended pressure can be time-consuming, even with a battery-operated tire pump.

Hone your tire-changing skills and make sure your jack is operational and your spare tire is pressurized. Your jack is a powerful tool for getting your car off a big rock or anything else that might keep the weight off your wheels.

If your car breaks down irreparably, stay with it unless it's obvious you can walk for help. In an emergency you can call attention to yourself by using the car's horn, lights, and mirrors. The spare tire, when doused with gasoline, burns with copious black smoke for a long time. If you need shelter from the sun, dig out enough room under your car to comfortably lie on your insulated sleeping pad. Store water in your body, not in your water bottles. Don't drink radiator water unless it contains only water, and filter it, when possible, if you do.

CONCLUSION

In Desert Solitaire, Edward Abbey offers us a powerful insight into the nature of the desert wilderness: "Despite its clarity and simplicity . . . the desert wears at the same time, paradoxically, a veil of mystery. Motionless and silent it evokes in us an elusive hint of something unknown, unknowable, about to be revealed. Since the desert does not act it seems to be waiting—but waiting for what?"

Searching for that "unknowable" is what keeps me going back to the desert again and again. I hope you'll join me.

Recommended Reading:

Desert Solitaire
Edward Abbey
Ballantine Books, 1968

A Sierra Club Naturalist's Guide: The Deserts of the Southwest
Peggy Larson
Sierra Club Books, 1977

California Deserts
Jerry Schad
Falcon Press, 1988

HIGH TEMPERATURE STRATEGIES

It makes good sense to stay out of the desert during summer, yet I found myself some years ago frustrated at being "locked out" of my favorite desert areas for three or four months each year. (I had to camp in the mountains, for God's sake!) So a friend and I began to develop strategies that would make summer desert backpacking not only feasible but actually enjoyable. The San Diego chapter of the Sierra Club established a new specialty rating—"high temperature"—for the effort, and I now lead an annual summer backpacking trip whimsically called the Iron Wo/Man Melt Down in the neighboring desert. For two days we hike and scramble around from breakfast to dinner, with brief rest stops, under the blazing sun.

What follows are the methods by which we manage to keep our cool under such conditions. While I am not at all encouraging you, the reader, to try to duplicate our feats, the strategies expressed here are nonetheless quite applicable to the hot and dry conditions often found elsewhere in the arid West. I wish to emphasize that the hazards of the summer desert travel are severe and should never be taken lightly.

Conditioning: Good aerobic conditioning is a prerequisite for any kind of high-temperature exercise. During the three weeks before our trips we practice "heat conditioning" in conjunction with normal exercise. Evidence of proper heat conditioning is profuse sweating. If the weather won't cooperate, then we wear sweat clothes or other heat-retaining clothing while exercising to induce heavy perspiration. This practice trains the body's sweat glands to dilate quickly in response to overheating, and the blood to circulate near the skin so as to liberate the body's internal heat. Psychological acclimation to heat is another benefit of heat conditioning. We become more comfortable with the feeling of simply being very warm. Forty-five minutes per session, three or four days per week seems to be adequate. Fluids are never withheld while exercising or afterward; ignoring thirst is a dangerous practice.

Clothing: In a high-temperature environment, head-to-foot clothing offers protection from the radiant heat of the sun, and from high winds that might evaporate perspiration too quickly. White, loose-fitting, cotton clothing and a white, broad-brimmed hat does the job well. In the absence of wind some air circulation is needed to evaporate moisture from the skin, and thereby cool it. Consequently, we cut slits or holes in our clothing where the sun doesn't shine—from armpits to elbows, from crotch to knees. Holes in the hat also help. Shirts that can be easily opened in the front when walking with the sun at your back are a real advantage. Skirts, we've found, solve the air-circulation problem too, though they're awkward when climbing or scrambling (of course, no one but ourselves has to put up with our crazy appearance!).

Electrolyte Maintenance: The body must have a proper balance of electrolytes to function at peak efficiency. The electrolytes we're most concerned with are potassium, sodium, magnesium, and calcium. These, of course, are lost in part through perspiration. Normally you replace any losses by eating a normal diet. But being active at high temperatures means perspiration losses of up to two gallons per day, and consequently a very rapid loss of electrolytes. Fatigue and muscle cramps are the typical signs of electrolyte depletion.

The solution is to use one of the commercial sport drinks or "thirst quenchers" designed to replace electrolytes. We recommend Gookinaid ERG (Electrolyte Replacement with Glucose), a product sold in ready-to-mix powder form. Gookinaid's "isotonic" mix insures that it is quickly absorbed by the body, and the extra glucose (sugar) gives a boost of energy. Other sport drinks may be overly sweet or too concentrated; however, you can experiment with dilutions.

Emergencies: Even if you do everything right, you can overheat. We make a point of closely watching each other for signs of heat exhaustion. In fact, a victim is often the last to notice the adverse effects of an overheated body and brain. Early signs are fuzzy thinking (slurred or incoherent speech perhaps) and a loss of balance and surefootedness.

We act very quickly if this happens: We steer the victim to a shady spot, or create our own shade with the lightweight tarps each of us carries. We place the victim on three or four of the "sit-upons" (small, insulating pads) we carry, and use the others as fans if the air isn't moving fast enough. We remove excess clothing to ensure the maximum cooling effect of evaporation. If a water source is nearby, we immerse the victim (if possible), or we shuttle water from the source to pour over the victim's body. If there's no water source nearby, then we at least "mist" the victim using the two or three spray bottles we carry. Meanwhile we coax the victim into drinking as much fluid (laced with electrolytes) as he or she can take.

Caution!

If you'd like to try high-temperature hiking or camping, then work up to it slowly. Start in the spring, with trips in the 90s (Fahrenheit, that is). Try camping near your car, and experiment with hikes that take you only a short distance away. Never let yourself become isolated from a source of water—either stay close to a stream or spring, or carry a supply that is adequate for any emergency as discussed earlier.

Chapter 13

Special Skills:
Rock Climbing

Chuck Bennett

"*Choosing to play this game in the vertical dimensions of what is left of wild nature makes us climbers.*"

—Yvon Chouinard, *Climbing Ice*

A s you begin to expand your horizons and seek new places to travel to and explore, you will encounter new obstacles—a summit that seems to be unscalable, a waterfall or pour-off in a canyon bottom that defies your attempts to bypass it, or perhaps an ancient Indian ruin in a canyon wall that seems beyond your reach. Usually, there's some way of dealing with challenges like these. In attempting to overcome these difficulties, you go beyond the stage of backpacking and enter the world of rock climbing.

LEVELS OF DIFFICULTY

More than one classification system exists which describes the level of difficulty of a climb. However, the most widely used classification system in this country is the Yosemite Decimal system:

Class 1: Walking

Class 2: Scrambling, with occasional use of the hands for balance. Little or no exposure[1].

Class 3: Easy climbing. Extensive use of the hands as well as the feet is required. Exposure is moderate; some climbers may wish to be belayed[2].

Class 4: More difficult climbing. Hand and foot holds are smaller and the exposure is greater. Belaying is necessary for safety.

Class 5: Holds are smaller and the exposure is great. Belaying is necessary and the placing of "protection" (protective equipment such as chocks, camming devices, slings and carabiners tied to solid anchor points) is required. Fifth-class climbing is subdivided into categories 1 through 13. At the upper end of the scale the categories are further subdivided into A, B, and C. These subdivisions reflect increasing levels of difficulty—the higher the number, the greater the difficulty.

Class 6: Climbing requiring artificial aid. The climber's weight is supported by standing in stirrups which are attached to pitons, bolts or chocks. This is necessary because of the extreme steepness (vertical or overhanging) and smoothness of the rock.

SPECIAL EQUIPMENT

An extensive array of special equipment has been developed for the sport of rock climbing. Some of it enhances the climber's technique, but much of it is designed to maximize safety.

Climbing Shoes

Climbing shoes are constructed to provide maximum adhesion to rock surfaces, with a stiffness sufficient to allow "edging" (standing on a very narrow projection or ledge with the edge of the shoe) yet with enough flexibility to allow the climber to have a good feel for the rock underfoot. The soles are made of a sticky rubber compound and feature a wide rubber band (called a rand) that wraps around the shoe just above the sole. Shoe uppers are usually constructed of thin leather with fabric reinforcement inside. Climbing shoes are normally worn with a very thin pair of socks or no socks at all, allowing a very tight fit. Many climbers prefer shoes one-half to one size smaller than their normal size. While sacrificing some comfort, the climber then has a better "feel" while moving over the rock.

---

[1] Exposure in climbing means the likelihood of serious injury or death in the event of a fall that is not arrested.

[2] A climber is belayed when his fall can be arrested by the action of a teammate. See page 142 for a full description of the technique.

Ropes

Climbing ropes are of a special construction called kernmantle (Fig. 13-1). In this design, a large number of small synthetic fiber strands (the kern) are contained within a woven outer covering (the mantle). Most climbing ropes used in this country are 11 millimeters in diameter, a little less than $1/2$ inch. Common lengths are 150 feet and 165 feet.

Figure 13-1: Kernmantle rope

Climbing ropes require special care. Since they're constructed of synthetic fibers, prolonged exposure to ultraviolet radiation (sunlight) will damage them. Exposure to any petroleum product will also damage them. When a rope is not being used it should be stored in a dark, cool, dry place. During use, stepping on or pinching the rope should be avoided; this could drive small dirt and rock particles into the weave of the rope, possibly cutting some of the small fibers. Ropes are designed not only to hold a climber's weight, but also to sustain a climber's fall. Falls, however, can place a serious strain on a rope. After a fall, the rope should be inspected carefully to determine if it is still safe to use for climbing. Usually a rope is retired[3] after a serious leader fall.

Harnesses

Most climbers use a sit harness or a combination of sit harness (Fig. 13-2) and chest harness while climbing. These

Figure 13-2: Sit harness with rope attached

harnesses allow the climber to easily tie into the rope and to distribute his or her weight evenly—a big advantage in the event of a fall. Harnesses are constructed of 2-inch nylon web material stitched together. The harness has some provision, usually two loops of web, for the climbing rope to be attached. The preferred method of attaching the rope to the harness is a Figure-8 knot.

Some climbers prefer to use a swami belt instead of a harness. A swami belt consists of enough one- or two-inch tubular nylon web material to circle the waist several times. The ends of the web are joined with a water knot, and the climbing rope is then tied into the belt. This method does not distribute one's weight as well as a harness in the event of a fall, but it's better than a third method—merely tying into the rope with a bowline-on-a-coil (page 143).

---

[3] A rope that is "retired" is no longer used for rock climbing.

Slings and Carabiners

A typical sling consists of loop of 1-inch tubular nylon webbing. The ends of the webbing are joined either by stitching or with a water knot. Slings are used in conjunction with carabiners to connect the protection to the climbing rope. Carabiners, resembling oversized safety pins (Figure 13-3), are constructed of lightweight, but strong aluminum alloy.

load is placed on the device, the arms are pushed out with more force, tightly jamming the device against the rock surfaces. The greater the load, the more tightly the cams are forced against the rock. These versatile devices will accommodate a wide variety of crack widths.

Figure 13-3: Carabiners

The spring-loaded gate (hinged bar) on a carabiner allows the climber to "clip into" a rope or a sling. Carabiners come in a number of shapes, but the most common are the oval and the "D" shape.

Chocks, Nuts and Other Wedging Devices

Chocks, nuts and camming devices (Fig. 13-4) are metal shapes inserted into cracks and openings in the rock to provide solid anchor points or protection. Chocks and nuts are typically wedge-shaped and have a loop of either cable or small-diameter kernmantle rope attached. The chock or nut is placed into a crack or opening in the rock, a carabiner is clipped into the loop, and the rope is then clipped into the carabiner. Often two carabiners and a sling are used to clip the rope to the chock or nut.

Camming devices feature a spring-loaded mechanism which is compressed and then inserted into an opening in the rock. The spring tension holds the opposing arms of the device in place. As a

Figure 13-4: Chocks (upper), nuts (middle), and a camming device (lower)

Descenders

Descending hardware facilitates rapid descent after a climb is completed. For safety and comfort, descenders must be used with a sit harness or a sit/chest harness combination. The most commonly used descender is the "figure eight," whose shape resembles the numeral 8. The rope is passed through and around the device and friction between the rope and the device enables a controlled descent.

Figure 13-5: Figure-eight descender in use

Ascenders

Ascenders clamp onto the rope and allow the climber to climb the rope itself, a laborious process. They're used in aid climbing (Class 6). Another use of the ascender is in self-belaying when a fixed rope is used.

CLIMBING TECHNIQUES

Climbing techniques can be logically divided into four basic categories—balance climbing, stress climbing, down climbing and rappelling. Regardless of the technique being used, a good climber always tries to maintain a smooth, continuous movement. He or she "flows" over the rock. Desperate lunges are not a part of effective rock climbing. In fact, most climbing can be compared to walking (as opposed to hopping or jumping) on level terrain, except that the movement is vertical instead of horizontal.

It's also worthwhile to emphasize that in most rock climbing the rope is used primarily as a safety device. With the exception of Class 6 (aid climbing), climbers do not haul themselves up a mountain by rope. Rather they climb the mountain as if a rope were not there; they rely on the rope to catch a slip or fall.

Balance Climbing

Balance climbing is like walking up a steep succession of steps. The body remains upright with its center of gravity over the feet. Hands are used for balance, however the climber does not lean into the rock. As the climber progresses, he or she continuously searches for the next hand holds and foot holds. Three points of support are always maintained—either two hands and one foot or two feet and one hand are always firmly on the rock. Only one hand or one foot is moved at a time, assuring balance at all times. No great muscular strength is required for balance climbing, since the climber's weight is carried by the legs.

Foot holds can range from tiny protrusions in the rock to wide ledges. Usually the edge of the boot or climbing shoe is used on a small foot hold. A climber should never use a knee on what should be a foot hold. This is poor form, but more importantly the climber will usually want to use that same spot for a foot stance. Both foot and knee cannot occupy the same place at the same time.

In balance climbing, hand holds are used primarily to maintain balance. Often these holds are very small. Hand holds near shoulder level are the easiest to use and afford the best support. Hand holds are either "cling holds" or "pressure holds." Cling holds are the most secure and easiest to use. In pressure holds the palm of the hand is brought to bear against the rock and friction provides the glue.

If a hand or foot hold appears questionable, the hold should be tested before the weight of the body is entrusted to the hold. Exert force in the direction of load while maintaining balance on the three points of contact. If the force fails to dislodge the hold, shift the weight gradually onto the hold.

Stress Climbing

When suitable hand holds or foot holds are not available, the climber can rely on other techniques to allow further progress. In stress climbing, a combination of opposing forces maintains balance and facilitates movement. The techniques of stress climbing rely a great deal on muscle strength and are therefore very tiring, especially if required for a long period of time.

Chimney stemming is a typical example of stress climbing (Figure 13-6). A chimney is two vertical walls facing each other that are approximately one to three feet apart. The most common method of chimney stemming involves placing the back against one wall of the chimney and the feet against the other wall. One foot is moved upward and then the back is moved up. Then the other foot is moved up, followed by upward movement of the back again. The opposing forces of the feet and back

against the rock walls hold the climber in the chimney. The climber's body, which is exerting these forces, is considered to be under a stress.

Another stress-climbing technique is the lie back (Figure 13-7). This can be used when a crack is too small to accommodate a climber's body or too large to support some kind of jam hold. Both hands grip one side of the crack and both feet are placed against the other side of the crack. The hands pull and the feet press against the rock. One hand or one foot is moved at a time allowing upward motion. This very tiring technique is most effective if the hands and feet are not close together. Lie backs are especially useful on inclined cracks, on large flakes, and at the edge of large slabs.

Jam holds (Figure 13-8) force the hand, arm, foot or leg into a narrow crack so as to jam the body part against the rock, thus maintaining balance or permitting upward movement. These holds must be done with caution to prevent injury and to assure that the body part can be extricated from the hold.

In cross holds or opposing-pressure holds, the fingers of both hands are inserted into a crack and the climber pulls

Figure 13-6: Chimney-stemming technique

Figure 13-7: Lie back technique

each hand in opposite directions. In the undercling, another opposing-pressure hold, the hands are used to pull or lift up while the feet are pushing down—as in a lie back. This technique allows a climber to traverse a down-sloping ledge.

Down Climbing

Down climbing is not easy—in fact it's usually more difficult than up climbing. The climber often can't see hand and foot holds clearly. Many holds can't be tested adequately from a position of safety. Furthermore, the climber is more likely to be fatigued during the descent of a mountain than its ascent.

The techniques used in up climbing are employed in down climbing, only the action is reversed. An additional technique is the use of a rope loop. The rope (or a suitable sling) is looped around a solid rock outcropping and then used to lower oneself. This is only practical for short drops, however.

Rappelling

Rappelling is a way of descending a rope smoothly and relatively quickly. Novice climbers often think rappelling is glamorous and are sometimes careless. This can lead to tragic results, since there's no easy way to climb back up a rope if something goes wrong. Rappelling is exhilarating, but it's also probably the most dangerous activity associated with rock climbing.

In rappelling, the descent of a climber is controlled by friction between the climber's body and the rope, or between

Figure 13-8: Foot jam (left), fist jam (middle), finger jam (right)

Figure 13-9: Dulfersitz rappel

a descender device (like a figure-eight) and the rope. Usually the rope is doubled, allowing it to be passed through the anchor point so it can be retrieved after the descent.

The anchor point for the rope must be strong enough to support the intended use. Preferred anchors are solidly rooted trees or rock protrusions. Also there must be some room below the anchor for the climber to place his body and begin the rappel. Anchors should be doubled up to assure fail-safe protection In that case, each of the anchors must be capable of carrying the entire load of the climber. If the rope passes over any sharp edges, it must be padded to prevent fraying (or even severing) during the rappel. If chocks, nuts, or other pieces of hardware secure the anchor, there should be at least two, and preferably three. No two pieces of hardware should be placed in the same crack.

Another consideration in safe rappelling concerns rope length. Before beginning a rappel, the climber must be absolutely positive that the rope is long enough to reach a safe stance at the conclusion of the rappel. It is also a good idea to tie a figure-eight knot about three feet from the end of the rope. The knot

cannot pass through the descending device, so it prevents the climber from sliding off the end of a too-short rope.

If mechanical descenders are not available, a technique called the Dulfersitz rappel (Figure 13-9) can be used. This is normally used only for low-angle or short descents as the rope friction on the body can be very uncomfortable and sometimes painful.

When setting up a Dulfersitz, the climber faces the rock and straddles the rope. The climber then reaches down and behind and picks up the double rope with one hand, and lifts the rope over his head to the other shoulder. In this arrangement the rope, after going around the hip, passes across the climber's body and over the opposite shoulder and around to the back. The rope at the rear of the climber is grasped with the "controlling" hand, which is used to control the speed of descent.

During any rappel, the climber should lean back into the rope, keeping his or her feet more or less perpendicular to the rock surface and keeping the feet apart to provide lateral stability. It's a good idea to keep a finger between the two ropes to prevent them from twisting.

SAFETY TECHNIQUES

Rock climbing demands constant vigilance and an awareness of hazards. The dangers of climbing fall into four categories: falling, being hit by falling rock, being stranded, and climbing with people who don't know what they are doing.

To reduce the likelihood of falling, a climber should always be looking ahead, carefully selecting the route. As we mentioned earlier, the climber should balance with the weight on the feet. Three points of contact with the rock should be maintained and each hold should be tested. A smooth rhythm should be maintained when in motion. It is important to remember, though, that all rock climbers who test their limits (even many who don't) will fall sooner or later. That's where ropes and protection come in (see next section).

To avoid being hit by falling rock, try to climb on good quality rock, avoid routes where rockfall is frequent, and learn to climb without dislodging loose rocks. Good quality rock should be sound, tight, and free of loose flakes or pieces. On most routes you'll encounter some loose rock, so hard hats should be worn. Always warn climbers below you of falling rock by yelling "rock!"

To avoid the occurrence of anyone on a team getting stranded, the leader must carefully select the route so as to avoid pitches beyond the ability of the weaker climbers. A cardinal rule for any climber is: Never climb a pitch beyond your ability (or nerve) to descend. Don't step into a position from which you cannot move forward or back. Being caught "spread eagled" is both embarrassing and dangerous. Good judgement also dictates that a climber turn back if the route ahead becomes too difficult for one's abilities and equipment, or if hazardous weather conditions prevent safe climbing.

The last safety technique is not really a technique at all; rather it's just common sense. You should always climb with people who are knowledgeable and possess the required skills, equipment, and good judgement. This is especially true for those new to climbing. Most major cities and popular climbing areas have climbing schools that cater to the needs of novices. Climbing schools can often be judged by the length of time

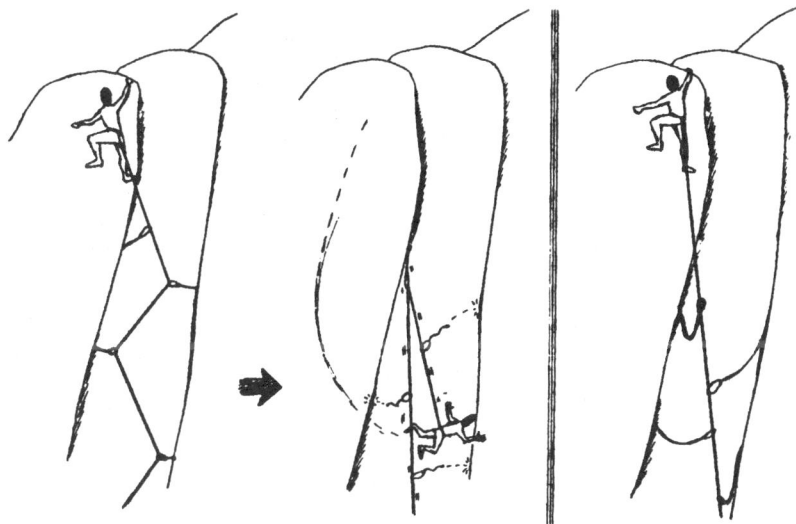

Figure 13-10: Incorrect placement of protection (left) causes protection to pull out or "unzip" during a fall. Drawing at right shows correct placement; the rope stays in a straight line.

they have been in business, and by their safety record (it's important to ask). If you are unable to attend a formal climbing school or class, then ask around in the climbing community before selecting the people you'll learn from. Good climbers will teach you the basic skills, and also impart to you the kind of attitude that promotes survival. With poor or reckless climbers, you're likely to pick up some bad, and potentially unsafe, habits.

Placing Protection

Chocks, nuts, and camming devices are the principal equipment used by climbers to assure their protection in the event of a fall. Correct placement of this "protection" (Figure 13-10) insures that a climber is held securely in the event of a fall. The climber must consider the direction of the force placed on the protection during a fall, and carefully choose a solid bearing area for the protection. The rope should run in a straight line between the climber and belayer to prevent excessive friction or rope drag. The protection should be placed in a narrowing crack and firmly seated. When placing protection, ease of removal should also be considered.

Use of the Rope; Knots

The purpose of the rope in normal climbing (up to Class 5) is to guard against serious injury in the event of a fall. The rope is there for protection only; the climber does not climb the rope or use it to haul people up.

Certain knots have proven useful in climbing situations (see Figure 13-11). These knots are effective because they're easily tied, do not weaken the rope, and are easily untied, even when the rope is wet. The most commonly used knot is the figure-eight, used for tying a climber's harness into a rope. It is also used for securing the rope end to the protection and to secure the belayer to the belay point.

Another type of knot is the bowline-on-a-coil. This is a rather complicated knot used to tie a climber into the rope when a harness is not used. The water knot is used to tie webbing together. The fisherman's knot ties two ropes together; and the prussik knot, a constricting knot tied with a small-diameter loop of rope around the main climbing rope, can be used in lieu of a mechanical ascender. All of these knots have an important place in climbing and should be practiced until they can be tied under the most adverse conditions. Out on the rock, a climber may need to tie knots such as these under the worst conditions of darkness, wet, and cold, and even when in pain.

Belaying; Climbing Signals

The word belay originated as a nautical term meaning "to stop or fasten by winding around a pin." Belaying in rock climbing means to protect the climber by wrapping the rope around the body of the belayer or by passing the rope through a mechanical device such as a figure-eight. This arrangement produces the necessary friction to halt or arrest the climber in the event of a fall. It means that a falling climber on the rope will not be jerked to a sudden halt during a fall, as he would if the rope were tied directly to an anchor point. Belaying is one of the most important skills in rock climbing. A climber literally places his or her life in the hands of the belayer, so the person playing the role of the belayer must be well trained and constantly alert while on the job.

The belayer feeds out or takes in the rope, providing sufficient slack to allow the climber free movement while at the same time keeping the rope tight enough to minimize the distance the climber would drop should a fall occur.

The most commonly used belay stances are the sitting hip and the standing hip (see Figure 13-12). The sitting hip belay is considered the strongest and most secure technique. In that position

Water knot

Double fisherman's knot

Double figure-eight knot

Prussik knot

Bowline-on-a-coil

Figure 13-11: Some knots for climbing

Figure 13-12: Sitting hip belay (left); standing hip belay (right)

the belayer (who is securely anchored) faces the direction of the climber and braces his or her legs against the rock. The rope passes around the belayer's upper hips, ensuring adequate friction on the rope.

The standing hip belay is less secure, but useful where there isn't enough room to sit. When standing, the belayer has only two points of support in addition to the anchor point. In a standing hip belay stance, the belayer must align himself in a straight line between the anchor point and the climber. The feet should be placed well apart with one foot forward in line with the rope.

Rock climbing is normally done in teams of two climbers. The first climber is the "lead climber" and the other is the "belayer." The lead climber places protection as he or she progresses up the route of the climb. As the protective devices are placed and secured, the rope is clipped into them. The difficulty of the climb and an assessment of the risk of falling determines how frequently the protection should be placed. Normally this would be 10 feet or less. Meanwhile the belayer is in a safe stance below, ready to apply friction to the rope in case the leader falls.

When the lead climber reaches a safe stance (before the end of the rope is reached), he or she places protection to form an anchor for a belay. At this point the lead climber becomes the belayer for the teammate who now climbs along the same route and removes protection while progressing upward.

Climbers and their belayers communicate through a standard set of oral signals. These phrases, which have been in use for decades, assure that miscommunication does not take place. The phrases are short and are given in a loud, clear voice. They're used automatically, even when the actions of the climber or belayer appear obvious. Some examples of the most commonly used signals are given on the next page.

Climber: "Belay on?"
Belayer: When ready replies "Belay on!"

Climber: "Ready to climb."
Belayer: "Climb."

Climber: "Up rope." (when too much slack is in the rope)
Belayer: "Up rope" (indicating that the command has been heard and is being executed)

Climber: "Tension." (a request for the belayer to tighten up the rope until the climber can be felt by the belayer)
Belayer: "Tension." (indicating the belayer has heard the command and is applying tension)

Climber: "Off belay." (indicating the climber has arrived in a safe position and the belay is no longer required)
Belayer: "Belay off." (confirming the signal)

In the case of a climber's fall, a strong pull on the rope is felt almost immediately by the belayer. (The climber should yell "FALLING!" so that the earliest possible warning is given.) In response, a belayer using a body belay swiftly brings the braking hand (which holds the rope) across the body, wrapping the rope around the hips and lower body. The frictional force between the rope and the belayer's body (or a friction device) arrests the climber's fall. Because this frictional force is often very great, a belayer using a body belay should wear sufficient clothing to prevent the rope from abrading the skin or flesh. Many climbers also wear leather gloves while belaying. This combination of adequate clothing and hand protection prevents rope burns. In practice, belaying is not as easy as it may sound. Rock climbing clubs often set up belay practice sessions in which novices can learn and test their skills.

BOULDERING: GYMNASTICS ON THE ROCKS

Bouldering, or rock climbing without severe exposure, is a rapidly growing sport closely allied with the more traditional forms of rock climbing. Bouldering climbs are rated in difficulty using the Yosemite Decimal system described earlier. For many climbers, bouldering offers the most difficult kinds of gymnastic challenges associated with rock climbing without the need to travel to remote mountain peaks. It can be done right next to roads and campgrounds in the national parks, and at sites close to many metropolitan areas.

Some climbers view bouldering as an end in itself; others practice the sport to prepare for technically similar, but much longer efforts on the big walls of the Sierra Nevada and other mountain ranges. Bouldering, however, should never be considered a casual sport. A fall on one's head or back from a height of only a few feet can be just a dangerous as a foot-first slip down a high cliff. Belaying may be needed for climbs on the larger boulders.

CLIMBING ETHICS

In recent years, climbers have adopted a rigid ethical code both promoting safety and discouraging damage to the environment. More than 20 years ago, pitons (steel pins pounded into cracks for protection) were standard items for the ascent of rock walls. But pitons, if they were removed from the rock at all, tended to chip out and widen cracks, thus changing the nature of the rock climber's environment—the rock itself. So pitons were replaced by reusable devices like nuts and chocks, whose effects on the rock are usually negligible. Today, the ethical climber tries not to deface the rock by adding bolts or any other permanent hardware or by chipping additional holds. The goal is to leave the rock unchanged and equally as challenging for the climber who follows.

BEFORE YOU BEGIN
ROCK CLIMBING

This chapter is only a brief introduction to rock climbing. It is not intended as a "do-it-yourself" guide for the novice. This chapter should not be substituted for a rock-climbing course or suitable guidance from experienced climbers. It is wise for the beginning rock climber to recognize that this sport has some very real hazards, and that it should not be practiced without proper instruction.

Recommended Reading:

Ropes, Knots & Slings for Climbers
Walt Wheelock
La Siesta Press, 1985

Basic Rockcraft
Royal Robbins
La Siesta Press, 1985

Advanced Rockcraft
Royal Robbins
La Siesta Press, 1985

Chapter 14

Special Skills:
Winter Mountaineering

Dave Ussell and Bob Feuge

"The same law that shapes the earth-star shapes the snow-star. As surely as the petals of a flower are fixed, each of these countless snow-stars comes whirling to earth . . . these glorious spangles, the sweeping of heaven's floor."

—Henry David Thoreau

T he mantle of white enshrouding the winter landscape is simultaneously an invitation to experience one of nature's most beautiful spectacles and a warning to be more wary and respectful than usual of the dangers that await the unprepared. Fortunately, preparations are not as difficult as they may first appear.

An outing in the snow is enhanced by breathtaking scenery, a virtually unspoiled wilderness, and a dearth of insects and dangerous creatures. The stillness and tranquillity of the winter landscape is seldom spoiled by hordes of fellow travelers. The winter traveler is not restricted to staying on trails, if, indeed, trails can be found at all.

SPECIAL CLOTHING AND EQUIPMENT

Winter travel places stringent demands on clothing and equipment. Certain advantages claimed for equipment used during the warmer three seasons can be more pronounced when the same equipment is tested during the fourth season. A case in point is the performance of internal- versus external-frame packs. An internal-frame pack's streamlined design sheds snow, hail and wind more easily than an external frame pack does. Its body-hugging shape does not impair the wearer's balance as much as an external-frame pack. With no exposed metal, internal-frame packs are easier and safer to handle with bare skin under extremely cold conditions.

Winter Clothing

We put on clothes to retain body heat in cold conditions, and wear less to allow for evaporative cooling in warmer conditions or when generating a lot of heat through exercise. The winter traveler must be prepared for both, and must do so with a limited wardrobe that is multipurpose and efficient. Thus the layering system discussed in earlier chapters becomes critically important.

The winter traveler should be prepared to put on any combination of layers that
* trap warm air
* hold in body moisture (when not exercising heavily)
* keep winds from removing body heat
* resist the passage of water from outside to inside
* allow ventilation and encourage the passage of moisture from inside to outside (when exercising)
* allow freedom of movement
* provide some protection from abrasion and penetration

These layers, ideally, would be light in weight, low in cost, and easily repaired.

Several synthetics do a good job of letting body moisture escape from the skin. The names of some commonly available examples are polypropylene, Capilene, pile, bunting, Synchilla, and fleece. Wool is the only common natural fiber that can provide significant warmth when it's wet. Most kinds of wool are too scratchy to be considered an acceptable choice for underwear. Capilene and polypropylene are some of the most popular choices. Some synthetic underwear may have a tendency to retain body odors, even after laundering.

For warmth, almost any material that traps air and minimizes its motion can be potentially useful. Wool, duck or goose down, and synthetic materials such as Quallofil, Polarguard, and Hollofil work well, with various advantages and disadvantages. The synthetics have the advantage of providing some warmth when wet, whereas down provides more warmth for the same weight, but is ineffective when wet.

To block the wind, a nonporous synthetic shell (outer garment) is best. There are many materials suited to this task, including nylon, Taslan and Goretex. The design of the shell should include adequate provision for ventilation. Jackets or parkas lined with an outer shell are fine for urban use, but they don't offer enough versatility for use under changeable winter conditions. Consider as an alternative a pile jacket and a separate shell garment. This affords comfort in moderately cold conditions (using just the jacket) and/or in windy conditions.

The use of vapor-barrier materials, such as plastic, urethane-coated nylon, or rubber, can be advantageous in certain situations. When the temperature is extremely low, a vapor-barrier layer under a jacket can add as much as 15°F of apparent warmth, although effective ventilation must be assured by such features as underarm zippers for use while you're exercising. Vapor-barrier mittens and socks are useable over a much wider range of temperature and activity. A simple way to test the effectiveness of vapor barriers is to wear plastic bread bags between your inner and outer socks. Your feet may feel slightly clammy, but will most likely stay warmer while out in the snow.

With the right combination of long underwear, a layer or layers of insulating garments, and a wind- and rain-resistant shell, comfort can be achieved under almost any conditions. Of course, it must be remembered that heat losses also occur from the extremities and from the head—more than 30 percent from the head alone. Polypropylene liner gloves and a ski mask or balaclava are good first layers. On top of those should be insulating layers consisting of a wool/polypropylene hat and gloves or mittens. A hood and nonporous overmitts can be used for extreme conditions. Hoods work best when they are attached to a jacket or parka. Outer gloves should have a non-slip surface in the palm area and a large gauntlet with a tightening arrangement to minimize drafts. It is common practice on winter expeditions to keep gloves on lengths of cord attached to the wearer in some way to avoid loss if they are removed for any reason.

It's worth mentioning that sometimes winter conditions can be more dangerous on warmer days. Sunshine or higher temperatures may cause snow to melt on contact with your clothing. If seams are not sealed properly or the outer material is porous, your clothing may absorb a lot of water, which then greatly reduces the effectiveness of your insulation when the sun drops and the temperature starts to fall.

Packs

Proper gear and clothing is often neglected by winter mountaineering novices who, by not taking extra clothing and other items, foolishly count on near-perfect weather and no delays. It's better to take along a larger day pack or backpack than what you would need for the warmer seasons. This reduces the temptation to leave important things behind and makes carrying the extra load more comfortable.

For cross-country ski touring in particular, a pack must allow the arms to move freely past the body while poling. When loading a backpack for overnight use, put the heavy items close to the back, not near the top. Pack medium-weight items at the bottom, and afterward stuff the lighter items anywhere they'll fit. Use plastic bags or coated nylon sacks to protect all items from snow and to group items by use.

Boots

Boots used for winter mountaineering should keep the feet dry and warm. A hiker should never try to keep feet warm by putting on more socks to the extent that circulation is reduced—that will only make the feet colder. Conventional leather boots must be sealed with a sealer specifically designed for that purpose. Gaiters (the knee-high kind are best) are helpful for not only keeping boots dry from the outside, but also for keeping snow from spilling into the boots from the top. Certain expensive gaiters have such features as full boot-upper coverage, Gore-tex material, and some insulation.

On long trips, even properly sealed boots can become soaked. What do you do then? A neophyte might handle the problem of wet boots by merely setting them aside in camp and putting on some warm booties. By morning, the boots would be frozen solid. A better choice would be to slowly dry the boots near a campfire. Another alternative is to put on a dry pair of inner socks, and then vapor barrier socks (plastic bags will do). On top of that, put on your outer socks (hopefully dry ones) and then the wet boots. "Steam" has been seen on boots handled like this within a few minutes, although it is unreasonable to expect the boots to completely dry by this method. To further the drying process, you can either place the boots in a plastic bag and sleep with them, or put a trash bag in the bottom of your sleeping bag to protect it and sleep with your boots on. You may not have the most comfortable of nights, but life will be easier in the morning.

Plastic mountaineering boots with removable inner boots are an excellent choice for the fourth season. They're rugged, warm, and waterproof, and will easily accept crampons, gaiters and snowshoes. The inner boots alone can be worn in the tent. On the negative side, they're fairly stiff, heavy, and expensive. Stiffness in a boot can be an asset in many climbing situations, however. Even when walking on flat terrain, the snow "gives" a little, which compensates for the lack of flexing in the boot.

Walking in deep, soft snow with a pack and boots alone is an exhausting process. With each step a hiker can sink to as far as the crotch, and forward progress is excruciatingly slow. This is called post holing. The solution is to lower your pressure on the ground by spreading your weight over a larger area. You can either wear snowshoes or skis. It's also possible to lighten or eliminate any load on your back by placing your gear in a lightweight sled specially designed to be towed behind a skier or snowshoer.

Cross-country skis, unlike snowshoes, require special boots. When you shop for skis, you're really looking for a system of skis, bindings, boots, and poles. Each kind of ski boot is designed for use with a particular type of binding, and bindings are attached to the skis by special tools. Your outfitter can help you sort through the many options and help you choose the right system.

Ski boots for day tours or ski backpacks should be durable and warm, have good torsional rigidity yet some forward flex, and should extend just above the ankle bone to provide lateral support and ankle protection. Boots with uppers made of Gore-tex or other synthetic fabrics are OK for light uses; leather boots are much better, as long as they're treated for waterproofness with the appropriate silicone or beeswax sealant.

Snowshoes

Snowshoes are usually selected based on the user's weight (with gear) and the type of terrain to be covered. Snowshoes with an upturned lip are best for powdery snow. Flat and open terrain allows larger snowshoes to be used. In steep, rough, or brushy terrain, the large snowshoes are more of a hindrance than a help. Smaller snowshoes with various lip curvatures are available for these conditions. Your local outfitter can advise you as to appropriate sizes and types of bindings. Older snowshoes consisted of little more than a wooden frame with a rawhide weave. Many newer snowshoes have a lightweight aluminum frame, reinforced neoprene pad areas, quick disconnect bindings, and a fixed or movable toothed grip for climbing slopes.

Cross-Country Skis

Cross-country skis are designed to grip the snow when one's full weight is applied, and to slide smoothly on the snow when less weight is applied. This allows you to "kick and glide" forward on the snow. Proper ski length and stiffness is important since the middle, or "kick" part, of the ski bottom must be in contact with the snow during the kick, and should be off the snow during the glide. Generally, the length of a properly fitted ski should reach from the floor to the wrist of your raised arm. You should also stand on the skis: a piece of paper should easily slide under the kick part of the ski when both skis are equally weighted, but each ski should touch the floor when all your weight is on it.

For ski travel in mountainous terrain, you'll need "off-track touring skis." These have a narrow "waist," a wider "tail," and an even wider "tip." Skis without these characteristics are suited for use on groomed tracks or race courses, but not for true cross-country travel. For general ski touring, skis should have enough "camber" (flex) so that they can be pressed together, bottom-to-bottom, with one hand.

Unless you are willing to spend the time required to gain enough experience in waxing, start out skiing with no-wax skis—skis with a relief pattern on the bottom to grip the snow when kicking. This term is a bit of a misnomer, since even they can benefit from the application of a glide wax (paraffin candle wax will do) to the tip and tail portions. Waxable skis, with no relief pattern, require the application of a "kick wax" on the kick portion of the ski to provide the needed grip.

Metal-edged skis are best for technical demands of steep, icy slopes, but they are usually not required for skiing in softer snow. Metal-edged skis are heavier and less flexible, and wet snow tends to freeze and stick to the metal.

If you're going to be wearing a heavy pack, you may need to have skis that are either wider (to provide additional flotation) or metal-edged (for stability).

"Skins" are an optional but very useful aid in ski touring. Today they're made with mohair (goat hair), nylon, or polypropylene fibers. One side has short hairs facing one direction, and the other side has a reusable adhesive.

When the sticky side is applied to the bottom of the skis, the hairs grip the snow (but not ice) and keep you from backsliding when climbing steep hills. Skins, of course, prevent efficient gliding, but this can be an advantage when it's necessary to keep your speed down on steep downhills.

Ski poles are essential to maintain balance, and also to assist with forward propulsion. Aluminum alloy poles, preferably a high-grade aircraft type, are best. If bent, they can usually be straightened in the field. Fiberglass poles, while cheaper, can shatter. Generally, the poles should just fit under your underarms when the tips are touching the floor.

Ice Axe

For winter mountaineering, there are not many pieces of equipment as useful as an ice axe. For a person falling on a steep slope, the ice axe is the only piece of equipment that can arrest the slide in a rapid and controlled manner.

Select a longer axe if your travels are on mostly gentle inclines, and a shorter one if you'll be climbing a lot. Consider that your "height" will change a bit when you sink into the snow while walking. Lightweight, metal ice axes are very strong, moderately priced, and require little maintenance. But they're always cold to the touch under winter conditions. Carbon-fiber axes are strong and absorb shock well, but are very expensive and not so forgiving if a boulder should bounce off the shaft. Ice axes with wooden shafts are less strong and less expensive than the others. Hickory is usually preferred to ash.

Gouges in wooden or synthetic axes are greater cause for concern than in metal. Holes should never be drilled in axes for any kind of attachment. Most ice axes already have a hole in the head for utility use. The axe should be kept free of rust and deposits, and sharpened when needed. Sharpening of the pick, adze, and spike should be done with a file rather than a grinder, so as not to cause excessive heat that could affect the temper of the metal.

Crampons

For icy conditions, there's no substitute for crampons, boot attachments whose sharp, metal points are designed to penetrate and grip hard snow and ice. Crampons are attached to boots with either a full strap binding or a step-in attachment that slips over the toe end welt of the boot and attaches with a strap around the ankle.

CRAMPONS

Crampons typically have ten primary (downward-pointing) points and two forward-pointing points for climbing. Like the ice axe, they should be kept sharp at all times. If you use them for aerating your lawn in the summer, don't forget to clean and sharpen them afterward! Protective sheaths for the points

are commercially available, but can usually be improvised with tape and old inner tubes, or something similar.

Sleds

There are a few decisions to make in selecting a sled for toting gear. All of the standard considerations of weight, material, cost, and ease of operation and maintenance apply. In addition, some ridges or runners of some sort (which function like that of a keel on a sailboat) must be on the bottom to allow easy forward motion and tracking, but limit lateral motions. A special, semi-rigid harness must be used to maintain the separation of traveler and sled when descending.

Special Climbing Gear

Winter climbing involves most of the usual rock-climbing gear discussed in Chapter 13. Unique to winter climbing are the ice axe, ice screws, and "deadmen." Ice screws, take the place of pitons, nuts, and chocks for use as anchors on ice. A deadman should not be confused with a dead man. Both happen to be difficult to move, but a deadman is simply a big, flat object that resists movement perpendicular to its plane. If driven into consolidated snow at a slight angle, like a tent stake, it becomes very good anchor. The angle should be such that increased pull on the deadman only serves to drive it deeper into the snow, anchoring it more firmly.

DEADMAN ANCHOR

Sleeping Equipment

Sleeping equipment for winter mountaineering should be maximized for warmth. It may be worth 5-15° of extra warmth if you use an optional vapor-barrier or flannel liner. An obvious and easy way to increase insulation, if you really need it, is to wear some or all of your insulating layers of clothing inside your bag—assuming there's enough room inside the bag.

A weight-conscious backpacker who happily takes a lightweight, ³/₄-length sleeping pad for the other three seasons, should not skimp on a pad for winter use. Much of a sleeping person's body heat escapes downward into snow if there isn't enough of an insulating barrier.

Many people like to connect two sleeping bags together to share intimate sleeping quarters. During cold-weather campouts, however, this can be less practical, especially for restless sleepers since warm air easily escapes and cold air rushes in. Attaching sleeping bags together in the winter should be reserved for emergencies involving hypothermia, where it may be necessary to help warm up a victim by body contact. It's a good idea for a group of winter wilderness travelers to have at least one pair of mating sleeping bags.

Special Items

Certain items not normally needed on most three-season trips may be of special use on winter trips. A lightweight snow shovel can help speed up tasks such as digging trenches or snow caves for shelter. An aluminum snow saw is indispensible for cutting blocks used for igloos.

Altimeters can be of critical importance if it's necessary to navigate in white-out or poor-visibility conditions. As discussed earlier, they can also be used to keep track of barometric pressure and thus changes in the weather.

Weather radios can be a good tool, but remember that batteries must be in top condition to perform at reduced temperatures. In remote areas, the signal strength of the nearest station may not be adequate for good reception.

Most normal sunglasses are not adequate for snow travel in the bright sunlight. In addition to a pair of normal sunglasses for use in shady conditions or on overcast days, you should have glacier glasses. They feature extra-dark lenses and opaque panels on the sides to keep out glare.

If you're going to include equipment to cover an expedition's special needs, you must simultaneously add repair items to keep that equipment in working order. Consider taking extra fasteners and lightweight tools for equipment such as snowshoes, rope to lash things together and for making splints, and possibly hose clamps, duct tape and wire for general repair of a variety of equipment.

WINTER TRAVEL TECHNIQUES

Over Snow and Ice

When traveling on a hard crust of snow or ice, an ice axe and (in more extreme cases) crampons become necessary tools.

When carrying an ice axe that isn't needed for emergency use, you can tie it to your pack, or carry it in either of two ways: Grasp the shaft at the balance point with the tip forward and the pick to the rear and down. Or use the ice-axe as a hiking stick with your palm resting on the head of the axe directly over the shaft with the pick forward [see page 151 for ice-axe terminology].

Walking

Carrying

Ready Position

Self-Arrest

Ready Grip

For | ward

In the ready position, the ice axe is ready for emergency action. Hold it so that the pick is to the rear. Then lift the axe until it is diagonal across your chest and grasp the lower part of the shaft with the opposite hand. Normally the axe head is in the uphill hand. The wrist strap is always used in the ready position to retrieve a lost axe if necessary. The ready position allows you to immediately go into a self-arrest maneuver that will minimize sliding after a fall.

During a slide or fall on snow or ice you must drive the pick hard and quickly into the surface to stop the slide. This must be done while simultaneously keeping the point off of the surface. If the point snags, it has a tendency to pull out the pick. If you are wearing crampons, it is important that they don't become snagged either.

During most falls, speed builds up rapidly, so quick reflexes are mandatory. Personal instruction and considerable practice is necessary for learning the various ways of self-arrest for the various types of falls. An ice-axe does little good, and may even do harm, to a person unskilled in its use.

On steeper slopes with snow that is consolidated but not too icy, you can use your ice axe as a kind of anchor during ascent, planting its point in a new spot ahead of you after every step or two. If you're wearing boots, you can kick-step by driving the toe of your boot far enough into the snow to form a level platform you can step up on.

On steep, hard-packed snow or ice, you'll either have to resort to wearing crampons or chop-stepping. Chop-stepping utilizes the adze of the ice axe to cut a small platform for weight transfer. In either case, you must be roped together with others or be belayed in a similar fashion to that described in Chapter 13. Much more information on advanced techniques such as these can be found in some of the books listed at the end of this chapter.

When descending a steep slope, all of the same conditions for ascending must be considered with some additions. Descending has the nice feature of being less exhausting. Unfortunately the tradeoff is that it can be much harder to locate secure footings.

If the slope is not too steep, you can use a plunge-step technique to walk downhill, or you can "glissade" down. A glissade is nothing more than sliding on one's feet or backside to the bottom of a slope, but using an ice axe (in a ready position with point dragging) as a kind of brake and rudder. In the plunge step, compaction of snow does the

Sitting Glissade

The Plunge Step

braking. The descent becomes a bouncy and somewhat animated jaunt down the slope with the ice axe ever ready to handle a fall.

Glaciers present problems not encountered in most other hiking, not the least of which are the crevasses (cracks) that develop when a glacier flows over a convex surface. Some crevasses are visible, while others may lie under a thin veneer of snow, ready to swallow the incautious traveler. Even when "on the level," all members of a climbing party must be tied into a rope so that if one drops into a crevasse, the others can use their ice axes to arrest the fall. The rescue of that climber is an advanced, but necessary technique that must be mastered by prospective glacier travelers.

Cross-Country Skiing Techniques

There are many ways for the cross-country skier to move around the back-country. The diagonal stride technique is a good way to get around on the flats or on gently rolling terrain. This is the technique that most resembles walking, except that you slide your feet instead of lift them. At the same time, you get extra propulsion by planting one pole at a time in the snow and pushing back and down on it.

Proper position is important to avoid fatigue and falls. Keep the knees a little bent and your body's center of gravity above the ski bindings. The bent knees serve as a shock absorber that cushions

the effects of moving over uneven snow.

The step turn is the basic technique for changing direction. The step turn is carried out just like you were walking and turning at the same time, using your poles for balance. However, each step can only give you a small amount of turn because you cannot cross your skis without risking a fall.

Wedge or snowplow techniques can help you control your speed or turn while going downhill. You put your feet apart at greater-than-shoulder width and turn your ankles in so that the inside edges of the skis form an arrow pointing forward. By applying more pressure with one leg or the other, it's possible to veer right or left.

When skiing downhill, don't bend over toward the front. This puts your head in a vulnerable position—it may hit your ski tips or another solid object if you fall. Instead bend your knees deeper when going faster. The lower position lowers your center of gravity and makes it easier to recover from being out of balance. If you must fall, then try to do so either to the back or to the side, with both legs together and bent. Don't try to do the instinctive thing, which is to try to catch the fall on a hand or elbow.

When choosing a route on skis, look for areas where the snow has been softened slightly by the sun. Try to stay away from shaded spots where an ice crust can occur. Avoid embedded rocks and trees—holes may lie next to them. Also try to pick routes away from windblown or icy patches (these often have a sheen), and always be aware of avalanche hazards. With experience you'll be able to "read" the snow, and pick the most efficient and safe routes.

A host of advanced techniques (best left to personal instruction or references such as those at the end of this chapter) can be used for both ascending and descending on skis.

CLOTHING AND SHELTER

It is very important on any winter outing to have at least two sets of clothing, particularly those garments that stay close to your body, such as long underwear. At all times, at least one set of clothing should be dry or at least in the process of being dried. Few things can ruin a winter trip faster than wet, cold clothing!

You should wrap your extra dry clothes in plastic bags and seek opportunities to dry moist or wet clothing when your travel itinerary and/or sunshine permit. Many tents have loops inside to accommodate stringing up clothes lines. It is remarkable how good a job a candle lantern can do for drying clothes under adverse conditions.

Shelters in the winter wilderness can range from easily moveable "four-season" tents to semipermanent igloos to emergency snow caves. Any shelter—even a cozy cabin—may require frequent attention if snow is falling thick and fast. It may be necessary to go outside often and dig out entrances or doors, clear ventilation holes, or brush off accumulated snow from tent walls.

Tents

Four-season tents are generally heavier to carry, but their safety and comfort in the winter environment are well worth the extra weight. Compared to ordinary tents, they usually have:
• a weather-resistant tunnel for entering and exiting the tent (more than one entrance is desirable).
• a vestibule for cooking and storage of gear.
• a structural design that withstands severe winds and resists collapse when weighted by an accumulation of snow.
• a design that maintains an adequate separation between the tent's inner walls and its outer, waterproof shell, or "fly." This improves ventilation, reduces condensation on the inner walls, and improves the tent's insulating ability.
• enhanced water resistance.

Regarding the last point, some tents designed for use in the snow lack a sewn-in floor. This allows ski poles to be used as tent poles, and it also reduces the likelihood of a fire in the tent due to a cooking mishap. The lower edges of this type of tent should buried in the snow to eliminate drafts.

The flimsy tent stakes you may use for summer camping are practically useless in the snow. You'll need wide, strong, lightweight aluminum stakes, or you can improvise in the field and make your own "deadman" tent stakes: Tie a 2-foot section of $1/8$-inch or thicker rope to each staking grommet on your tent, and tie 6-inch or longer pieces of rigid material (thick tree or shrub branches will do) to the other ends of the ropes. Dig a shallow pit in the snow for each deadman and bury it with rope attached. By compacting the snow above and around each deadman with your boot, you can create anchors almost as rigid as blocks of ice. If the snow is powdery and compaction is inadequate, you can try pouring water into the snow above the deadmen to freeze them in. Very secure deadman anchors can be difficult to remove; you may have to use an ice axe or snow shovel, or chip away at the snow above them by kicking with your boots.

When choosing a tent site, avoid spots beneath trees that have (or potentially could collect) large amounts of snow. High winds or a rising temperature could dump that snow on you. Never pitch a tent with an entrance facing the prevailing wind, otherwise falling or drifting snow will pile up there.

Once your tent is pitched, you may want to set up some kind of comfortable quarters outside for cooking and eating—if the weather is good. You can use a snow shovel (or improvise using pots and pans) to scoop out a two-tier trench to be used as a kind of picnic table. In a larger group, it's fun to construct a circular trench with an island in the middle.

Igloos

There's no doubt igloos are the most luxurious accommodations a traveler can fashion in the winter wilderness. A well-built igloo with warm bodies inside can maintain a temperature well above freezing, regardless of the weather outside. Igloos are amazing absorbers of sound as well. Very little outside noise can penetrate the walls.

An igloo can make a wonderful base camp for longer trips, but it should not be the shelter of choice when time, energy, or daylight are in short supply. A group may require two or three hours to build one, assuming at least one experienced person will direct the operation.

First, a flat site with a thick base of consolidated snow is selected as a "quarry." Then, members of the party stomp on the quarry site to compress the snow as much as possible. It may be helpful to wait an hour or two to let the snow consolidate further after compaction.

Blocks of snow are cut from the quarry using a snow saw, carried to the igloo site, and placed in an ascending spiral pattern. The first level, or "race," should be about 6-8 feet in inside diameter—or larger if the builders are experienced. The blocks must lean inward, slightly on the first race, and more severely on successive races. The curve in the walls must begin almost immediately or else the top will become too high to install the final wedge-shaped ceiling blocks. Gaps between the blocks must be chinked with loose snow. With a little foresight, blocks can be cut from the quarry so as to sculpt outside dining quarters.

When the igloo dome is completed, a short tunnel must be dug under the wall of the igloo (not on the side of the prevailing wind), with its exterior end below the floor level of the igloo. That will help prevent warm air from escaping. A hole is then punched in the top of the roof for ventilation. A single candle can provide all the light you need, even on the darkest nights. If you must do any cooking inside, make absolutely certain there's plenty of ventilation.

Emergency Shelters

In the event you are caught unexpectedly in the winter wilderness without a tent, you can fairly quickly create your own emergency shelter. In a real pinch, a large trash bag can be used as a kind of emergency bivvy sack. Compact emergency bags made of "space age" material can be purchased and carried with your first-aid kit for such possibilities.

Other solutions may exist in the form of caves or crevices in rocks for short-term shelter. While bivouacking, it's helpful to assume a fetal position to minimize your body's surface area in contact with the cold environment.

Snow trenches can be quite easy and quick to construct, especially if you have a shovel or items that will scoop snow. A snow trench is little more than a rectangular pit dug into compacted snow. Dig to a sufficient depth and length to accommodate yourself and whatever gear you wish to keep inside, but don't make the trench so wide that you can't cover it easily. Snow blocks can be cut to form an inverted "V" for the roof. Gaps should be chinked and a ventilation hole must be installed if you seal the whole thing. Ideally, you would dig a tunnel with an entrance lower than the sleeping enclosure to keep out cold-air drafts. If that isn't possible, a horizontal entry with a wind block can be fashioned.

Snow caves can be described as igloos built from the inside out. Select a place where a thick blanket of consolidated snow lies against a slope—except where an avalanche might occur. Start by digging straight in and then up, where you can hollow out a sleeping platform. When finished, poke a hole in the roof for ventilation.

Several of the references at the end of this chapter describe in detail the various kinds of emergency shelters.

COOKING

There are some significant differences between cooking and nutrition during summer camping and during winter camping. If the weather forces you to cook inside a tent, you must make sure there is enough ventilation, especially if a blanket of snow surrounds you. You must also be aware that all tent materials will burn. Be extremely careful to control the size of the flame, and keep the stove in a location near the doorway or inside the vestibule, if your tent has one. If your stove becomes warm or hot underneath, don't place it on the tent floor, as it will melt the snow underneath and possibly tip over. Instead you can place it on a small insulating pad, piece of wood, or other stable platform.

In addition to adding more fat to your diet for calories and warmth, heated foods and hot drinks should be an integral part of every meal. As mentioned earlier, alcohol is a depressant that can actually make a person lose body heat faster under cold conditions, so its excessive use must be avoided.

Refueling liquid-fuel stoves can be dangerous under subfreezing temperatures, because stove fuel remains in a liquid state down to about -40°F. Also, fuel evaporates very rapidly, causing a pronounced chilling effect even at room temperature. Fuel can cause instant frostbite if spilled on bare skin at very cold temperatures. Always wear nonporous gloves when pouring fuel under these conditions.

In the winter, it may be impossible to locate a source of flowing water. Thus you will often be forced to collect and melt snow. Because snow occupies so much more volume than water, this is a tedious process. On clear days, you may be able to obtain some water by exposing snow-filled water bottles (dark-colored bottles work best) to sunlight, but this is slow. Melting snow with a stove is much faster, but uses considerable fuel. When planning for your fuel needs, consider both the extra demands of cooking in a winter environment and the need to melt water.

On subfreezing nights, water bottles left outside, and often inside, a tent will freeze up. If you can, put those bottles inside your sleeping bag with you to keep them warm. A second choice would be to bury those bottles in the snow outside, where ambient temperatures often stay close to the freezing point, which is probably much warmer than in the air. Make sure you can locate the bottles in the morning though.

HAZARDS AND INJURY AVOIDANCE

During winter travel, you must always be concerned about special hazards and the possibility of injury. Here are several:

Hypothermia

Hypothermia (formerly called "exposure") is the decrease of core body temperature to a level at which normal muscular and cerebral functions are impaired. Hypothermia occurs most rapidly in cold and windy environments, especially if wetness is a factor. In the winter environment, hypothermia is brought on by immersion in cold water, thin clothing, physical activity or struggle to the point of exhaustion, slim body mass, or a combination of these. Particularly when clothing gets wet, it no longer insulates effectively, thereby promoting a rapid loss of body heat to the environment. Again, this is why it is important to have an extra set of dry clothing with you.

Mere temperature readings are not always a reliable indicator of the severity of the cold environment. The wind-chill index (tabulated on the opposite page) provides a better guide for cold, windy conditions. When wetness is a factor, the effective temperatures are even lower.

It's important to recognize the signs of hypothermia, both in yourself and in your companions, so that remedial actions may be taken immediately. The

WIND CHILL TABLE							
Wind Speed (in mph)	**Actual Temperature in °F**						
Calm	40	30	20	10	0	-10	-20	-30
	Equivalent Wind Chill Temperature in °F						
5	35	25	15	5	-5	-15	-25	-35
10	30	15	5	-10	-20	-35	-45	-60
15	25	10	-5	-20	-30	-45	-60	-70
20	20	5	-10	-25	-35	-50	-65	-80
25	15	0	-15	-30	-45	-60	-75	-90
30	10	0	-20	-30	-50	-65	-80	-95
35	10	-5	-20	-35	-50	-65	-80	-100
40	10	-5	-20	-35	-55	-70	-85	-100

symptoms and treatment for hypothermia are discussed in Chapter 17—First Aid.

Frostbite

Unlike hypothermia, frostbite is a local effect, readily affecting extremities such as fingers and toes, or the tips of the nose and the ears. When exposed to cold temperatures (or wind-chills), blood vessels in these areas tend to shrink, reducing or cutting off circulation. That lowers the skin temperature in those areas. With continued cooling, the tissue freezes and the frozen area enlarges and extends deeper. The tissue is injured by ice crystals in the frozen area, by dehydration, and by disruption of osmotic and chemical balances in the cells.

Frostbite can occur in any cold, winter environment but it is usually associated with inadequate clothing, reduced food consumption, exhaustion, injury, or a combination of these factors. A good preventative measure is vigorous physical activity (if that's possible). When the body tries to cool itself, blood flows to the extremities where it circulates and sheds its heat. For more about frostbite signs and treatment, see Chapter 17.

Dehydration

Though it may seem unlikely, you can become dehydrated during winter conditions, particularly at higher altitudes. This is because cold air and also thin air contain little water vapor. Every time you inhale and warm the air inside your lungs, moisture is taken up by that dry air. Every time you exhale, that moisture is lost to the outside environment—you can see it in fact.

Since the sensation of thirst may not be strong in a winter environment, a conscious effort must be made to consume enough fluid during your travels. Hot liquids, of course, are best, but cold water is fine as well. Don't eat snow unless you become overheated from exertion. In that case only small quantities are of any use, as it requires a great deal of energy (body heat) to transform snow into water.

If you are consuming enough fluid, then you should feel the need to urinate at least every few hours (preferably more often). If you're not properly hydrated, then symptoms of dehydration may come on, such as fatigue, dizziness, and a feeling of faintness.

Sunburn

The winter environment presents some unique challenges pertaining to excessive ultraviolet radiation. Clean, dry, thin air allows ultraviolet energy to pass more easily than thick, warm and humid air does. Snow and ice act like a mirror that directs the UV upward to such uncovered areas as the cheeks, ears, nose, lips, and chin. Even the inside of the nostrils can burn. Keep this in mind when applying sun block.

Avalanche

Avalanches can consist of simply snow, or snow mixed with rock, mud, or earth, depending on the season and location. They represent probably the most serious hazard for the winter wilderness traveler. They can occur almost without warning, carry a hapless victim down a steep slope at high velocity, and bury him or her beneath tons of icy material.

An avalanche can only occur where snow has collected on an inclined surface, and where the snow cover, built up in layers, lacks the necessary cohesion to stick together. Cohesion depends on the
• steepness of the slope
• crystalline nature of the snow of adjoining layers
• temperature change over time
• depth of the snow mass

As temperatures rise and fall, and as new snow is added or snow melted, the snow cover can become either more stable or less stable. When unstable conditions exist, the slightest mechanical force—even the sound pressure of sonic booms, thunder, or gunfire—can set off an avalanche. A traveler walking or skiing across such an unstable slope can easily trigger them also.

There are basically two types of avalanches: loose-snow (sluff) avalanches and slab avalanches. Loose-snow avalanches occur when snow accumulates on a slope that is steeper than the maximum "angle of repose." This loose snow may be made unstable by light, fluffy snowfall falling onto the slope, any loss of cohesion between new snow and old, and lubrication between layers produced by percolating meltwater or rain. These conditions cause a chain reaction, starting with a small amount of moving snow that snowballs into a much larger, ominous mass of sliding snow and debris. In spring and summer, loose-snow avalanches are often caused by wet snow falling on top of cold, dry snow. The wet snow, which fails to stick to the layer underneath, can be destructive, even at low velocity, because it is heavy. In fall and winter, loose-snow avalanches consist of powdery snow that packs less punch because of its lighter weight.

Loose-snow avalanche

Slab avalanche

Slab avalanches are the most destructive of all. They consist of a layer or layers of snow that break off and slide as one large block, pushing other snow in front. The slab breaks loose suddenly, often accompanied by a loud crack like that of a gunshot. Tons of icy debris then accelerate down-slope. The larger slab avalanches are capable of flattening forests and buildings.

Avalanches of both kinds tend to recur periodically in the same steep gullies or chutes, called avalanche paths. Each path has three segments: a "release zone" at the top where the avalanche begins and the snow accelerates; a middle section, or "track," where the snow maintains a steady velocity; and a "run-out zone," where the snow decelerates. The top two zones are the most hazardous.

Large avalanches originate in release zones with slopes between 30° and 55°, although small avalanches, or sluffs, will start tumbling from slopes as steep as 80°. Open, smooth slopes are more dangerous than those covered with rocks, trees, or brush, because there's little in them to anchor the snow cover.

In avalanche-prone terrain, try to stick to ridgelines wherever possible. Especially avoid a mountainside with a broad release zone and a funnel-like chute underneath that would concentrate the sliding snow. Always be on the lookout for evidence of past avalanche activity, like icy debris or smashed trees at the foot of a steep slope.

Avalanches can start on both concave and convex slopes, although more avalanches originate on convex slopes where the slow creeping of icy snow produces tension. On or near a ridgeline, always avoid the lee side of a cornice (a wave-like feature in the snow caused by prevailing winds—see illustration below). Stay on the windward side of a cornice to avoid dislodging it and starting an avalanche.

If you are crossing a slope, and cracks are seen to radiate from your tracks, or there's a "whoomping" sound, then you're on an unstable slope. Either turn back or make your way quickly to a safer position.

Over 80 percent of avalanches occur during or immediately after a major snow storm. If a recent storm has brought 3-6 feet of new snow in a short time, then a strong possibility of avalanche exists. Aside from that, rapid changes in temperature (particularly warming) will destabilize layers in the snow cover and increase the chances for an avalanche.

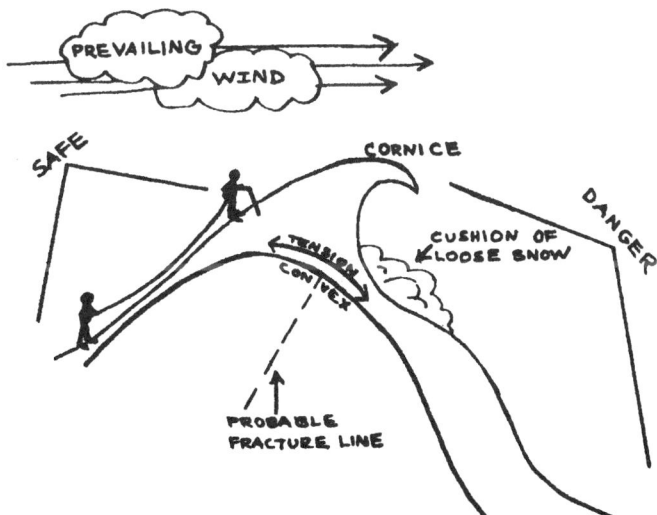

If you are forced to travel across the paths of potential avalanches, try to observe as much of the following as possible:

• Space your party so that each person can be seen by as many people as possible.
• Loosen belts and straps that could encumber your attempt to dig out of an avalanche.
• Cross hazardous areas one at a time.
• Walk across hazardous areas (rather than ski) if the snow is not too soft. Ski tracks tend to release slab avalanches.
• Wear warm clothing and carry emergency items in your pockets.
• Carry shovels and ski poles that can be used as snow probes.
• Use avalanche cords, securely tied to all members of your party, and carry avalanche beacons or "electronic rescue transceivers."

If you do get involved in an avalanche:

• [If on skis] try to steer out of the avalanche area. If you can't, then jettison your poles, skis, and pack.
• if you are caught up in sliding snow, try to "swim" to stay on the surface. Some experts believe the backstroke is the best technique (see illustration below).
• When the sliding snow begins to slow, lunge forward. Reach up with one hand and also spread your legs. An arm or leg sticking out of the snow will enable rescuers to find you more quickly. Use the other hand to create an air pocket in front of your face for breathing.
• Once halted, the snow will settle and harden. You probably will not be able to move nor be heard if your head is buried. Relax to conserve oxygen, and await rescue.

Rescue efforts must be fast and efficient. It goes without saying that each member of the party should be knowledgeable and trained in the techniques of searching or probing (with poles) for buried victims. Two good sources for avalanche information are listed in the following pages.

Recommended Reading:

Ski Touring in California
Dave Beck
Wilderness Press, 1980
   (Contains instructional material as well as a collection of Sierra Nevada
   ski tours for beginning through advanced skiers.)

Harsh Weather Camping
Sam Curtis
Menasha Ridge Press, 1987
   (If you are a fair-weather camper, this book will either convert you or kill you.
   Curtis has experienced all the joys and hardships of winter camping.)

The ABC of Avalanche Safety
Edward R. La Chapelle
The Mountaineers, 1985
   (A detailed look at all the things that can go wrong in avalanche country,
   and how to avoid them.)

Mountaineering: The Freedom of the Hills
Ed Peters, editor
The Mountaineers, 1982
   (Includes extensive coverage of snow and glacier travel.
   A classic in its field.)

Snowshoeing
Gene Prater
The Mountaineers, 1988
   (Includes a well-illustrated section on snow camping.)

Cold Comfort
Glenn Randall
Nick Lyons Books, 1987
   (No other book addresses the issue of avoiding cold
   so succinctly and completely.)

Additional Reading:

Cross Country Ski Gear
M. Brady
The Mountaineers, 1987

Free-Heel Skiing
P. Parker
Chelsea Green Publishing Co., 1988

Avalanche Safety for Skiers and Climbers
Tony Daffern
Rocky Mountain Books, 1983

Cross Country Skiing
Ned Gillette
The Mountaineers, 1988

Mountain Skiing
V. Bein
The Mountaineers, 1982

Backcountry Skiing
L. Tejada-Flores
Sierra Club Books, 1981

Ski Camping
R. Watters
The Great Rift Press, 1989

Hypothermia, Frostbite and Cold Injuries
J. Wilkerson
The Mountaineers, 1986

Cross Country Skiing Right
B. Hall
Harper and Row, 1985

Chapter 15

Women in the Wilderness

Carolyn Wood

"All my life through, the new sights of Nature made me rejoice like a child."

—Marie Curie

Wilderness travel allows women to explore and enjoy new environments, face challenges outside the routines of urban living, and develop new personal dimensions. All this is certainly true of men as well, but for many women there are significant physiological differences to consider. Societal expectations concerning the roles of women may impact a woman's wilderness experience, too. This chapter addresses these special concerns and offers practical solutions from women who love and enjoy the wilderness.

PHYSIOLOGICAL AND PSYCHOLOGICAL CONSIDERATIONS

The average height of a woman in the United States is 5'4" as opposed to 5'10" for men. Size affects the length of your stride and your pace. It can also affect the availability and selection of equipment. When crossing over rough terrain, shorter legs may put you at a slight disadvantage for hopping streams or scrambling over boulders.

Women are, on the average, significantly lighter in weight and have less muscle mass than men do. This may affect how much weight you can carry when backpacking. When determining this, you should figure a "load-to-body-weight-ratio" of about $1/3$. That means, for instance, that a 60-pound pack is a maximum load for a 180-pound person, while a 40-pound pack is about the most a 120-pound person should handle. This, of course, assumes both people are in good physical shape. The 20-pound difference in pack weight is obviously significant. If you are a lighter person, you may have to think twice about the personal gear you'll take, and you may not be able to realistically handle the same quantity of community gear that others handle. Equitable sharing of gear in a group of people of various sizes and abilities doesn't mean that every person must carry the same load.

In general, women do not use oxygen as efficiently as men. Women have fewer red blood cells per unit of blood. This is important because red blood cells carry oxygen to the muscles where the oxygen is used to produce the energy needed for motion. Women also have a higher proportion of body fat and a lower proportion of muscle mass than men. Women, because of their smaller size, usually have a smaller heart, lesser blood volume, and lesser lung capacity. All this means that the average woman must work a little harder than the average man for most activities involving motion. It's important to note, however, that a woman's response to physical exercise is equal to a man's, and that improvements in training can far outweigh any differences in the average physical abilities of men and women.

Women are more likely to have an undetected iron deficiency, even in the absence of anemia. This condition can delay the removal of lactic acid from the muscles during exercise, causing you to tire easily. You may want to have your blood tested for iron deficiency. Iron supplements can take care of slight deficiencies.

In general, women have a smaller mass and therefore less "heat capacity" (ability to store heat) than men. As a result, some women have difficulty keeping warm in cold weather. This means that careful attention to clothing and dressing in layers is very important. When exposed to cold it's a good idea to eat small carbohydrate snacks frequently. You'll need the extra, quick energy.

In any group of men and women, there may be significant psychological differences—such as preferences for certain kinds of activities—between the two sexes. Quite often, for instance, women like to take time to absorb the surrounding environment, while men often like to "get somewhere and do something." By recognizing these differences, you can help build a trip that can cater to all. For example, on a layover day one group may choose to linger and carefully explore the immediate area, while another group may be off to bag a peak.

CONDITIONING

Conditioning for wilderness travel is no different than conditioning for any other athletic pursuit. The better your physical condition, the more enjoyable the experience. One concern novices frequently express is whether or not they will be strong enough to keep up with the group. Until recently, the average woman had not received much encouragement to pursue athletic or physical challenges, nor had a chance to test her strengths. With a good conditioning program, however, a woman's endurance can equal a man's. Adopting an effective program (see Chapter 3) not only builds the necessary physical strength, it also builds self-confidence.

Since women have wider pelvic structures and looser knee ligaments, they're more prone to alignment problems of the knee cap. Exercises that strengthen the muscles surrounding the knee are recommended.

Many women have the necessary lower-body strength needed to support the weight of a heavy backpack, but they lack the upper-body development that most men have. Upper-body muscles are used particularly when lifting or putting on a pack. Various techniques can overcome any difficulty. For instance, you can use a rock or tree to prop up the pack when putting it on or taking it off. You can also increase the strength of your upper body through weight training. Even a modest program can yield impressive gains in strength.

MENSTRUATION

The decision whether or not to travel in the wilderness during menstruation depends on your experiences at home. If cramping and flow are normally no problem, you'll find your menstrual periods in the wilderness are only slightly inconvenient. By taking self-sealing plastic bags for used sanitary products, extra tissues, and moistened towelettes to maintain personal freshness, you'll handle any situation with aplomb.

During the menstrual cycle, certain hormones are released which may cause a general loosening of many of the body's ligaments, resulting in lower back, knee, or arch pain. Since the weight of a pack can aggravate a backache, you may want to use pain reliever. such as aspirin or ibuprofen, to relieve the discomfort.

Disposing of your used sanitary products can be accomplished in several ways. The best way is to simply bag all used items securely and carry them out. You can burn them when and if a campfire can be built. You can burn at least some of the items in a remote location, but you must be very careful about this in fire-prone areas. Wildfires have been inadvertently caused by campers who tried to burn items like toilet tissue in the wild, but had them blow away and ignite dry brush.

Always pack in a full supply of sanitary products! Even women with menstrual cycles like clockwork may find that altitude, heavy exercise, or just plain excitement can alter the normal pattern. Even if you don't end up using most of your tampons or sanitary napkins, there may be another, less-well-prepared woman in the group who might be very grateful for your foresight.

In the event you are caught short of supplies, extra panties, socks, T-shirts, bandanas, or handkerchiefs can be used. Fold the piece of cloth to fit, and secure to underclothes with safety pins, if they're available. If you have an allergy to wool, don't use wool socks or you may find yourself with two problems to overcome!

Is it foolish to go into an area frequented by bears during menstruation? There appears to be no clear answer. Experiences vary. Plenty of women have visited bear country while menstruating with no incident. Bear-keepers at zoos report no additional precautions are taken, or recommended, during menstruation. On the other hand, there have been several reports of menstruating women being fatally mauled. Whether their scent was stronger at that time and attracted the bear, or whether it was the fact that their paths just happened to cross, no one will ever know for sure. A basic precaution is suggested in the book *Bear Attacks*[1]: wear tampons, not external pads.

EQUIPMENT

For women 5'4" and under, a major challenge is finding boots, clothing, sleeping bag, and pack that fit well. The good news is that a much larger selection is available now than several years ago.

Regarding boots, the first thing to know is that the majority of boots manufactured are patterned on men's "lasts," or models of the foot. More and more companies, however, offer boots designed on women's lasts, which are typically narrower, especially in the heel. A snug heel will prevent your foot from sliding around in the boot and causing blisters. When shopping for boots ask the clerk which brands have women's lasts. Don't let anyone suggest you can adapt your feet to men's boots by lacing the boots tightly or adding extra socks.

When choosing a backpack, consider the following: Most women need a pack frame that arches away from the head and buttocks. A pack designed for a man's slimmer hips and buttocks tends to tilt forward on a woman, bumping her in the head with each step. A pack designed for a woman is also shorter between the waist and shoulder, has contoured shoulder straps (to keep the pack riding closer to her narrower shoulders), and a suspension that allows most of the weight to be carried on her hips. The last factor is important because it takes advantage of woman's lower-body strength and relieves pressure on the shoulders. Most internal frame packs are designed to do this.

Some backpack brands come in a variety of torso lengths. For the 5'4" or shorter woman, ask for the shorter lengths. The challenge offered in pack selection is how to get a good fit for the smaller body size and still buy a backpack with a reasonable capacity. Pay attention to the loading style—some styles are more efficient than others.

Day-pack selection is a lot less critical. You may want one that has a wide waist belt and rides on your hips comfortably. This could even be a convertible fanny pack—a belt-riding pack that can be unzipped and enlarged to create a larger, conventional day pack.

Petite women are faced with the challenge of finding smaller sizes of thermal underwear, rain gear, and even shorts suitable for outdoor use. Outdoor shops tend not to stock a wide variety of small sizes, since the demand is relatively low. Don't give up, though. Sizings are often notoriously inconsistent. If there's nothing suitable, then talk to the store's buyer about placing a special order. A competent buyer will know which manufacturers offer extra-small clothing and gear. Be prepared to wait some time for your special order. Think twice about accepting a child's size as a substitute. Children's clothing is often made of lighter weight material.

Sleeping bag choices for the petite woman may be quite limited, too. Even so, it's important to get a short bag for two reasons—less weight and more warmth. In an overly long bag, you'll have more trouble keeping your feet warm. Again, children's bags probably won't be a very good solution. They're usually too narrow at the hips, and don't offer the features or quality of an adult bag.

---

[1] *Bear Attacks: Their Causes and Avoidance,* by Stephen Herrero, Nick Lyons Books, 1985

PERSONAL ASSERTIVENESS

Inexperienced persons often don't ask questions or attempt to participate in making trip decisions because they may believe everyone else already knows the answers. In addition, some women may think that men know more about the outdoors simply because they are male.

Actually, being a novice means you need to ask questions about anything you don't understand. That includes what is a "hot spot" on the foot; how to set up a tent; how to start, use, and refuel a stove; and how to use a map effectively. Don't hesitate to speak to the leader about a pace that's too fast, or when you need to stop for a pack or clothing adjustment. Taking care of such needs immediately, rather then delaying them, will save time in the long run.

Don't leave your powers of reasoning and judgement at home just because you are in an unfamiliar situation. When you're appropriately assertive, you become a responsible member of the team. You take responsibility for yourself as well as others. It's surprising how many men who are novices feel resentful over their female partner's expectation that they know how to handle everything. By the same token, men with plenty of wilderness experience are sometimes equally unhappy when they are expected to do all the thinking and call all the shots.

TOILETING

Because most of us are so accustomed to the accessibility and ease of use of modern bathrooms, "toileting" in the wilderness can be a major area of concern. The techniques of eliminating body wastes and maintaining privacy—especially when part of a group—can be problematic.

As we've seen in Chapter 8, disposing solid wastes in a small "cat-hole" in an area well away from water sources is a sound procedure. The specific technique best for you, however, will come by trial and error. The squat position may be difficult if you are accustomed to only sitting in chairs and if you wear high-heeled shoes. Squatting can become unbearable if maintained for a long time. If there's a tree with low, strong branches nearby, another technique is to hold on and balance over the hole. If you can find a small log or a rock in a private spot with soft soil beside it, you can dig a hole there and use the log or rock as a kind of a toilet seat while extending your buttocks over the hole. A third technique is to dig the hole near something you can lean back into. This is tricky and it is better to put something soft between your lower back and the log or rock to prevent scrapes. A fourth technique is to try balancing with your hands behind you and your feet in front of the hole.

When it's cold in the evening, a good way to stay warm is to consume a hot drink before going to sleep. Of course, input equals output. If "nature calls" routinely around 2 a.m. at home, then it likely will in the wilderness, too. Since the bathroom won't be a convenient few feet away, one technique is to use a "tent bottle" along with a special funnel designed for a woman's anatomy. (Some backpacking shops and mail-order companies carry these funnels.)

Set up your private indoor bathroom before you go to sleep: Set aside a one-liter plastic bottle with a narrow top. (If you've spray painted the bottle, except for an area masked from top to bottom, then you've clearly marked your bottle and also provided a clear space to view its contents. A one-liter bottle handles about two average "pees.") Have your funnel, a small pack of tissues, a couple of pre-moistened towelettes, a self-sealing plastic bag, and your flashlight (a headlamp works best) nearby. Stay off your sleeping bag when first practicing the technique. After filling the tent bottle, screw the top back on immediately! Let the tissues catch any drips from the funnel and then leave the funnel out to dry. Stash the tissues and towelettes in the plastic bag. Next day empty the bottle, rinse it if possible, and let it air out.

Many women (as well as men) report that half of their internal plumbing system refuses to function smoothly while on wilderness trips. Of course, no one ever dies from a few days of constipation. In some cases this is due to a change of diet. Many women, however, are susceptible to "inhibition constipation," which is probably triggered by being uncomfortable about toileting in the outdoors. Inhibition constipation can be overcome by first understanding that you are not the only one who has experienced it. Try drinking something warm shortly after waking up. Take the time to find a pleasant spot far enough away from camp that affords absolute privacy. Allow yourself plenty of time to relax and let nature take its course. If you're on a trip with a tight schedule, then plan to wake up earlier so you'll have enough time. You can even prepare your latrine the evening before. Be careful where you dig a hole, though. You won't want some unsuspecting member of your party tripping in the night.

PREGNANCY

Pregnancy is physiologically normal. But from conception onward, the body undergoes profound adjustments. While pregnancy is no reason to avoid wilderness travel entirely, certain considerations deserve mention. Miscarriages, most common in the early stages of pregnancy, and premature labor, in the later stages, can pose serious complications in isolated areas. Before undertaking any wilderness travel while pregnant, be sure to discuss it with your physician.

In the later months of pregnancy, maintaining balance while walking or scrambling may be a problem. A walking stick may help somewhat. Knee ligaments become looser in late pregnancy, contributing further to instability. Falls, especially on the abdomen, are a serious risk.

Because the pregnant woman provides oxygen to the developing fetus as well as herself, her heart must work harder, even when she's resting. There are more demands on nearly every muscle and organ in the body as well. The pregnant woman must carefully monitor her level of fatigue, and scale back any plans for strenuous travel. During the later months, it may be either uncomfortable or impossible to wear a full-size backpack. In that case, a day pack may have to be substituted.

Meal planning for a pregnant woman has to take into account her special nutritional needs. She may need to double her protein intake and increase her consumption of milk products.

Studies have shown that pregnant women living for long periods at altitudes of 8000 feet and up tend to experience increased blood pressure, problems with breathing, water retention, and swelling of the hands and feet. It is not known if such effects are apparent, or detrimental, for short-duration trips. Certainly, any pregnant woman should carefully monitor herself for any adverse symptoms brought on by a high altitude, and be prepared to descend to a safer level if necessary. Certain drugs and chemicals commonly used by mountain travelers, including Flagyl for giardia, Diamox for high-altitude symptoms, and iodine for water purification, should not be taken during pregnancy.

OTHER CONCERNS

An intrauterine device (IUD) should never be inserted just prior to going into the wilderness. The cramping and/or bleeding following insertion may last days. One out of every four or five women will spontaneously expel or need to have the device removed for intolerable side effects. If you use an IUD, allow plenty of time to adjust to it before venturing far from medical help.

Menopause can bring on a different set of considerations for the outdoorswoman. Until the menstrual cycle has been absent for a full year, there's always the possibility of having an unexpected episode. Estrogen therapy can result in a return of menstrual-like cycles. In either situation, it's important to pack in the usual supply of sanitary products, and pain medications, if necessary, until the change is complete.

If you're troubled by "hot flashes" during menopause, getting overheated only makes the problem worse. Avoid hiking in hot weather if you can, make use of shade during rest breaks, and stay well hydrated by drinking plenty of liquids. On group trips, inform the leader of your needs.

Bone thinning (osteoporosis) is a health problem for all aging people. For women, a high rate of bone loss seems to be associated with menopause. Thinner bones are more likely to break, possibly in rugged areas that might be far from medical facilities. If you know you are at risk for osteoporosis, you can adapt by keeping your pack weight to a minimum and perhaps foregoing trips to remote areas. If carrying a backpack causes low back or hip pain, you can still continue to enjoy the wilderness by day hiking.

You may want to add certain supplies to your medical kit such as vaginal suppositories for yeast infections, and antibiotics for urinary-tract infections. Vaginal suppositories need to be kept cool, so pack them where they will be least exposed to heat.

Finally and emphatically, don't stick to a low-calorie diet while undergoing strenuous, long-duration exercise. Uphill backpacking can burn 500 or more calories per hour. This energy can come from body-fat reserves, but this is an inefficient and dangerously uncomfortable process. There's nothing wrong with a low-calorie intake on layover days or days with moderate exercise, but eat heartily on the days your body requires extra energy. If you're on a medically supervised liquid diet program, consult your physician to determine how to adjust your program.

FEMININITY

Femininity, as defined by Webster's, involves the "qualities or attitudes characteristic of women and not shared by men." How to retain one's personal sense of femininity is a concern for some women. The answer is elusive, because the concept of femininity depends on one's cultural background.

Feeling comfortable with one's self certainly promotes any woman's sense of femininity, no matter how she defines it. For women traveling in a wilderness environment, there may be more to feeling comfortable with one's self than mastering the necessary skills of wilderness travel and camping. It may also involve bringing along something special that makes a woman feel revitalized at the end of a long day.

Many experienced outdoorswomen have found their own special ways to rejuvenate their spirits and retain a sense of femininity. For some, the extra something may be sandals and a bathing suit. A small amount of perfume, scented moisturizing cream, lipstick, or even makeup does the trick for others. (Remember, though, that scented products can attract insects and bears.) Post earrings or a colorful bandana can lift tired spirits. Weighing little, these items are impractical on the trail, but welcome at day's end when it's time to unwind and relax.

Trekking in the wilderness and enjoying outdoor activities does not mean giving up attitudes or things that may make a woman feel feminine. To the contrary, meeting physical challenges and exploring new worlds of beauty expands personal horizons, enhances self-confidence, and strengthens femininity.

Recommended Reading:

Woman in the Woods
Kathleen Farmer
Indiana Camp Supply Books, Inc., 1976
  (Somewhat dated, but encouraging and practical.)

Hiking the Backcountry: A Do-It-Yourself Guide for the Adventurous Woman
Jackie Johnson Maughan and Ann Puddicombe
Stackpole Books, 1981
  (Excellent, in-depth treatment.)

How to Shit in the Woods: An Environmentally Sound Approach to a Lost Art
Kathleen Meyer
Ten Speed Press, 1989
  (Not a joke—it contains everything you need to know.)

Children in the Wilderness

Marianne Ringhoff

"We are the world, we are the children..."

—Diana Ross

Hiking and camping with children can be most enjoyable for all concerned. Kids are natural explorers, filled with enthusiasm and curiosity. When you're accompanied by little ones, your world seems a bigger and more wonderful place. By sharing in their experiences, you become like a child yourself—liberated from the cares of adulthood, at least temporarily.

Children learn quickly by observing, and they readily imitate your behavior. Be a positive role model. Also be receptive to your children's moods. Tailor your activities, whenever possible, to their interests. A successful outing—one that is both enjoyable and a learning experience—is one that your children may remember for the rest of their lives.

DESTINATION AND ROUTE

The trip destination should be appropriate for both your children's and your own interests, and not beyond the scope of your experience and training. Do include your kids in the process of planning. Ask them what they would like to see and do. Plant the seeds of anticipation. Start by gathering information about the places you'd like to visit. Aside from queries to tourist bureaus and parks, try your local library. Consult or borrow geographic, natural history, and guide books. Some libraries now have video departments with tapes offering previews of the popular parks. Let the kids participate in the decision-making process.

FOOTWEAR

When choosing footwear, remember that kids don't just walk. They will invariably spend much of their time running, jumping, and climbing. Don't hobble them with boots that are too heavy and uncomfortable. On the other hand, you'll want shoes with enough support to handle rocky or uneven ground.

High-top sneakers often work fine, especially for the younger child starting out on short, easy day-hikes. Once the child is ready to hike longer distances or over rough terrain, though, the proper choice of footwear becomes important.

Today you can choose among a wide variety of lightweight hiking boots in children's sizes. These boots break in quickly, offer good foot support and traction, and sell for a moderate price. They're comfortable and stylish enough to be worn at home or school as well. Don't forget to allow a break-in period—wear them on at least a couple of shorter walks or hikes before the main event.

When choosing a boot size, consider your child's rapidly growing feet. Have your child try on boots using two socks on each foot—medium and heavy weight. There should be enough room to wiggle the toes but not enough room to allow the heels to slip when the boots are snugly laced. Have the child squat down to check for heel slippage, and have them walk down an incline to check for cramped toes in front. Check that neither the big toe nor the little toe gets pinched on the side (boots with square toe-boxes usually prevent this problem).

Before the trip, make sure that toenails are clipped short. On the trip, carry foot fleece (soft wool) for placing between the toes if needed, and moleskin for "hot spots" and blisters. Check your child's feet during rest stops, and be receptive to any complaints. Don't allow a hot spot to develop into a blister—apply moleskin at the first hint of redness and discomfort.

CLOTHING

Temperatures can change quickly in the wilderness. Dry, sunny conditions on a south-facing slope can instantly turn into damp, chilly conditions on a north-facing slope with the rounding of a single switchback on the trail. A single thundercloud blotting out the sun's rays produces an instant nip in the air. Taking off extra clothing in warm weather is a minor inconvenience. But not having enough clothing in cold conditions can precipitate an emergency situation.

A three-layer clothing system works well with children, as with adults. Generally, the first layer is for comfort, sun protection, and a small amount of insulation. The second, insulating layer retains body heat, while the third, protective layer sheds rain and wind. Pile on or remove the layers as appropriate. Remember that a child's body has a larger surface area to mass ratio than an adult has, therefore a child loses body heat more rapidly. Warm headgear (a knitted cap or balaclava) and mittens are lightweight, essential items for cold conditions.

For sunny conditions, don't forget to protect your child's delicate skin from the sun's ultraviolet radiation. That means long-sleeved tops, a wide-brimmed hat or a cap with a bill, and sunscreen on all exposed parts of the body such as the back of the hands. Collecting all this specialized clothing may be quite costly. But kids' clothing seldom wears out before being outgrown, so your child can be the recipient or the donor of hand-me-downs. Consider sewing identification labels into your child's outdoor clothing; this could be helpful for searchers if your child ever becomes lost.

DIAPERS

This essential item for very young ones merits considerable creative thought. For an extended trip, cloth diapers are less bulky to carry than disposables. They can be used with diaper liners which usually contain most of the waste. You can bury the waste as an adult would, and wash (not directly in a stream or lake, but well away from the water) and reuse both the liner and cloth diaper. If disposables are used, they *must be carried out*. If a disposable's inner lining is cotton, it can be removed from the plastic and burned. The plastic itself should be carried out.

"Biodegradable" diapers are appearing on the market. However, in the harsh climate of many wilderness areas it may take years for them to disintegrate. Even if you bury them deeply, animals may locate and dig them up. Ask yourself how you'd feel if you discovered the remains of diapers at a prospective campsite.

SLEEPING BAGS

Children sleep "colder" than adults, so the choice of a sleeping bag should reflect that fact. Usually a child will sleep warmer in a lighter, more compact mummy bag than in a roomier, rectangular-style bag. Some children cannot tolerate the confinement of a mummy bag. Most junior-size bags fit children up to about 5 feet in height. The leftover length, if any, can be tied off or tucked under as a mattress. When choosing between down or synthetic fill (see Chapter 5), take into account the issue of bed-wetting as well. Down bags lose their insulating qualities when wet, and they are difficult to launder.

To prevent a child from creeping out of a sleeping bag at night, cinch the top cord down to shoulder size. Any extra cord can be secured in such a way to prevent the child from getting tangled up in it, yet allowing easy access if it's necessary to open the bag in a hurry. One effective way is to wad up the excess cord into a plastic film cannister. The tight-fitting lid will pinch the cord, keeping it inside.

PACKS

Any child old enough to walk can wear a pack. Start out with a small "play" daypack for your toddler. You can put special toys and snacks into it for trips to the park or to the babysitter. The child gets used to carrying things on his or her back, and feels helpful to boot.

Most kids old enough to use daypacks for school can easily graduate to a pack with a rigid frame. Junior-size, external-frame packs often have adjustments that will accommodate a fair range of growth. When checking for fit, load up the pack and adjust the straps so that the waist belt lies on the hip bones.

The weight of the pack should be borne by both hips and shoulders. A well-padded waist belt may be needed for a thin child; a broad frame will be necessary for a heavy child. Make sure there are no buttons, zippers, or extra folds on the pressure areas of the hips that may cause chafing. See how easily the pack's closures (zippers, cinch cords, velcro) allow your child to get at items stored inside.

Shoulder straps should attach to the frame about one or two inches below the top of the shoulders. While on the trail, check from time to time to see if the pack is riding comfortably. Sometimes the waist belt will slip down below the hips and result in too much weight on the shoulders.

CARRIERS

One of the best ways to get children interested in the outdoors is to start early. For pre-toddlers, this usually means that you'll be purchasing a child carrier. Newborn infants, who lack the ability to hold their heads up, should be transported in a sling-type carrier worn on the front of the parent's body. From roughly age 4 months and up most children are comfortable in a standard backpack-type carrier. The better models have a capacity of up to 40 pounds. In addition to providing a good view of the surroundings, the rocking motion of a carrier can soothe even the crankiest baby.

When shopping for a carrier, make sure you try it on with the child in it. Have someone check for pinching on the child's arms and legs. Look for any stray belts, buckles or snaps that can get into little mouths. Some kind of head support is desirable if the child is very young. Make sure the pack is comfortable and does not throw you off balance when you walk.

The child in a backpack-type carrier should face forward with head high enough to see over your shoulder, but not higher than your head. When on the trail, avoid the possibility of the child climbing out by making sure all belts are securely fastened and snug. Some carriers feature a "kickstand" that will support the pack upright on the ground. In that position, the pack can serve as a high-chair in camp, but you must never leave your child unattended in that way.

FOODS

Get the kids involved in the fun of pre-trip menu planning. Consider their likes and dislikes, and try out the meals before your trip. Kids burn up an amazing amount of energy during a trip, and therefore they always seem to be hungry. That means plenty of snacks should always be available to feed to them. Chocolate-covered raisins, peanuts, candy, granola bars, and fruit rolls are tasty, nutritious in varying degrees, and rich in the calories that kids need on the trail. Have the kids mix their own gorp at home before you leave. You may be surprised what they put in it!

Weight and packaging of foodstuffs is especially important on family trips. Your younger kids won't be able to carry the weight they use and consume, and that will add to your burden. Remember the importance of fluids—bring plenty of water with you if none is available along the trail.

For the main meals at camp, quick and easy preparation is an important consideration, particularly if you run into bad weather. Finger foods will keep the little ones busy while you are preparing the main course or courses. Encourage the older ones to get involved in the kitchen chores. It's amazing how kids will do things willingly in the backcountry that you can't get them to do at home!

HEALTH AND SAFETY

Have you ever had a child hand you some beautiful arrangement of vegetation that just happened to be poison oak? Kids are so adventurous they can get into just about anything before you realize it.

With some instruction beforehand, your children will know that if they see "leaves of three," they should "let it be." But if they do blunder into poison oak (ivy or sumac), you can wash the affected parts of skin with a mild soap. That will reduce or eliminate the allergic reaction that usually follows some hours or days later. If a rash does appear, old-fashioned calamine lotion helps relieve the itching. Don't allow your kids to use sticks for cooking; they may be from poison oak plants or contain toxins.

Syrup of Ipecac in your first-aid kit is useful in inducing vomiting if your child has swallowed something poisonous. The Sawyer Extractor, a suction device, is useful for treating poisonous snakebites and all kinds of insect bites and stings.

Be sure to keep your children's immunizations, such as tetanus, up to date. While on the trip, sunscreen applied to all exposed skin will prevent much potential misery. Perhaps the most important, but often overlooked, preventative measure is constant vigilance. You and your children must develop a sense of awareness of each other, and of the hazards that exist in the wilderness.

CONDITIONING AND PREPARATION

Children may be physically more resilient than adults in some ways, but they still need plenty of conditioning prior to a big trip. It's important to properly prepare a child's mind as well.

Walking is the easiest form of conditioning. Walk to the park, walk around the neighborhood, walk on the beach, climb some hills. Stick to a routine—walk in bad weather as well as good. But always make it fun. Let them catch raindrops and look for a rainbow. Sneak in a natural history or science lesson while you're at it. And practice some of the routines you'll follow when on the trail; for example, shedding and adding clothing as the weather changes. Children have short attention spans,

so vary your routines to keep things lively. March to a song, count trees or fence posts, spy on birds, or challenge them to a race. This is a good opportunity to give them some freedom—let them choose the direction of travel, or let them play tag on the beach or in the park. Pique their curiosity and follow through in answering their questions.

In your pre-trip planning discuss the agenda with your child. When planning for a day-trip, allow for some exploratory time. On an extended trip, be sure to allow for one or more layover days. The immediate area around a campsite can seem like a whole universe to a little one. Let the child gain some familiarity with the surroundings; allow him or her to bond with nature.

SURVIVAL TRAINING

The most important aspect of pre-trip planning is teaching your children how to avoid getting lost, and what they should do if they do get lost or separated. In a larger group of kids, the "buddy system" works well. By having children pair up, each buddy always knows the whereabouts of the other. If someone leaves the group for any reason, he or she must tell the buddy and also the parent or leader.

On the trip, each child should carry at least one item of bright-colored clothing, a whistle, and a plastic trash-can liner in addition to other items that might be in his or her pack. The first two items are quite effective for signalling to would-be rescuers, while the third serves as emergency shelter.

Children should be taught that the first thing to do when "lost" is to STOP—Sit, Think, Observe, and Plan. They should be secure knowing that their parents, and possibly others, are out looking for them. They must realize that the farther they wander, the more lost they will become.

Project Hug-a-Tree (see Resources at the end of this chapter) offers an excellent program to schools and clubs on basic survival for children. By "hugging a tree," a lost child avoids panic and does not wander aimlessly. The child is trained to blow a whistle rather than use his voice, and to listen for any response. If an aircraft passes overhead, the child "makes himself big" by wearing brightly colored clothing and lying flat in a clearing. The child is trained to use a plastic trash-can liner as a sunshade and, with a hole cut in it, as an impromptu shelter from rain and cold.

What should *you* do if your child is missing? First, don't panic! Second, use a whistle to call to your child. If there's no response, retrace your steps and mark the spot you last saw your child. If there's no further response to signalling, send for help. Include information such as your child's physical description, his clothing, the type of footwear, and the point the child was last seen.

If you're smart, you will have prepared, back at home, a tracing and imprint of the child's boot or hiking shoe. Here's a good way to do it: Place a piece of paper on soft ground. With your child wearing his hiking shoes, spread ink on the lugs or sole pattern of either the left or the right shoe. Have the child carefully step on the paper with the inked shoe and leave it in place while you make a pencil tracing of the sole rim. To clean the sole afterward, blot it with a rag and then let your child scuff through some sand or dirt.

See Chapter 18 for more information on search and rescue techniques.

ON THE TRIP

As long as your child has had adequate preparation, the real trip will be just another adventure, though a bigger one. Remember that having shorter legs means more steps must be taken, so your child will probably tire more quickly than you do. Start out slow, then gradually increase the pace to match the ability of the least able child in your party. Don't let the more energetic ones run ahead of the group—you'll never be able to keep track of everyone that way.

By all means, make the trip interesting and educational. Start good wilderness habits (safety, conservation, picking up after one's self) early—they will last a lifetime. Aim for a positive experience with nature. Share observations and feelings, and be responsive to your child's interests. Use games to energize and to calm. Bring photocopies or printed material on plants, animals, and animal tracks. Encourage questions, and if you don't know the answer, try to find it together. Most important, don't push. Let nature be the teacher.

Recommended Reading:

Finding Your Way in the Outdoors
Robert L. Mooers, Jr.
(Easy reading with the use of many diagrams.)

The U.S. Armed Forces Survival Manual
Edited by John Boswell Rawson
Wade Publishers
(A complete guide to survival in any circumstance.)

Starting Small in the Wilderness
Marlyn Doan
Sierra Club Books, 1979
(A good introduction for the beginning family hiker.)

Backpacking With Babies and Small Children
Goldie Siverman
Wilderness Press, 1986
(Practical information, with answers to questions you usually forget to ask.)

Resources:

Project Hug-a-Tree
6465 Lance Way
San Diego, CA 92120
(Send a self-addressed, stamped envelope for free information.)

Camp Fire
4601 Madison Ave.
Kansas City, MO 64112

Some manufacturers of children's equipment:

The Baby Bag Company
P.O. Box 566
Cumberland Center, ME 04021

Gerry Baby Products
12520 Grant Dr.
Denver, CO 80233

Tough Traveler, Ltd.
Geneva Road
Brewster, NY 10509

Suggested Children's Games:

Sames and Differents
This game involves things of various shapes and sizes, such as leaves, rocks, trees and clouds, that bear some resemblance to each other. Have the child look at one object, then have him discover another object that is similar in some way.

Nature's Shapes
With heavy paper, cut out different shapes, such as circles, squares, rectangles, and triangles. Have the child match the shapes to natural features, small and large.

What am I?
Blindfold the child in a safe area. Have him use all the senses except sight to discover the world around him. Ask questions like: "What do you hear?" "How does that feel? Soft? Rough? Sticky? Wet? Smooth? Warm? Cold?" "What does that taste like?" (Use edible foods, of course.)

Next Stop
Count steps to the next rest stop or destination. Identify a point ahead on the trail, and allow the child to hike "on his own" to reach it. Let your child measure the time taken during a rest stop—a great way for him to learn how to tell time and get a sense of the passage of time.

Night Walks
Visit a place at night that you saw earlier in daylight. What is different about it? This may be a little scary for some kids, but most love it.

Chapter 17

Wilderness First Aid

Carol P. Murdock and Carl W. Trygstad

"Give me health and a day and I will make the pomp of emperors ridiculous"

—Emerson

Once you step past the threshold of the wilderness, you trade the conveniences of swift medical attention for the uncertainties of adventure. It is essential, then, to be familiar with the elements of basic first aid, as well as the particular problems and medical complications that may occur in outdoor situations. We strongly urge that anyone venturing into the wilderness take an American Red Cross Standard First Aid course, along with either the American Red Cross or American Heart Association Cardiopulmonary Resuscitation (CPR) course. On trips to remote areas, at least one person in the group should have advanced training in first aid.

This chapter briefly addresses a wide variety of medical concerns pertinent to those who travel in the wilderness environment. More complete sources of wilderness first-aid information are listed at the end of this chapter.

BEFORE YOU GO

The one procedure that most benefits the wilderness traveler in advance is the tetanus immunization. Tetanus spores are found everywhere and can be introduced into the body through even minor wounds. With prior immunization, tetanus is quite preventable. Adults should have a tetanus booster every 10 years. If you sustain a puncture wound, cut, or burn in the wilderness and are not sure of your immunization status, you should seek medical advice as soon as you return home. A variety of other immunizations are recommended for trips to foreign countries, but these are not normally needed for wilderness travel in the U.S.

WHAT TO TAKE

First-aid kits can range from sophisticated to very simple, but what you need depends upon the length of your trip and how far you'll be from medical help. A skimpy kit—suitable for certain day hikes or short, overnight trips—could include only band-aids, gauze wrap, some 1-inch cloth tape, a needle for removing slivers and thorns, moleskin, aspirin tablets, and a pencil and notepad. After gaining some experience you will become aware of additional items, appropriate for your type of trip, that you should be adding to those above. If you purchase a packaged first-aid kit, you'll probably want to eliminate some items and add others to suit your needs, and also repackage the items to save weight. Any lightweight, sealed container, such as a plastic carton or container, will do.

The following list, containing items for a rather complete kit, is appropriate for extended trips into remote areas—up to two weeks. Supplies are adequate for a group of four people. These supplies, of course, would not be adequate for the long-term treatment of victims with serious injuries or illnesses. After first-aid is rendered to such victims, evacuation from the wilderness and treatment at a hospital is the appropriate course of action.

RECOMMENDED ITEMS	QUANTITY	USE
Band-aids, 1/2" or 3/4"	20-30	For cuts and abrasions
Cloth tape, 1" roll	1	To secure splints
Gauze wrap, 2" roll and 4" roll	1 each	To secure dressings
Gauze pads, 4" size	6-10	To cover abrasions
Moleskin or molefoam, 6" square	1	To prevent and treat blisters
Triangular bandage, 36"	1	Multiple uses
Elastic wrap, 4"	1	To support sprains and secure dressings
Aspirin, 5 gr (325 mg) tablets	30-50	For pain and fever
Antibiotic ointment, 15 mg tube	1	To prevent skin infections
Antihistamine, 8 mg chlorpheniramine or 25 mg Benadryl tablets	6-10	To counter allergic reactions
Decongestant with antihistamine tablets	6-10	For nasal congestion
Ibuprofen 200 mg or Tylenol with codeine 1/2 gr (32 mg)	6-10	To treat pain
Iodine solution, 2% tinture or 10% Betadyne	1 oz	For wound disinfection
Thermometer	1	To measure body temperature
Lip balm with sunscreen	1 tube	To prevent sun damage
Insect repellent	1 oz tube	To discourage insect bites
Wire-mesh splint	1	For a cervical collar or splints
Sawyer Extractor	1	Removal of venom from insect/snake bites

In addition, the following are suggested medicines taken from a recent medical journal article [Vol. 78, No. 2, August 1985 *Post Graduate Medicine. Travel Medicine.*] Each of the first three items requires a prescription.

SUGGESTED ITEMS	QUANTITY	USE
Cavit (obtain from a dentist)	7 gm tube	For tooth fillings
Acetazolamide (Diamox), 250 mg tablets	14	For acute mountain sickness
Phenergan (Promethazine), 25 mg suppos.	4	For nausea and vomiting
Imodium, 2 mg tablets	12/person/week	For diarrhea
Neo-Synephrine	15 gm tube	Nasal congestion, sinusitis, nasal bleeding
Bacitracin-polymixin ointment	30 gm tube	For burns, abrasions, blisters
Sudafed tablets	12-24	For nasal congestion
Corticosteroid cream	15 gm tube	For rashes, swelling and itching from plant contact or insect bites

FIRST AID IN THE FIELD

Despite the best planning, injuries and unexpected illnesses can occur on trips. Although it is hoped that these difficulties can be quickly remedied and the trip continued, sometimes a trip has to be aborted. The participants may need to devote all their efforts to returning to the trailhead (or other exit point) quickly and safely. A careful plan to assess the extent and nature of the illness or injury is needed in order to determine whether or not the trip can continue, and what future course of action to take.

Assessment of an Injured Person

If the stricken person is conscious but does not seem to know you, the first thing to do is to identify yourself as someone who is able to help. A simple statement such as, "I'm Mary. I'm trained in first aid and I want to help you," will decrease the anxiety of any victim of serious injury or illness. If the victim is moveable, but not in a safe position, he or she should be moved to a safer environment.

The history of events leading to the accident or ill health of the victim should be obtained if possible. Questions such as, "Where do you hurt?," "Are you having difficulty breathing?," and "What happened?" or "What do you think is wrong?" can bring out useful information not only about what happened, but also about the current state of the victim. If you obtain satisfactory answers to these questions, then you can plan what to do next.

If there is no response by a stricken person, then immediately invoke the "ABC" procedure of basic life support:

A—*Airway*. The airway must be open and free of debris. Often, better positioning is all that is needed. Keep the neck of an unconscious victim supported and straight with in-line traction. Remember, however, that the victim of a fall may have a neck fracture, so any manipulation of the head must be done carefully.

B—*Breathing*. If the victim does not breathe spontaneously, then start rescue breathing.

C—*Cardiopulmonary Resuscitation*. If there is no pulse, begin CPR.

The ABC procedure sketched above is documented in the CPR-course workbook.

For a conscious victim, a complete survey should be undertaken to determine the extent of injury or the severity of illness. This is the "secondary survey" described in the American Red Cross First Aid workbook. Where appropriate, this should include checking the pupil size and response to light, feeling the neck for tenderness, and observing the chest motion as the victim takes a deep breath. All tender areas should be examined for fractures or bleeding. Communicate with, and try to calm, the victim. The movements, pulses, and sensations in all extremities should be investigated.

All information, especially breathing rate, pulse rate, and responsiveness should be written down. It is more important to note changes than it is to be preoccupied with detail. Keep the victim warm, stop any bleeding with direct pressure, and splint all fractures to prevent further motion.

In general, evacuation is necessary for any victim who is unconscious, has bone fractures, has difficulty breathing, has a serious eye injury, or has pain that does not respond to simple measures such as taking aspirin or ibuprofen.

The following list summarizes the proper sequence of action in the event of a serious accident or illness borne by a member or members of your party:

1. Approach the victim safely without jeopardizing your own safety.

2. Restore and/or maintain breathing and heartbeat.

3. Control any heavy bleeding.

4. Examine the victim carefully (secondary survey) after the above problems are controlled.

5. Decide where and how you (or others in your group) will obtain help.

6. Write down the following information before going (or sending someone) for help: the name of the person or group reporting the accident (if a sponsored trip, include the phone number of the parent organization); the name, address, and home phone number of the victim (or victims); the date and time of the accident and the nature of the accident; the condition of the victim; first-aid treatment rendered; the exact location of the victim (it may be best to mark this location on a map). All written information, along with any map, is carried with you when you go for help.

7. When you reach help (by telephone, radio, or in person), find out whom you are talking to.

8. Convey all the pertinent information listed in #6 above, taking special care to give explicit map directions to the site of the victim, including any information about where rescuers could get lost.

9. Give an estimate of how many rescuers you think may be required and the expected difficulty of the rescue.

10. If you have notified any other agencies, reveal that information.

11. Have the person to whom you gave the information repeat that information to ensure it was understood. And finally, if you're on the phone, let the other party end the conversation. *Never hang up first.*

While waiting for help at the site of the accident, the person (or persons) remaining with the victim should

• continually monitor the victim's condition.

• protect the victim from the environment and from further injury.

• supply any necessary liquids, foods, or further first-aid treatments, as applicable.

• provide emotional support in a tactful way.

• maintain a written log of any changes in the victim's condition and of any treatment given.

In any emergency situation, one person should take charge. This person can be the leader of the group or the person with the most medical knowledge or experience in first aid. This person can designate responsibilities and assign tasks. Everyone should stick to his or her plan. Only changes in the victim's condition or weather should alter that plan.

Shock—A Commonplace Complication

Shock occurs when the circulatory system fails to provide enough blood and oxygen to vital parts of the body. It can occur as a result of trauma, bleeding, burns, heart attack, breathing difficulties, spinal cord damage, infection, diabetes, and extreme allergic reactions.

In the wilderness, early recognition of shock is essential because shock can progress rapidly, and treatment is limited. Early signs of shock may include feelings of anxiety. Other symptoms may include a rapid, weak pulse; altered consciousness; lethargy; stupor; and slurred speech.

The best treatment for shock is simply the correction of the cause, if that's possible. Stabilize suspected neck fractures (see Figure 17-1); perform rescue breathing and administer CPR if necessary; control bleeding; splint fractures; and treat allergic reactions.

Figure 17-1: Stabilization of the neck using rolled-up articles of clothing and a bandana

Whether the cause is treatable or not, you can provide first aid for shock by keeping the victim warm and comfortable. A victim in shock may lose body heat even in weather conditions that seem warm to you. Victims should be kept flat, except those with heart and breathing problems who should be allowed to sit up. Reassure and comfort the victim. Avoid any rough handling, and monitor the victim's condition by frequent physical evaluations. Give fluids to the victim unless medical assistance will arrive shortly, and as long as the victim is not unconscious, having convulsions, vomiting, or clearly has an injury requiring surgery.

A severe allergic reaction known as anaphylactic shock can occur from insect bites, medications, or foods. The symptoms are itching or burning skin (especially on the face and chest), flushed skin, hives, swelling of the face and tongue, blue lips, a tight feeling or pain in the chest, and breathing difficulties. There may be a weak pulse, dizziness, faintness, or even coma. The treatment is to maintain an open airway. If available, give Benadryl orally while the victim is still able to swallow. Those known to be allergic to specific substances should carry either an Epipen or Anakit injection kit available by prescription.

MEDICAL PROBLEMS IN THE WILDERNESS

Abdominal Pain

Abdominal pain is frequently encountered in the wilderness. Most of the time it will resolve itself spontaneously. The objective in assessment is to decide which types will go away, and identify those for which the victim should be evacuated. Constant pain is usually more significant than intermittent pain. Pain around the umbilicus, or a pain that shifts from one place to another, is generally less significant than pain located at one of the corners of the abdomen.

Vomiting is usually an attempt by the body to rid itself of toxins. Small amounts of fluid, and Phenergan (see first-aid kit list) will help. Persistent vomiting, and vomiting associated with head injury requires evacuation. If several people on an outing start to vomit at the same time, think of food poisoning (which will usually resolve itself) or altitude sickness.

Diarrhea may occur in the wilderness, especially if the water supply is impure, or the food is spoiled or contaminated. Most diarrhea can be treated with modification of diet, fluid intake, and possibly Imodium. If there is fever or blood present in the stool, the condition is more serious and an attempt to evacuate the victim should be made. Diarrhea promotes dehydration, so large amounts of fluid may be needed to restore the fluids lost in watery stools.

Appendicitis is always a feared cause of abdominal pain. There is usually a history of vague discomfort or pain around the umbilicus which then moves to the right lower part of the abdomen. A low grade fever, constipation, loss of appetite, and nausea are common. These victims should be evacuated as soon as possible.

Heart Attack

Heart attack (or myocardial infarction) is the death of a section of the heart muscle from lack of blood and oxygen. There are other conditions that can cause chest pain, but this condition is the most life threatening. Signs and symptoms may include chest pain, which can be denied by some victims. Other victims may describe this pain as an ache, a feeling of being squeezed or crushed, or a heaviness in the center of the chest behind the breastbone. The pain may spread to one or both arms, shoulders, neck, jaw, or back. It lasts longer than two minutes and is not relieved by rest. Other symptoms may include sweating, nausea, or shortness of breath. Treat by having the victim stop what he or she is doing and rest quietly. Rescue personnel must be notified as soon as possible. CPR may be required suddenly and for long periods of time. CPR should be started at the scene on all cardiac arrest victims and continued until resuscitation is successful, the rescuers are exhausted, rescuers are placed in danger, there is failure to respond to prolonged efforts, or definitive care is provided. CPR should also be started in other cases of cardiac arrest besides heart attack; i.e, from hypothermia, suffocation in an avalanche, lightning strike, and smoke inhalation.

Stroke

Stroke is a name applied to a group of disorders that disrupt the blood supply to a part of the brain. It can be caused by either a ruptured or blocked blood vessel in the brain. Signs and symptoms occur suddenly. The specific symptoms depend on which part of the brain is involved. A victim's face may be flushed and warm, with perhaps a grayish pallor. The pupils of the victim may be unequal in size; often one eyelid droops. There may be weakness or paralysis on one side of the body. The victim may lose speech. Breathing can be slow and of a "snoring" type. The victim may be unconscious and lose control of bowels and bladder.

Treatment is of a protective kind. Keep the airway open and anticipate the need for CPR. Handle the victim gently and don't move him or her more than necessary. Keep the victim warm and if unconscious, position the victim on his/her side with an arm supporting the head so secretions drain from the side of the mouth (see Figure 17-2).

Figure 17-2: Positioning of an unconscious victim

Diabetes

Diabetes is a chronic disease resulting from a lack of insulin. Two major problems can happen with diabetics. One is diabetic coma (too much sugar) and the other is insulin shock (too much insulin or too little sugar).

Signs and symptoms of diabetic coma happen slowly. The victim may complain of a dry mouth and thirst, or experience excessive urination, abdominal pain, and/or vomiting. The skin is dry, red, and warm. Pulse may be weak and rapid. The victim's breath smells very "fruity" or sickeningly sweet. If left untreated, confusion and then coma result. Treatment consists of keeping the victim warm and evacuating him or her to a medical facility.

Insulin shock occurs rapidly, usually from a diabetic on insulin skipping meals or overexercising. Signs and symptoms include dizziness and headache; aggressive behavior abnormal for the victim (similar to alcohol intoxication); complaints of intense hunger; pale, cold, and clammy skin; and profuse perspiration. Symptoms can progress and lead to fainting, convulsions, and finally, coma.

Insulin shock must be treated immediately. If the victim is conscious, give two pieces of hard candy, half a candy bar, or six or seven Lifesavers. You can also give a 4-ounce glass of orange juice, apple juice, or milk. The symptoms should improve in about 20 or 30 minutes. If they do not, give another dose of sugar. If the victim becomes unconscious, you can sprinkle sugar under the tongue or use one of the commercially prepared gels made for this purpose. If in doubt that the condition is either diabetic coma or insulin shock, give sugar. It will help for insulin shock and won't aggravate the symptoms of diabetic coma much.

ENVIRONMENTAL HAZARDS IN THE WILDERNESS

Attacks by crawling, flying, biting and/or stinging creatures can range from being a nuisance to life-threatening. Exposure to allergens in certain plants or overexposure to the sun can be incapacitating or at least misery-inducing. These and other environmental hazards can usually be avoided by being aware of the potential dangers. Here, we'll focus on treatment for some of the more important problems:

Bites

Relatively few rattlesnake-bite victims in the United States actually die from the effects of the venom, primarily because most are able to reach help relatively quickly. The seriousness of a rattlesnake bite depends on the amount of venom injected (some bites are actually "dry"); the species of the snake; the condition of the victim; and other factors. Where venom has been injected, there is immediate swelling, warmth, and pain. Later, tingling or numbness around the victim's mouth may develop and nausea and vomiting may occur. The victim may become weak, feel faint, sweat, and have a weak, rapid pulse. Breathing difficulties, muscle twitching, and paralysis can follow in

time. The use of a suction device (such as a Sawyer Extractor) to remove some of the venom can be somewhat effective if performed immediately. Five or more minutes after the injection of venom, it does little good. The only lasting treatment is that given by a hospital.

While being evacuated, or awaiting rescue or professional medical help, a rattlesnake-bite victim should be kept at rest so as not to speed up the movement of venom through the body. Some physicians advise the use of a constriction band two to four inches above the bite to prevent the spread of venom. A constriction band is not a tourniquet—it is tied loosely enough so that one's fingers can fit underneath it. An extremity can be splinted and kept at heart level for comfort. Do not use ice, pressure dressings, or make incisions around the bite. Any rings or the jewelry the victim is wearing near the site of the bite should be removed, since a great deal of swelling can occur.

Ticks are common in wooded areas and attach themselves to a victim's skin, usually under the clothing, in order to draw blood. They can transmit diseases such as Rocky Mountain spotted fever, Colorado tick fever, and Lyme disease. The best method of removal is to grasp the tick close to the skin with a pair of tweezers and pull gently. Avoid crushing or puncturing the tick and do not grasp it with your bare hands. After removal, disinfect the site and wash your hands. If parts of the tick break off in the skin or symptoms of any of the above diseases appear (fever, headache, red-spotted rash), seek advice from your physician.

A black widow spider's bite produces pain similar to a pin prick, slight burning, and redness at the site. Local tissue reactions vary, with some victims exhibiting an immediate one- or two-inch area of blanching around puncture wounds surrounded by redness. Other victims have no significant reaction at all. If a large amount of venom has been injected, the victim develops painful muscle cramps that rapidly spread to the entire body. The victim may be anxious, restless, and may complain of weakness and sweating. Most people recover without help over the course of one or two days. However, children and the elderly are most likely to have serious reactions. Treatment consists of applying ice to the bite and immediately transporting any victim with symptoms to the hospital.

Initially, brown recluse spider bites cause very little pain. They often develop a characteristic red blister within one to five hours, surrounded by a "bull's eye" of whitish-blue discoloration. Generalized reactions include itching, a rash, chills, fever, nausea, vomiting and headache. The damage from these bites is caused by tissue destruction, which can take place weeks or months after the bite. These victims should be seen by a physician, who will either give drugs or remove the tissue surgically.

Bees, wasps, and hornets cause injury by attacking the victim and leaving a stinger with venom sac attached to it. The immediate reactions are pain, swelling, redness, warmth at the site, and itching. Some victims may experience a severe allergic reaction called anaphylactic shock. A stinger can be removed by scraping it from the skin with a knife edge or other keen edge, taking care not to squeeze out more venom from the sac (Figure 17-3). Chilling the sting site brings relief.

Figure 17-3: Since a bee's venom sac may still be attached to the stinger (upper magnified view), it should be scraped free of the skin (lower magnified view) without squeezing the sac.

Several kinds of flies, mosquitoes, and fleas can cause irritating bites with local skin reactions. Treatments called Afterbite, Campho-phenique, or a cold application are helpful in relieving the discomfort. In situations of heavy insect populations, try to keep all skin covered with thick clothing or netting. Chemical repellents containing a 75-95% concentration of DEET applied liberally to the skin and clothing work best. Some adults may experience skin irritation and/or rare severe side effects. Do not use a stronger than 15% concentration of DEET on children under age 6. In those cases, protective clothing and netting may be the only defenses.

Scorpions have a thin tail with a stinger on the end that can inflict a painful sting. Most in the United States are nonlethal and produce a reaction similar to a wasp or a hornet. These bites can be treated by applying an ice pack or chilling the bite area in some way. One species lethal to humans is found in northern Mexico and less commonly in parts of the Southwest American desert. The sting from a lethal species may initially go unnoticed. In five to sixty minutes pain develops and may be severe. Tapping the area lightly produces a tingling or prickly feeling, and the affected area becomes quite sensitive to touch. Children, who are most susceptible to the reaction, experience elevated blood pressure. Any victim experiencing these symptoms should be transported to a hospital as quickly as possible.

Rodents such as mice, squirrels, chipmunks, raccoons, and marmots occasionally carry rabies, and also the fleas that can spread this disease to other mammals. Avoid any wild animal that appears tame or friendly. If you are bitten, clean the wound with soap and water and seek medical care. Don't attempt to befriend or feed animals in the wild.

Rashes

Poison oak is a three-leafed bush found throughout the western states whose sap contains a resin producing an irritating allergic reaction on the skin of susceptible individuals. The onset of a rash may appear anywhere from one hour to two or three days after exposure. Many "favorite" treatments abound, but all serve only to relieve the irritation. Lotions such as calomine or Caladryl are soothing and help dry the rash and control itching. Antihistamines control itching but can cause drowsiness. Severe involvement may require the use of oral medication prescribed by a physician.

Susceptibility to poison-oak rash varies widely among individuals. Those who are particularly allergic should become familiar with and avoid contact with the plant. After contact, the resin must be removed from the skin within about 10 minutes, or the reaction may occur. If possible, wash the skin with soap and water, and remove any contaminated clothing. If the resin stays on the skin, scratching can spread the rash from one area of the body to another.

Overexposure to Ultraviolet Radiation

Sunburn is caused by overexposure to the ultraviolet radiation of the sun. Overexposure can occur quite rapidly whenever the sun is high in the sky and at high altitudes, where the atmosphere is thinner. UV can penetrate thin clouds easily, and it readily reflects off of rock, soil, water, and especially snow. In most wilderness situations, virtually all persons (children especially) need protection from the sun in the form of sunscreening clothing or sunscreen lotions.

Sunburned skin becomes red and sensitive to touch, and the victim may experience chills after the sun sets. Besides the immediate damage, repeated overexposure to the sun produces degenerative changes in the skin that can eventually lead to cancer.

Treatment consists of relieving the discomfort and avoiding any further sun exposure. Apply cold, wet dressings to the affected areas if the skin is unbroken. Hydrocortisone preparations are also effective if applied early, but sparingly. Aspirin may prevent some of the inflammation if taken early.

Snow blindness is a sunburn of the cornea, typically brought on at high altitudes where intense ultraviolet reflects from snow and strikes the surface of the eye. Symptoms include excessive tearing, swelling, and redness in the eyes. About eight to twelve hours after exposure, the victim may complain that the eyes feel irritated and gritty. There is also headache and a decrease in vision.

Do not let the victim rub his or her eyes. Cover the eyes with cold compresses and keep them closed. Re-check the eyes in 24 hours. If they are infected, leave them uncovered and have victim wear sunglasses. Early and frequent application of ophthalmic ointment or drops help relieve pain.

Burns

Burns are damage to the skin caused by heat, chemicals, or radiation. The signs and symptoms depend on the degree of burn sustained. With a first-degree burn, the skin appears red. A second-degree burn is red with blisters and may be swollen for several days. A third-degree burn involves several layers of skin and is white or charred in appearance with broken blisters and evidence of damage to underlying structures. In a third-degree burn there may be no pain if nerve endings in the skin have been destroyed.

The severity of burns can also be described in terms of the percentage of the body affected. To estimate the percentage of body surface involved, use the palm of your hand—it represents about one percent of your body's surface area.

First-degree burns are treated with cold water applications. A cool wet T-shirt or clean cloth can be applied to a burn that does not have a broken skin surface. Second- and third-degree burns have broken skin. Do not use ointment, spray, or any home remedy on these burns. With a third degree burn, do not remove adhered particles of clothing. Instead, bandage over the burns and cover with any clean dressings (sterile if available). Elevate hands, feet or legs if involved. When the face is involved, maintain an open airway with the victim sitting up. You may apply cold packs to burn areas but not directly on the burn. If the victim is conscious and not vomiting, you can give one of the commercially prepared electrolyte fluid replacements (Gookinaid, Gatorade etc.) slowly in small amounts. If burns cover a joint, are near the eyes or genitals, are deep, or the victim is over age 50 or under age 5, evacuate to medical help. Burn victims have a high risk of going into shock from fluid loss.

Lightning

Lightning injuries can occur from direct strikes, secondarily after another object has been hit, or from ground current. Many people can be struck at once, causing multiple victims.

The first assessment should be to check for breathing and heartbeat. The victim may need prolonged CPR before checking for further injuries. Other common problems include spider-like burns, fractures, and temporary paralysis. These should be treated accordingly.

Blisters

Blisters are caused by friction, which results in an accumulation of fluid under the skin. The most common place is on the feet, from poorly fitted boots or shoes.

The first sign of a blister is a "hot spot" which appears red and is tender to touch. If untreated, fluid forms and the skin covering the fluid may break and leave a very sensitive, irritated, open bleeding area.

Treat blisters early in their formation by covering with tape or moleskin. Products called Newskin or Second Skin can be used to coat the friction area and protect it against further rubbing. Do not open a blister unless there is a danger of it rupturing or if it interferes with walking. Before opening a blister, wash your hands and clean the skin with soap and water or disinfectant. Sterilize a pin over a flame, holding the end of pin with a cloth. Puncture the edge of the blister, not the top, and drain. Cut a hole in a piece of moleskin and apply it to the skin *around* the blister (Figure 17-4). For further protection from friction you may want to put a piece of molefoam over the blister itself.

Figure 17-4: Managing a large blister

Overheating

Heat cramps are caused by the loss of electrolytes (sodium, potassium, magnesium, and chloride) from the body during heavy exertion. They often occur in warm weather or after prolonged strenuous physical activity. They are usually characterized by severe, spasmodic contractions in one or more of the large muscles of the legs.

Treat heat cramps with rest, gentle massage, stretching, and by drinking lots of fluids containing electrolytes. For a cramp in a calf muscle, straighten out and support affected leg, grasp the foot at the toes and pull slowly and gently. Never pound or twist a cramped or sore muscle.

Heat exhaustion is caused by the inability of the body to dissipate heat and the loss of electrolytes during strenuous exercise in a hot, humid environment. Heat exhaustion and heat stroke are thought to be the same phenomenon but of different severity.

Signs and symptoms of heat exhaustion include fatigue, faintness, dizziness, and nausea which may lead to vomiting. The victim's skin becomes pale and moist. The heart rate and temperature are normal, however. Immediate treatment for the victim includes rest. Give the victim electrolyte fluid replacement, or water if that is all that is available. Apply wet cloths to the victim and fan vigorously. When the victim is rested and feels improved, activity can be resumed.

Heat stroke, a very serious condition, is caused by dehydration and the loss of the body's ability to dissipate enough heat in a hot environment. The onset of heat-stroke symptoms can be rapid. The victim becomes confused, loses coordination, and may become unconscious. The skin becomes hot and dry, and the body temperature rises to 102°F or higher. There may be shortness of breath, diarrhea, and seizures.

Treatment must begin at once. Stop all activity and protect the victim from the source of heat. To provide shade, you may have to place the victim under some vegetation, or make your own shade by holding a tarp or ground cover above him. Remove the victim's clothing, wet him down, and fan vigorously if there is no wind. If water is limited, sponge the victim, especially under the armpits, behind the neck, and in the groin. Give liquids only if the victim is conscious and able to swallow. Recheck the victim's temperature every 30 minutes and continue cooling until his temperature is down to normal. Do not give aspirin products or stimulants. After the victim's condition has stabilized, medical help should be sought.

Chilling

Frostbite is an injury produced by severe cold in which flesh freezes. It is caused by exposure of a body part to cold air, wind and/or snow. The extent of injury is categorized as either simple, superficial or deep frostbite depending on the symptoms and on the depth of tissue damage. The method of treatment depends on the depth of the frozen tissue.

Simple frostbite (or frostnip) commonly affects the hands, feet, face or ears. The earliest signs are a sensation of cold or pain with redness of the affected skin. As freezing progresses, the tissues become whiter and all sensation is lost. The victim may not be aware of the problem until someone indicates that there is something unusual about their skin color.

Simple frostbite is treated by slowly warming the affected area, either with your own bare hands, blowing warm air on the site, or if fingers are involved, holding them in your armpits. Complaints of tingling or a burning sensation during recovery is normal. Never rub snow on frostbitten areas—this promotes further chilling. Never expose frostbitten flesh to a source of extreme heat, such as directly above a campfire! Superficial frostbite affects deeper tissues and the skin appears white and waxy. The area will feel frozen on the surface but will still have its normal pliant texture when you press on it. Begin rapid rewarming of the area only if there is no chance of refreezing. The entire body should be kept warm during and after the treatment. Rapid rewarming procedures are described in *Medicine for Mountaineering* (see Recommended Reading at the end of this chapter). Protect the superficial frostbitten area by covering it and handling the affected part gently. As soon as possible, transport the victim to a medical facility with the affected limb slightly elevated.

Deep frostbite or frozen limbs have the feel of a frozen piece of meat and have no resilience when touched. The skin turns mottled or blotchy and is white, then grayish yellow, and finally grayish blue.

Deep or severe frostbite should not be treated under field conditions. Walking out on frozen feet does less damage than inadequate rewarming and refreezing. If the victim is unable to walk, the victim will have to be carried.

Hypothermia is a generalized cooling of the body's core temperature to a point where the body can no longer generate its own heat. It can happen within a matter of minutes in the case of immersion in cold water, or over a period of hours following the onset of cold, wet weather conditions. Even in temperatures well above freezing, hypothermia can come on as a result of inadequate clothing and shelter. Physical exhaustion and wet clothing accelerate the process. Children and the elderly are particularly predisposed to hypothermia.

To avoid the later, serious stages of hypothermia, be alert for early signs and symptoms, such as undue fatigue, weakness, slowness, apathy, forgetfulness, and confusion. These symptoms may be observable by others, but the victim himself may not be aware of them.

Hypothermia is classified as either mild or profound. The victim of mild hypothermia usually experiences little or no change in mental ability, with either a normal or slightly impaired coordination for activities such as walking. The victim may be shivering and typically has difficulty manipulating buttons, zippers, and boot laces. The victim may also be somewhat lethargic, and his speech may be vague, slow, and slurred.

It is important to recognize these signs and to begin treatment immediately. Get the victim out of the wind, rain, or cold environment, and remove any wet clothing. Protect the victim from further heat loss, especially from the head and neck. Give the victim warm liquids (but no alcohol). Complications from mild hypothermia are minimal, and those stricken by it can resume their activities when warmed up.

A victim who advances to profound hypothermia experiences a definite change in mental status. The victim may be apathetic and uncooperative; shivering is replaced by muscle rigidity. All movements become erratic and jerky. As the victim's core temperature falls further, he becomes irrational, loses contact with his surroundings, and falls into a stupor. If untreated, he eventually lapses into unconscious and then dies from cardiac arrest or other complications.

In addition to the treatments given for mild hypothermia, handle the victim gently when removing clothing and giving care. Do not rub the extremities to stimulate circulation. Instead, place wrapped warm rocks or hot-water-filled bottles around the victim to accelerate the warming process. If possible, place the victim in a sleeping bag in contact with two other people. Continue warming the victim until evacuation to a medical facility is possible.

In practice, such treatments in the field can be problematic, since other members of a party may be afflicted by varying degrees of hypothermia as well. In bad weather it is essential that all members of a party stick together, so that each member can look after the others' welfare.

Altitude Illnesses

High-altitude illnesses have been recognized for many years, but they've become more common as more people experience rapid ascents into the mountains. These illnesses range from mild conditions of headache, nausea, and fatigue to the truly life-threatening conditions of high-altitude pulmonary edema (HAPE) and high-altitude cerebral edema (HACE). As with most conditions, prevention is much better than any of the current treatments.

The development of acute mountain sickness (AMS) is related to a person's physical activity, past acclimatization, rate of ascent, and the altitude reached. It is uncommon below 8000 feet, but occurs in 30 percent of persons abruptly exposed to 10,000 feet, and 70 percent of persons exposed abruptly to 14,800 feet. The most effective preventive measure is to remain at 8000-10,000 feet for a few days and then gradually ascend to the planned altitude. If ascent is less than 1000 feet per day above 10,000 feet the condition is not likely to occur. Another preventive measure is to avoid alcohol and sleeping pills.

The symptoms of AMS vary in severity in different individuals, but tend to be constant for a given person with each re-exposure to altitude. Symptoms usually begin from 6 to 28 hours after ascent. A throbbing, generalized headache; decreased appetite; nausea and vomiting; and general fatigue characterize this relatively mild illness. The symptoms have been compared to that of a hangover from an alcohol binge. They tend to gradually decrease as long as further ascent is postponed. A high-carbohydrate diet begun a few days before ascent may help to prevent or decrease these symptoms.

While most persons with AMS do well and can remain at 8000-10,000 feet, some persons will have more severe symptoms, or symptoms that begin at higher altitudes. These may include cough, shortness of breath, intermittent breathing, and difficulty with coordination. (To check for coordination, you can have the person try to walk a straight line putting the heel of the forward foot to the toe of the back foot.) Individuals with these symptoms should descend at least 1,000 feet to prevent further compications.

Conditions that may mimic AMS include dehydration, hypothermia, carbon monoxide poisoning, and severe infections.

HAPE is less common than AMS, but much more serious and potentially fatal. It strikes one or two percent of climbers above 12,000 feet and is most common on the second night at these altitudes. It, too, is related to rate of ascent, exertion, use of alcohol or sleeping pills, and cold. Early symptoms may include a dry cough, an increased pulse rate, and decreased exercise performance. Shortness of breath, bluish skin color, and a phlegm-producing cough occur as the condition progresses. In some cases, a victim of HAPE can lapse into coma or suddenly die without any warning signs at all. Although several forms of medication including diuretics and oxygen have been used, descent is the only uniformly successful form of treatment.

HACE represents a markedly more severe form of high-altitude illness. There is a progression of symptoms such as lack of coordination, changes in consciousness, severe headache, bizarre behavior, and coma. Descent is the only successful treatment.

Although slow ascent is the best prevention for high-altitude illnesses of all types, there are medications that can help when this is not possible. Acetazolamide (Diamox) in doses of 250 mg 12 hours before ascent will decrease the likelihood of AMS. (Acetazolamide is a sulfonamide; persons who have reacted in the past to sulfa drugs should not take it. Side effects include tingling of the lips and fingers and an altered sense of taste. Because it is a diuretic, water consumption should be increased after taking this medication.)

Dexamethasone (Decadron), a cortisone-type drug, can also be used at a dosage of 4 mg taken every six hours starting 24 hours before ascent and continuing for several days. Because there may be some serious side effects to this drug, it should not be taken unless under the direction of a medical professional in the group.

High-altitude illness is a preventable condition. Mild forms are inconvenient, but the more severe forms can be fatal. Slow ascent, especially above 10,000 feet with sleep at a lower altitude, use of Diamox, and avoidance of alcohol and sleeping pills will help to make your trip pleasant and safe.

TRAUMA

Bleeding

Bleeding is the loss of blood from the body' s circulation and can be either external or internal. Uncontrolled bleeding can quickly lead to shock.

The first step in controlling bleeding is the application of direct pressure to the bleeding site. A clean or sterile dressing is preferred but if not available, your hand can be used. If bleeding has been difficult to stop, do not remove the dressing but add more dressings on top of the first ones. If you do not suspect a fracture, you can elevate an extremity above the heart. Pressure points (places where an artery crosses a bone) can also be used to control bleeding but are not usually effective when used alone. Tourniquets should only be used when the loss of limb is necessary to save a life. The presence of the tourniquet should be clearly indicated on the victim.

A bruised, swollen, tender, or rigid abdomen are signs of internal bleeding. Penetrating chest or abdominal wounds, fracture of the pelvis and bleeding from the rectum or vagina are also likely to indicate internal bleeding. These victims should be evacuated as soon as possible.

Small bruises can be treated with cold compresses or cold water immersion for the first 48 hours along with a mild compression dressing.

Wounds such as lacerations should be cleaned with soap and water or a disinfectant. Grossly contaminated wounds can be irrigated with cooled boiled water or water disinfected using iodine or chlorine. Closing wounds with sutures should be avoided, but adhesive tape or sterile cloth strips may be used. Highly contaminated wounds should be observed for signs of infection (swelling, redness, warmth around the wound, and foul-smelling drainage). These wounds should be treated at a medical facility.

Fracture

Fractures are classified as either simple (no broken skin) or compound (bone protrudes through the skin). Signs and symptoms are pain, swelling, deformity, bruising, tenderness over the area, and inability to move the injured part. The victim may also say the sound of "snapping" was heard at the time of injury.

Treat fractures with splints to prevent movement. If it is a compound fracture, you may also have to place a dressing and bandage over the open area. Splints should be carefully padded and improvised from whatever is available. Practice splinting on an uninjured individual first before applying the splint to a victim. You can splint one extremity against an uninjured one if necessary. Use such items as Ensolite and pack waist bands (as cervical collars), wire splints, ice axes, camera tripods and parts of pack frames (see Figure 17-5).

Figure 17-5: Some methods of splinting with an ice-axe (top), an uninjured leg (middle), and a branch (lower)

Sprains, Strains and Dislocations

Sprains are stretched or torn tendons, ligaments, and blood vessels around joints. The ankle is the most common site of a sprain. Signs and symptoms are pain at the joint, tenderness, discoloration, and swelling.

A mild or moderate sprain may be treated by wrapping the joint with an elastic bandage in a figure-eight pattern and applying cold (snow or stream water). A more severe sprain (blue-purple discoloration below the ankle bone after 12-24 hours) should be elevated, wrapped with an elastic bandage, and not used to bear weight. The boot may be kept on as long as it does not interfere with circulation from swelling.

Strains are stretched or torn muscles, often occurring in the back. They are caused by lifting a heavy object improperly. Signs and symptoms include sharp pain, stiffness, and swelling. Treatment consists of applying cold over the area for 24 hours, rest, and use of pain-control medicines.

A dislocation is the displacement of a bone end from its socket. A common type involves the shoulder joint. Signs and symptoms include a pointed rather than rounded appearance to the joint and pain when at rest. This normally requires medical help, so if none is available in the field, then immobilize the affected joint, and remove the victim to a source of outside help.

If there is doubt about an injury being a sprain, strain or dislocation, treat it as a fracture.

CONCLUSION

Although this chapter covers many first-aid issues, it is far from all-inclusive. Anyone who spends time in remote areas should continue learning more about the problems specific to the wilderness. Our recommended reading list contains several books that will give you more help in preparing for emergency situations.

Recommended Reading:

Medicine for Mountaineering, 3rd Edition
Edited by James A. Wilkerson, M.D.
The Mountaineers, 1985.
 (Good for the avid outdoor enthusiast, but too technical for many.)

Medicine for the Outdoors
Paul S. Auerbach, M.D.
Little, Brown and Company, 1986
 (Comprehensive and easily understood by the layman. However, procedures for CPR and choking are outdated.)

Mountaineering Medicine
Fred T. Darvill, Jr., M.D.
Wilderness Press, 1985
 (Concise and easily understood. This should be carried in every backpacker's first-aid kit.)

The Pocket Doctor
Stephen Bezruchka, M.D.
The Mountaineers, 1988
 (Concise, compact, and written for those headed for foreign lands.)

Search and Rescue

Don Stouder

"Be prepared"

—Boy Scouts of America

I f everyone who ventured into the wilderness followed the Scout's motto, there would be little need for a chapter like this. But for many a circumstance—sometimes avoidable and sometimes unavoidable—people do get lost or injured in the outdoors. Thoughtful planning can often prevent these occurrences from ever happening.

People accustomed to living in remote places for several days at a stretch are usually well prepared to deal with adverse circumstances. Those who run into difficulty in the wilderness are more often casual users—day hikers, fishermen, hunters—who really don't travel very far from the nearest road or civilized place. With too little equipment and too little know-how, they risk getting into situations they can't handle.

Thoughtful planning—even for day trips—greatly reduces the risk of being stranded without help.

First, leave a detailed itinerary with someone you trust. Agree on a time of return (allowing plenty of room for changes in your schedule) and then do your best to meet the intended itinerary. Instruct your contact person to call for help if you do not return. Don't expect the Army to come charging after you on a moment's notice if you get stuck, but at least someone will be aware of your predicament and help will come eventually.

Second, never go into an unfamiliar area without the basic tools of navigation—map and compass—and the competence to use both effectively.

Third, carry the essential safety and survival items appropriate for your trip. For frequent, shorter trips, it's handy to put together a small "survival kit" or purchase a commercially available kit. No matter how well prepared you are, there's always the possibility of getting injured or lost.

BEING LOST, AND DEALING WITH IT

The old warning on railroad crossings told you to "stop, look, and listen."

That's not a bad idea, either, for the disoriented hiker. Assuming you've been separated from a group and become disoriented, stop and try listening for them. They may be signalling you. Call to them, or better yet, use a whistle. You can make some tentative movements toward where you think they went, or climb to a nearby high point for a better view. But don't wander about without a coherent plan.

If you aren't successful, then remember the cardinal rule: don't panic! If you've absorbed all the information contained in this book and are reasonably well equipped, then you know that everything you need to survive, perhaps rather comfortably, is at your disposal. The most important thing you need now is the patience to sit down and think clearly and calmly about your choices.

Should you sit still, make yourself comfortable, and wait to be found? Or should you attempt to find you way out? The alternative you choose would, of course, depend on many factors. Will the weather hold up? How long until sunset? How prepared are you for a bivouac? Do you have the proper navigational tools, and if so can you locate yourself on the map and navigate to a position of safety? What obstacles lie along the way? How long will it be before someone reports you as missing?

You may decide to stay put and let the searchers find you. If so, make yourself as conspicuous as possible. If the sun is up, build a smokey fire (but think very carefully about how you'll do this safely in wildfire-prone areas). To catch the attention of aerial searchers, lay out bright-colored clothing or camping gear on a hilltop or in a clearing. Rearrange the natural features of the landscape into some unnatural geometric form—if that doesn't take too much energy. Remember, three of anything (whistle blasts, gunshots) is the universal signal for distress. Use a signal mirror if you have one. Conserve your food, water, and strength; and protect yourself as best you can from heat, cold, and excess sunlight. At night, build a fire both to keep warm and to attract attention. Above all, know that when you are missed you'll be looked for. Relax.

If you're certain you can reach help by your own muscles and know-how, then be reasonable about it. Don't stumble through unknown terrain in the dark. Don't hurry across the desert in the midday heat if you need to conserve your water supply.

If you reach civilization before rescuers can find you, then your first order of business is to make sure that that fact is communicated to anyone who may be out looking for you.

THE CASE OF THE
MISSING HIKER

Discovering that a friend, relative, or member of your party is missing is a terribly unnerving experience. But again, there's never any excuse to panic. You must weigh the urge to do something immediately against the possibility that launching a search, or going for help, too soon may put the searchers, or the messenger, at risk. Take into consideration who is missing, and that person's experience, age, medical condition, whether or not the person has the proper equipment, and how long he or she's been unaccounted for. The appropriate time to initiate a search may depend on current or anticipated weather conditions, and the time of day.

First try to establish where the person was last seen (Point Last Seen, or PLS in rescuer's parlance). It's very important that the area near the PLS remain undisturbed so that future searchers can examine it carefully for clues such as tracks and scents. Shouting or other noises should be tried first to see if the lost person responds. This should be followed by a brief search of the trails or other possible places a person could have gone in the area around the PLS.

Those who are searching should stay in pairs and keep communicating with others as much as possible. Each searcher should be on the lookout for clues such as footprints or personal belongings. If there's no indication of success after about two hours, then it's time to "call in the cavalry."

Fortunately for outdoor enthusiasts in the West, most areas are served by volunteer rescue teams. Some are part of the local sheriff's or parks department, while others are independent groups. As a rule, the individual rescuers are required to participate in extensive training and qualifying sessions. Most teams are linked together in an organization called the Mountain Rescue Association, which sets standards for training and facilitates mutual assistance when needed. To summon the help of a rescue team (not only to help find a lost person, but also to evacuate an injured person) you must notify the local law-enforcement authority, be it the county sheriff, park ranger, or other authority. (Where applicable, the emergency telephone number 911 is the fastest way to reach the right agency.)

If the distance to the nearest source of help is large, send at least two well-equipped persons. They must carry detailed information about a lost hiker's identity, PLS, equipment, and condition, if known. (For a detailed list of information messengers should carry about injured persons, see Chapter 17.) Since the authorities may have questions about a lost person's personality, attitude, and other psychological factors, it is best to send a messenger who knows the lost person well.

When the search and rescue team arrives, let them take over. Allay your considerable anxiety with the knowledge that they know their business better than anyone else.

Studies of lost persons and search missions have revealed some very interesting statistics.[1] These are shared here

---

1 The following information is from a study done by William G. Syrotuck and published as "Analysis of Lost Person Behavior."

to help guide those who may be faced with searching for a lost individual.

Generally there are three broad categories of circumstances in which people become lost:

Predetermined or Known Location

The missing person, when lost, was at a known or semi-familiar location such as a campground, picnic area, popular fishing area, home, automobile, etc. This category usually involves children and the elderly. Kids tend to be inquisitive and wander off, while the elderly may wander off, become confused, and simply not remember the way back. Senile persons may attempt to "return" to some fondly remembered place from their past. In this category
• 34% followed a road, pathway, or trail
• 33% went cross-country
• 25% went down a drainage ditch or a path of least resistance
• 8% were found stuck in hazardous terrain

En Route

The lost person was traveling in the company of one or more persons along a road, trail, stream, or other known route of travel; and at some point became separated from the group. Often, such separations are caused by confusion about directions, or by the fatigue of a person who has to struggle to keep up with the group. Examination of these

cases showed that
• 22% stayed on a path or trail
• 61% left the main trail
• 11% got stuck in a hazardous area
• 5% had a medical problem

Wilderness

The victim had intentionally entered a wilderness area for recreation of some kind. Subjects in this category were mainly hunters seeking prey in off-the-beaten-path locales. But these statistics also apply to bird watchers, flower pickers, and photographers. Preoccupied with their own interests, these individuals often fail to pay proper attention to changing terrain, weather conditions, or the time of day. The data shows that
• 62% found and stayed on trails
• 23% remained in heavy brush or timber,
• 8% headed for the sights or sounds of people
• 4% were victims of hazardous terrain

CONCLUSION

Although no one relishes the prospect of being in an emergency situation, Murphy's Law dictates that if you visit the wilderness often enough something will go wrong sometime. With a little foresight and planning, you can reduce the risk of someone getting lost or injured in your group, and you'll be better prepared to act intelligently, either as a victim or a rescuer.

Recommended Reading:

Wilderness Search and Rescue
Tim J. Setnicka
AMC Books, 1980
(The "Bible" of search and rescue techniques.)

APPENDIX
Wilderness Basics Authors

A retired engineering manager, *Scott Anderson* was raised in a family that spent much vacation time camping in the western U.S. He was introduced to backpacking as a Boy Scout, and later did some backpacking while his son was a Scout member. His interest in wilderness travel was renewed when he took the Sierra Club's Basic Mountaineering (now Wilderness Basics) Course in 1983. He's been involved in the program ever since, presently as the snow camp coordinator.

Priscilla Anderson has had 14 years experience as a teacher in the public school system, and 6 years experience as a designer of training programs in the business world. She has enjoyed camping both as a child and as a parent, and she became an avid backpacker once her children had grown. She participates in the Sierra Club San Diego Chapter's Wilderness Basics Course and enjoys helping others appreciate the wilderness experience.

Jan Craven's fascination with nature began with childhood explorations on the grounds of the Philbrook Art Museum in Tulsa, Oklahoma. Aside from catching tadpoles in the ponds of the Italian garden, she fantasized about the life of the Plains Indians whose finely crafted artifacts in the museum's basement generated more excitement than the Renaissance art displayed upstairs. Family vacations in southern Colorado added hiking, fishing, pack trips, stargazing, and snipe hunts to the essentials of life. After a period when the demands of homemaking and career took precedence, her interest in the outdoors was rekindled by taking the Basic Mountaineering Course. This, along with Chapter Outing Leader training, provided her with the tools to handle the challenges and intrigues of the Southwestern deserts, mountains, and canyons. Hiking and backpacking continue to bring her great satisfaction, as well as lending physical, mental, social, and physical balance to her high-tech marketing career.

Chuck Bennett has been affiliated with the Basic Mountaineering Course as an instructor and outings leader for the past 13 years. He has also served as the course chairman for four years. His climbing experience includes bouldering in southern California, as well as climbing trips to the Sierra Nevada and to Pico de Orizaba in Mexico.

Hal Brody has been exploring the Southwestern deserts since 1980. Since becoming a Sierra Club trip leader in 1981, he has served as a Wilderness Basics Course leader, specializing in desert outings. For more than 7 years, he has carefully prepared and led qualified adventurers on summer desert trips. He shares his love and knowledge of the desert with his trip members in order to help them gain a deep appreciation of the desert, and to create environmentalists whose votes and political actions may help safeguard the remaining desert wilderness.

A geologist by training, *Nelson Copp* is pursuing a career in computer graphics. His many interests include bicycling, hiking, backpacking, and cross-country skiing. His leadership roles in the Sierra Club San Diego Chapter have included the Wilderness Basics map-and-compass coordinator, and the Bicycle Section outings and membership chair. Currently he's serving as the Chapter's outings leader coordinator and Leadership Training coordinator.

Mary Engles, R.P.T., has been a physical therapist in San Diego for 18 years. She has a masters degree in orthopedic physical therapy, and has been an avid cyclist, hiker, and backpacker for 20 years in spite of her own orthopedic problems.

Mike Fry has been hiking and backpacking since his early experiences with the Boy Scouts in the late '50s. He discovered lightweight equipment and the Sierra Club in 1968, took the San Diego Chapter's Basic Mountaineering Course in 1970, and has been an outings leader and environmental activist ever since. He continues to experiment with clothing, equipment, and nutrition to insure safe and enjoyable outings. Aside from his work as an electronics engineer, Mike spends about 60 days annually on backpack and cross-country ski trips, mostly in his native San Diego County, in southern Utah, and in the Sierra Nevada.

Robert L. (Bob) Feuge has lived in the Southwest for all of his life of 48 years, the last 22 years in California. A psychologist by academic training, he has been an avid hiker, backpacker, skier, and canoeist since childhood. Another of his avocations is Southwestern anthropology. Bob has been a member of the Sierra Club since 1986, and has been involved in various environmental issues dealing with land use in the San Diego area since 1973.

Keith Gordon is a former mountaineering store manager and a former instructor at the Aspen School of Mountaineering. In 1974 he unstrapped his rucksack and strapped into the cockpit, where most of his ascents are now made as a captain on corporate jets.

David S. Moser (age 44) has lived in the San Diego area since 1947. A physicist by education, he is an avid hiker, photographer, and amateur astronomer. He has been involved with the Sierra Club since 1983, and has held the positions of outings editor, outings coordinator, outings chairman, and chairman of the Wilderness Basics course for the San Diego Chapter. He has traveled to many points on the globe, and is disappointed that there isn't enough time to see them all.

Carol P. Murdock is a registered nurse by profession, a Red Cross Standard First Aid instructor of long standing, and a member of the Wilderness Medical Society. She has been a Sierra Club outings leader since 1975 and has led many day hikes, backpacks, mule trips, and bicycle rides. For more than 13 years, she has organized an annual, weekend-long Wilderness First Aid seminar for the San Diego Chapter. She is also responsible for coordinating and teaching a first-aid program for San Diego Chapter outing leaders and trainees.

Donald B. Stouder is a health and safety educator and an emergency medical technician. A native of New Jersey, Don has been a hiker and camper most of his life, and has been involved with rescue organizations for 13 years. He wishes to dedicate the contributions he has made in this book to his father.

While car-camping as a child, *Marianne Ringhoff* learned well the elements of outdoor living. From her mother she learned how to improvise with very little. From her father she acquired the wisdom of common sense and the love of traveling and exploring new areas. Her brothers unwittingly taught her the life of rough and tumble, and that a little dirt can be fun. Her children, now teenagers, have been camping and enjoying the outdoors since they were infants. Marianne has been active in the San Diego Chapter's Focus on Youth section, and has assumed a leadership role in the Wilderness Basics Course. She also participates in a Wilderness Survival for Children program. Professionally, Marianne is an Intermediate Care Unit nurse.

Jerry Schad introduces his students at San Diego Mesa College to the wonders of the natural world by way of courses in the physical sciences. He also guides hikers and bicyclists along thousands of miles of California roads and trails by way of his several guidebooks, and columns written for various publications. A Sierra Club outings leader since the late '70s, Jerry enjoys trips to the celebrated parks and wilderness areas around the West, as well as to the "vest-pocket wildernesses" that lie very near some of California's most populated areas.

Emily B. Troxell has taught a variety of subjects to audiences ranging from handicapped middle-school students to college students. She is currently an adjunct faculty member at Palomar College, but also works as an interpretive ranger at Cabrillo National Monument. At Cabrillo, she often relates the story of the gray whale, but her most enjoyable task is wading into the tidepools to tell of the lifestyles of the creatures found there. She believes that programs such as outdoor education for grade-schoolers and courses in wilderness appreciation for adults will help people better use and appreciate the world's natural places.

Eugene A. Troxell is an associate professor of philosophy at San Diego State University. He has taught continuously at San Diego State since receiving his Ph.D. in philosophy in 1966 from the University of Chicago. He is co-author of *Making Sense of Things*, published in 1976 by St. Martin's Press. His academic specialties include the philosophy of Wittgenstein, and ethics—particularly environmental ethics. He has served as president of the San Diego Ecology Centre, is an Aikido instructor, and counts among his avocations hiking, camping, and backpacking.

Carl W. Trygstad, M.D. is a senior consultant in urgent care and emergency medicine at Scripps Clinic and Research Foundation, La Jolla. He is a long-time member of the Sierra Club, and has spent many vacations backpacking in the Sierra Nevada and in other mountainous areas of the world.

David Ussell came to California by way of Canada and England, where he was born in 1949. His initial experiences with backpacking as a Boy Scout in Canada helped prepare him for a stint in the U.S. Army starting in 1971. Dave earned a B.S. degree in physics from San Diego State University, and furthered his interest in the outdoors by becoming involved with the Sierra Club San Diego Chapter's outings program and Wilderness Basics Course. He has held a variety of Sierra Club offices in recent years. Winter mountaineering is his favorite outdoor activity. His other interests include music, photography, science, computers, dance, drama, and people—especially children.

Olive Wenzel has loved the wilderness since she experienced its healing quietude as a small child. She's written many articles about nature's beauty, and is proud to have helped establish the Forest Fire Laboratory in Riverside, California.

Carolyn Wood, 41, has lived and traveled throughout the world. Introduced to backpacking through the Basic Mountaineering course in 1983, she has also developed an interest in outdoor photography, especially the macro-photography of wildflowers. Her interest in the differences between women and men in the outdoors developed from her own experiences and those shared by other outdoorswomen. She regularly gives a presentation entitled "Women in the Wilderness" for the San Diego Chapter's Wilderness Basics course.

A native southern Californian, *Ted Young* has long enjoyed visiting California's deserts in winter and the mountains in summer. His favorite kind of summer vacation is backpacking to a base camp above timberline in the Sierra Nevada and then spending the days hiking cross-country—ideal circumstances for refining map and compass skills.

INDEX